Contents

Part II National experiences

Series Editor's Preface

The study of regions and regionalism in Europe is undoubtedly a boom industry today. It is both an intellectual and political fashion to suggest that we are moving towards a 'Europe of the Regions'. This view is, no doubt, encouraged by the European Commission, which might be said to have an institutional interest in the development of a new level of legitimate government, as a means of by-passing the member states. Even if one rejects this somewhat cynical view, the process of European integration has often encouraged the revival of regionalism, if only because regions themselves have come to view Brussels as a pot of gold in a decade or so of resource squeeze imposed by their national governments. Brigid Laffan's discovery of the saying 'while you're in Brussels get us a grant' is fairly common throughout Europe! Thus, the setting up of Brussels offices by the regions is now an established and expanding phenomenon. Rightly or wrongly, European regions feel that the setting up of a Brussels office in order to directly represent their interests to the European institutions (in addition to using the member state channel) is a worthwhile investment.

This is, perhaps, the greatest paradox of regions in Europe. It is conventional wisdom that the growth of the European Union is caused by the declining power of nation states to control their own economies in the face of international capitalism and globalisation. Hence, nation states agree to gradually transfer sovereignty (or at least to 'pool' it) to the supranational level in an attempt to gain some purchase on the process of globalisation. Whilst no sensible person would argue that the nation state has ceased to be of significance in terms of the key questions of public policy, there has undoubtedly been a drift of power upwards. Nevertheless, Europeanisation seems to have encouraged, not weakened, the view that regions can be an effective level of governance. Indeed, Europeanisation has even encouraged nationalism in some of Europe's regions. For example, the Scottish National Party (SNP) has as its central platform an 'independent Scotland within Europe'. It sees this slogan as the best way of re-assuring doubtful Scottish voters that Scotland could break away from the United Kingdom, under the protection of the European Union. Thus, European integration, far from causing the demise of notions that we could have an effective and vibrant regional governance in Western Europe, has sometimes encouraged a greater degree of regional mobilisation. The actual (rather than the supposed) effects of the European Union on regions is one of the many key questions addressed in this volume.

One needs to be watchful for myths in politics, of course. As the editors point out in their introduction, since the early 1960s, there had been a revival of regionalist movements and pressures to strengthen democracy. This lead to forms of institutionalisation of regionalism in many countries and to many experiments in decentralisation – hence Mény's description of the 1970s in the decade of decentralisation. This promise seems to be unfulfilled today, however. Exogenous and endogenous events have meant that, as the editors suggest, there is not very much evidence that regions really have become an essential level of government in Europe. The story is one of much symbolic politics and institutional innovation and not much real redistribution of power between levels of government, other than to the supranational level.

Continuing the theme of the 'regional paradox', the volume also analyses the political economy of regulation issue and the idea that the only effective level of regulation, following the crises of the Keynesian welfare state and the emergence of Fordism, might be the regional level. Thus, regions might be seen as necessary to organise the infrastructure of economic growth in this more fluid period. Again, this seems generally not to have happened.

These paradoxes, and many others, are examined in detail in this volume. As the editors put it (adapting from Jessop) their central aim is not, as many other authors have done, to 'bring back the regions' but 'to put the regions in their place'. This is the key innovative contribution of this edited volume. It adds enormously to our understanding of the realities (as opposed to the myths) of the role of regions in the complex, multi-layered, 'networked' and multi-arena politics of the Western Europe today. It makes sense of the effects that several factors – such as globalisation, Europeanisation, new forms of governance structures involving changing patterns of public and private interactions – have on the role of regions in the system of governance in Europe. Via an extensive range of well researched and analytical case studies, the volume sheds much light on just why the promise of regional government in Europe has yet to be fulfilled. It is realistic and a well balanced study of the many promises and *relatively* few achievements. In challenging the notion of a 'Europe of the Regions', the volume concludes with a powerful argument that regions rarely succeed as a level of co-ordination or regulation of multiple actors and networks which characterise the new governance. These findings might depress many – but those who support the regional cause or seek to understand its fortunes will benefit greatly from the scholarship exhibited in this volume, as will all of those scholars and practitioners who seek to understand the process of governance in the new Europe.

Illustrations

FIGURES

TABLES

Contributors

Arnaldo Bagnasco is Professor of Sociology at the University of Turin and was Director of the journal *Stato e mercato*. He has developed a theory of the small enterprise in regional development and now works on class and capitalism. He has published in particular *Tre Italie. La problematica territoriale dello sviluppo italiano*, Il Mulino, Bologna, 1977; *Torino. Un profilo sociologico*, Einaudi, Turin, 1986; *La construction sociale du marché. Le défi de la troisième Italie*, Editions ENS-Cachan, Cachan (with C. Trigilia), 1993 and recently, *L'Italia in tempi di cambiamento politico*, Il Mulino, Bologna, 1996. He also edited (with Charles Sabel), *Small Firms and Economic Development in Europe*, London, Pinter, 1995.

Richard Balme is Professor of Political Science at Institut d'Etudes Politiques de Lyon, and also teaches at IEP Paris. He has edited (with P. Garraud, V. Hoffman-Martinot and E. Ritaine), *Le territoire pour politiques: variations européennes*, L'Harmattan, Paris, 1994 and *Les territoires du néo-régionalisme: coopération interrégionale et globalisation économique*, Economica, Paris, 1996. He wrote (with B. Jouve) 'L'Europe en région: la mise en œuvre des fonds structurels et la régionalisation de l'action publique en France métropolitaine', *Politiques et management public*, vol. 13, no. 2, June 1995; 'From regional to sectoral policies: the contractual relations between the State and the regions in France', in J. Loughlin and S. Mazey (eds) *The End of the French Unitary State? Ten Years of Regionalization in France*, London, Frank Cass, 1995.

Arthur Benz is Professor of Political Science and Government at the Martin Luther University of Halle Wittenberg. His publications concern the government in the federal systems, public administration and regional policy and European integration. He has published

Föderalismus als dynamisches System, Westdeutscher Verlag, Opladen, 1985; *Modernisierung der Staatsorganisation*, Nomos, Baden-Baden, 1990 (with J. Hesse); *Horizontale Politikverflechtung*, Campus, Frankfurt (with F. Scharpf and R. Zintl) and *Kooperative Verwaltung*, Nomos, Baden-Baden, 1994.

Mick Dunford is Professor of Economic Geography at the Centre for European Studies at the University of Sussex and editor of *Regional Studies*. He is co-author of *The Arena of Capital* (1983), *Capital, The State and Regional Development* (1988), *Rhône-Alpes in the 1990s* (1991), *Successful European Regions: Northern Ireland Learning from Others* (1996), *Industrial Change and Regional Development* (1991) and *Cities and Regions in the New Europe* (with G. Kafkalas) Belhaven Press, London, 1992.

William Genieys is a researcher at CEPEL (University of Montpellier). He has published 'Sociologie des élus régionaux en Languedoc-Roussillon et en Pays de Loire', *Pôle Sud*, no. 2, 1995 (with S. Derviche and J. Joana); 'Un janus notabiliaire, Yves Pietrasena', *Science de la Société*, no. 38, 1996; 'Les élites périphériques espagnoles face au changement de régime', *Revue française de science politique*, vol. 46, no. 4, 1996. Currently, he is completing a work on the socio-historical analysis of the institutionalisation process of the Spanish peripheral elites.

Michael Keating has been Professor of Political Science, University of Western Ontario since 1988. He has also taught at the University of Strathclyde, North Staffordshire Polytechnic, Institut d'Etudes Politiques de Paris, and the Virginia Polytechnic and State University in the United States. He is the author of eleven books and numerous articles on nationalism, urban policy and regionalism and the editor of four contributed works on regionalism in Europe among which are *The European Union and the Regions* (with B. Jones) Oxford University Press, Oxford, 1995 and *Political Economy of Regionalism* (with J. Loughlin) Frank Cass, London, 1996. His most recent book is *Nations Against the State: The New Politics of Nationalism in Quebec, Catalonia and Scotland*, Macmillan, London, 1996.

Patrick Le Galès is Senior CNRS research fellow at the Centre de Recherches Administratives et Politiques de Rennes and teaches at IEP Rennes and IEP Paris. He was Jean Monnet Fellow at the Robert Schuman Centre of the European University Institute in Florence at the time of writing. He has published *Politique urbaine et développement local, une comparaison France-Grande-Bretagne*, l'Harmattan, Paris, 1993; (ed. with Mark Thatcher) *Les réseaux de politique publique*, L'Harmattan, Paris, 1995, 'Du gouvernement des villes à la gouvernance urbaine', *Revue française de science politique*, no. 1, 1995; 'Regional economic policies: an alternative to French economic dirigisme?', in J. Loughlin and S. Mazey (eds), *The End of the French Unitary State? Ten Years of Regionalisation in France*, Frank Cass, London, 1995; 'Is the grass greener on the other side? What went wrong with the French regions and lessons for Britain', (with P. John), *Policy and Politics*, no. 4, 1996.

Christian Lequesne is senior research fellow at the Fondation Nationale des Sciences Politiques (CERI). He also teaches at the Institut d'Etudes Politiques de Paris and at the College of Europe at Bruges. His work is concerned with governance and public policies of the European Union. He is preparing a book on the EU Fisheries Policy. He has published *The State of the European Community: Policies, Institutions and Debates in the Transition Years* (with L. Hurwitz eds), Lynne Rienner, Boulder Co, 1991; *Paris-Bruxelles. Comment se fait la politique européenne de la France*, Presses de Science Po, Paris, 1993; *L'Union européenne: ouverture à l'Est?* (with F. de la Serre and J. Rupnik), PUF, Paris, 1994; 'La Commission européenne entre autonomie et dépendance', *Revue française de science politique*, vol. 46, no. 3, June 1996.

John Mawson is Professor of Urban and Regional Planning and of Public Administration at the University of Dundee. After lecturing at the University of Birmingham, he was chief executive of West Midland Enterprise Board. He acts as a consultant to numerous professional organisations and parliamentary commissions. He has published 'Contacts versus competitive bidding: rationalising urban policy programmes in England and France' (with P. Le Galès), *Journal of European Public Policy*, vol. 2, no. 2, 1995; 'The re-emergence of the regional agenda in the English regions: new patterns of urban and regional governance?', *Local Economy*, vol. 10, no. 4, 1996; 'The Government Office for the English regions', in S. Hardy, M. Hebbert and B. Mallone (eds), *Region Building*, Regional Studies Association, London, 1995.

Marco Oberti is a lecturer in Sociology at the University of Rennes 2 and a researcher at OSC (CNRS/FNSP). He has worked on local societies and social classes in Italy, and is completing a work on the Italian society (to be published by La Découverte). He has published 'Villes, quartiers et cité', in J. Roman (ed.), *Villes, Exclusion et Citoyenneté*, Esprit/Seuil, Paris, 1993; 'Le vote Front National à Mantes La Jolie' (with P. Le Galès and J.C. Rampal), *Hérodote*, no. 69, 1993; 'Analyse localisée, quartiers et cités', *Sociétés Contemporaines*, no. 22-23, 1995; *Le monde des étudiants* (with O. Galland), La Découverte, Paris, 1996 and has written several articles and chapters on urban exclusion.

Evelyne Ritaine is directeur de recherche at the Fondation Nationale des Sciences Politiques, CERVL, Institut d'Etudes Politiques de Bordeaux, where she also teaches. Her areas of interest are territories and public mediations in Southern Europe. She has published 'La modernité localisée? Leçons italiennes sur le développement régional', *Revue française de science politique*, no. 2, 1989; 'Territoire et politique en Europe du Sud', *Revue française de science politique*, no. 1, 1994; *Le territoire pour politiques: variations européennes* (edited with R. Balme, V. Hoffmann-Martinot and P. Garraud), L'Harmattan, Paris, 1994.

Stefaan De Rynck has been a researcher at the European University Institute of Florence, where he worked on the Belgian regions as actors of public policies. He has published articles on local government, the policy of regional development in Belgium, and the Committee of Regions. He has been a consultant for the European Union Structural Funds in the Flemish region.

Andy Smith is an FNSP researcher at CERVL (Bordeaux) and teaches at IEP of Bordeaux and Rennes. He has recently published *L'Europe politique au miroir du local. Les fonds structurels et les zone rurales en France, en Espagne et au Royaume-Uni*, L'Harmattan, Paris, 1996; 'A la recherche d'interlocuteurs . . . La Commission Européenne et le Développement territorial', *Science de la Société*, no. 34, 1995, (with M. Smyrl); 'The French case: exception or the rule?', *Journal of Regional and Federal Studies*, summer 1996; 'La Commission Européenne et les Fonds Structurels, vers un nouveau modèle d'action?', *Revue française de science politique*, vol. 46, no. 3, 1996.

Marie-Claude Smouts is directeur de recherche CNRS (Centre d'Etudes et de Recherches Internationales) and Professor at the Institut d'Etudes Politiques de Paris. She has written extensively on multilateral diplomacy, North–South relations and international relations. Currently she is working on modes of international regulation and the notion of governance. Her latest works are *L'ONU et la guerre. La diplomatie en kaki*, Complexe, Brussels, 1994; *Les organisations internationales*, Armand Colin, Paris, 1995; *Le retournement du monde* (with B. Badie), Presses de la FNSP, Paris, 1995, (2nd edition revised and updated).

Theo Toonen is Professor of Public Administration at the University of Leiden. He has notably published 'The unitary state as a system of co-governance: the case of the Netherlands', *Public Administration*, Autumn 1990; 'Change in continuity: local government and urban affairs in the Netherlands', in J. J. Hesse (ed.), *Local Government and Urban Affairs in International Perspective*, Nomos, Baden-Baden, 1991; 'Dutch provinces and the struggle for the Meso', in L. J. Sharpe (ed.), *Rise of Meso-Government in Europe*, Sage, London, 1993; 'Bestuur op niveau: regionalisatie in een ontzuild bestuur', *Acta Politica*, vol. 3, 1993; 'Federalism in the Netherlands: the federal approach to unitarism or the unitary approach to federalism?' (with B.J.S. Hoetjes and F. Hendriks), in Franz Knipping (ed.), *Federal Conceptions in EU Member States: Traditions and Perspectives*, Campus Verlag, Baden-Baden, 1994.

Vincent Wright has been an Official Fellow, Nuffield College, University of Oxford since 1977 after having taught at the London School of Economics. He also teaches widely in Europe and is a Fellow of the British Academy. His recent research is on privatisation, the reform of the public sector and the restructuring of the state in Western Europe. He is the editor of *West European Politics*. He has written extensively on the government and administration in Europe and notably in France. His latest books are (ed.) *Privatisation in Europe*, Pinter, London, 1994; (ed.) *Federalizing Europe?* (with J. Hesse), Oxford University Press, Oxford, 1995; (ed.) *La restructuration de l'Etat en Europe* (with S. Cassese), La Découverte, Paris, 1996.

Acknowledgements

This book[1] is the outcome of the conference 'Regions in Europe' organised in October 1995 at the Institut d'Etudes Politiques de Rennes by the Centre d'Etudes et de Recherches Internationales (CERI), Fondation Nationale des Sciences Politiques (Paris) and the Centre de Recherches Administratives et Politiques (CRAP), Institut d'Etudes Politiques de Rennes and University of Rennes I. We would like to thank all the colleagues who participated in the conference and those who contributed to the book.

We have acknowledged the support of the British Council, Paris, from the beginning of the project. We are grateful to the then Ambassador Sir Christopher Mallaby, the then director of the British Council, David Ricks and also Mrs Sharon Memis for her dynamic commitment.

We are very grateful to our directors, for their support and trust: CERI's two directors, Jean-Luc Domenach and then Jean-François Leguil-Bayart, CRAP's director, Erik Neveu as well as Marcel Morabito, IEP Rennes director. The preparation of the conference and the book owes much to various colleagues in Rennes and Paris. We wish to thank Hélène Arnaud (CERI), for doing the fund-raising exercise, Mireille Orhant (IEP Rennes) for the organisation of the conference. Sylvie Haas, Francine Biancardi, Karolina Michel and Sophie Béroud (CERI). Students from IEP Rennes are also to be thanked for their various contributions. We are especially grateful to Marylène Bercegeay (CRAP) for her essential role in the preparation of the manuscript.We owe much to her calm professionalism.

Last but not least, we acknowledge the financial support of CERI, CRAP, IEP Rennes, and the following institutions: the British Council, the French ministère-délégué aux Affaires européennes, the Centre National de la Recherche Scientifique, the University de Rennes I, the

Regional Council of Brittany, Rennes City Council and the newspaper *Ouest-France*.

Paris, Rennes, September 1997

NOTE

1 The French edition, *Les Paradoxes des régions en Europe*, La Découverte, Paris, was published in March 1997.

Introduction

*Patrick Le Galès and Christian Lequesne**

Regions in Western Europe made a comeback after the Second World War. For Perry Anderson, the appreciation of 'regions' in most European countries went hand in hand with the depreciation of provinces and 'provincialism'. To explain this 'invention of the regions', Anderson [1994] puts forward general processes relating to unequal economic development, cultural homogenisation, European integration and the calling into question of the supremacy of the nation. The establishment of stable frontiers and the easing of relations among European states also seem to have relaxed the constraint of mobilisation around a sacred nation, and allowed the development of the notion of region which is often associated with the strengthening of democracy, for example in Germany, Spain and Italy. Since the 1960s, the renewal of regionalist movements and pressures exerted within states to strengthen democracy have led in this way to forms of institutional regionalisation in a number of countries. This is why Yves Mény [1982a] could state that the 1970s were the decade of decentralisation. The 'long march' of European regions seemed all set to move ahead, basing itself on the functional logics of state reorganisation and pressures from regionalist movements.

Fifteen years later, this march does not seem to have led to the development of a regional level of government in most European countries. Three paradoxes are evident in this regard. The first paradox is that, although since the 1970s Europe has undergone an overall movement of regionalisation (in the sense of the reinforcement of intermediary levels) and above all, an increasing interdependence between different levels, recent developments in various countries remain remarkably differentiated [Balme *et al.*, 1995; Sharpe, 1993c] and the regions do not necessarily emerge as winners. Whereas fifteen

* Translation Uttam Bharthare and Claire O'Neal.

years ago there was much evidence to suggest that regions were to become an essential level of government, this evolution did not take place. Why do regions (in the sense of regional elected governments) not constitute a level of government in Europe?

From a *political economy* perspective, Carlo Trigilia [1989] identified a second 'paradox of the regions'. He pointed out that the crisis of the Keynesian welfare state, coupled with that of Fordism, explained the difficulties of regulating interests in the Western capitalist countries. For example, the regulation of social and health expenses seemed destined to necessitate the development of an intermediary level capable of closely adjusting to the reduction of funds, to negotiate the balance between supply and demand of health care, and to manage its political cost. At the same time, all the major Western countries have to face problems of inefficiency in all the main vertically organised sectoral policies in the social domain. Everywhere decentralisation and partnership are mobilised to try to remove this inefficiency. Consequently, for reasons linked to proximity, efficacy, rapidity of reaction, experimentation or innovation in the fields of training, health and social welfare, the region was destined to play an important role. At the economic level, only an intermediary level seemed capable of organising the conditions of economic growth, in particular, non-economic, invisible factors such as infrastructure, training, innovation and their diffusion. The region seemed necessary to regulate and structure economic interests and, thus, to organise economic development.

Having demonstrated this, however, Trigilia noted the absence of regions as a significant level of regulation of interest in Italy. This seemed to him to be the paradox of the Italian situation. He then pointed out Italian neo-localism, the regions' lack of political and legal resources and the absence of organised interests at a regional level. But this paradox is not specific to Italy alone. A similar observation can be made, at least for France [Le Galès, 1994], differently for the United Kingdom, as well as for non-federal states.

The third paradox relates to European integration which seemed to legitimise regions and reinforce their resources. Now, more detailed studies reveal differentiated effects [Smith, 1995; Hooghe, 1996b]. European governance is characterised by a multitude of networks and agencies, as well as a web of levels of government which give rise to a need for horizontal co-ordination. Within European multilevel governance, the different driving forces of which we are now beginning to understand, regions seemed to play a relatively important role and this sometimes led to the slogan 'Europe of the Regions'. Hence, most of the recent studies on regions have analysed the impact of European integration on regions and have studied regional mobilisation, particularly the creation of networks and forums of public action (see especially the two contributed works edited by Jones and Keating [1995] and Hooghe [1996b]). These political science studies have demonstrated that the inter-state paradigm which certain theorists of international political relations still apply to European integration [Moravcsik, 1993b] is not satisfactory, as the sharing of resources and legal powers between European, national and regional actors, calls into question the very idea of a hierarchy or of a recurring leadership of states [see Lequesne, 1996]. Following the example of studies of federal political systems [Croisat and Quermonne, 1996], they illustrated, moreover, that decision-making *at several levels* in the networks or sub-systems of specialised actors, was characterised by weak accountability, and this legitimacy problem could not be settled solely by a great increase in representative institutions. It also appealed to the conditions for the emergence of a 'public space of several levels' (Keating, Chapter 1 in this book).

While trying to draw lessons from the European integration process, it also seemed important to us to analyse regions from the comparative and national points of view, in order to better understand the impact of these processes. In fact, an increasing number of studies of these issues systematically favour a *top-down* approach from Brussels. While this facilitates challenging the centrality of the state as well as reifications associated with it [Marks *et al.*, 1996], and pushes aside the simplistic thesis of a new European political order based on the 'Europe of the Regions', it still does not allow the reifications associated, this time with the region. Regional dynamics are too often presented as something to be taken for granted, all the more so as the development of polycentric governance in Europe opened up the playing field, facilitated a large increase in networks and intergovernmental relations, and modified opportunity structures, a factor which favours the relative autonomy of regions.

Following several studies which have put forward regions, this book attempts, using Jessop's (modified) expression, 'to put the regions back in their place', approaching them from a variety of theoretical and empirical angles. In fact, for centuries, regions and cities in Europe have been organised within nation–states, and sometimes existed even before states (that is to say, before the creation of the Committee of Regions and the Structural Funds policy). Now, transformations affecting European regions are often attributed to the European Union whereas the effects of globalisation, economic reorganisation, the internal dynamics of nation–states and regional identity-seeking mobilisation are, for the moment, undoubtedly much more important in the development of the majority of European regions than EU policies, though this scenario might change. On the other hand, if we closely observe institutional dynamics, we can see that changes come about rather slowly. Even if the state stands back or is undergoing reorganisation [Wright and Cassese, 1996; Caporaso, 1996], the weight of politico-administrative national systems remains important in European governance [Lequesne, 1997]. This point does not constitute a conservative defence of the *status quo*, but pleads for exhaustive analyses that take into account the diversity of states and European regions in the ongoing process. If European governance does have an impact on the reorganisation of states and the transformation of European regions, this impact combines with others by modifying opportunity structures and the rules of the game.

This book is then a contribution to the analysis of reorganisation between states, regions, markets, civil societies, local governments, etc. The theoretical and methodological stance adopted explains the choice that guided us. The approaches adopted by the different authors go beyond the traditional paradigms of the study of centre–periphery relations, in which the study of the periphery is conceived only as a function of the domination of the nation–state – an approach very much present in studies on ethnic regionalism. Most of the chapters in this volume form parts of theoretical currents which are not centred solely on the nation–state, namely, the models of analysis of intergovernmental relations and political economy.

However, this work is not a new comparative analysis of legal competences and the powers of the regional institutions in Europe. Nor is it a critical study of EU regional policy. Both of these dimensions have already been extensively treated in social science literature [Charpentier and Engel, 1992; Hooghe, 1996b]. Nor is this book an anthropological work on the identity of regional cultures in Europe or a semantic analysis dealing with the production of regional discourse. As political scientists mainly interested in the *governance* of European societies, we have chiefly conceived this book in order to question the forms of political regulation that regions are in a position to operate on what, in the absence of a better expression, is called the European political space [Leca, 1996]. This choice fully explains why we have chosen to bring together in this publication not only political scientists, economists and sociologists working on European regions, but also specialists on international relations, the state and cities.

Conceived on a transversal mode, the first part of the book places the region in the global context of the market, intergovernmental relations and the international system. Michael Keating's chapter reminds us how difficult it is to define a region when it escapes all norms, thus rendering the exercise very daunting. In fact, under the generic banner of region, many territorial areas can be grouped which are defined not only by history or cultural communities (Scotland, Catalonia, Flanders), but also by the simple criteria of administrative and political organisation (Pays de Loire, most of the German *Länder*). Sometimes the term region is used simply to identify an economic area, such as the virtual areas in north-east London. Furthermore, this economic area does not necessarily draw on the notion of common borders as illustrated by the example of the 'four engines' (Baden-Württemberg, Catalonia, Lombardy and Rhône-Alpes), which were grouped by the functional necessity of economic performance. Michael Keating also points out that European integration legitimates such different forms of regional mobilisation that, for the moment, it does not allow the development of any real theory of regional mobilisation. Certain public and private regional actors are, in fact, formulating demands for endogenous economic development based on the support of the Community Structural Funds, just as they are trying to use the Single Market to secure a place in world-wide competition [Jones and Keating, 1995]. Furthermore, even if it seems irrefutable that European integration supports nationalist and ethno-regionalist movements that see the region as a source of historical and cultural identity, this causal link cannot be generalised. Certain autonomy-seeking and separatist movements (for example, the Flemish and Basque movements) perceive an outright contradiction between their strategy of national liberation and the European Union which reinforces the interpenetration of economies and societies, incarnating to a certain degree the universal against their quest for diversity. Marie-Claude Smouts also rightly reminds us that specialists of international relations use the notions of region and regionalism to denote different areas of exchange and solidarity on a multi-territorial and multinational scale. However, it would be somewhat reductionist to see these areas merely as the deliberate strategies of states endeavouring to design new territories (the European Union, APEC, NAFTA, the Visegrad group) to face the functional challenges of globalisation. Marie-Claude Smouts demonstrates, on the contrary, that the transnationalisation of societal flows made visible by the activity of businessmen, consumers, traders and migrant workers, generates the emergence, *from the bottom*, of spontaneous regions, that participate in a vast movement of the deterritorialisation of politics [Badie, 1995a].

The chapters by Andy Smith and Vincent Wright bring us to the 'how' and 'why' of the interaction and exchanges that regional actors develop with the host of other actors (European Union, states and sub-regional) in the European space in order to bring about political regulations, which are generally (somewhat loosely) called public policies. In the words of Richard Balme, it is a matter of grasping European regions, beginning with the system of 'enlarged intergovernmental relations' [Balme, 1994]. Andy Smith demonstrates that the sub-regional or local level remains the preferred level for using the Structural Funds in Spain, France and the United Kingdom, and hence again no causal link can be established between EU regional policy and the strengthening of regional authorities in these three countries. From a methodological point of view, his chapter recalls the usefulness of adopting approaches such as 'local orders' [Friedberg, 1993] or 'policy networks' [Mayntz, 1993; Rhodes *et al.*, in Hooghe, 1996b; Le Galès and Thatcher, 1995] to analyse the new forms of European governance. Unwilling to dissociate *policies* from *politics*, Smith insists that the study of public policies based on policy networks should be linked to inquiries on the very nature of European integration. The nature of states, the market and European societies could be added to Smith's inquiry. This is the analytical framework that Vincent Wright proposes in his chapter. When dealing with the question of European regionalisation, Wright grounds his argument on changes in states and carefully avoids the zero sum game that claims the demise of the state. He finds justification in the fact that the state does not have a monopoly on legitimate political regulation. However, one may wonder whether the devolution of this power to the regional (or European) level was not sometimes a strategy for state elites to get rid of expensive social problems at a time when budget austerity and opposition to taxes are widespread.

To consider the dynamics of regionalism in Europe without questioning the political capacity of regions [Keating, 1992b] from the point of view of civil society would certainly have been a lacuna. The chapter by Evelyne Ritaine on southern European countries does just that. Building on the work of Italian researchers, Ritaine observes that the historical construction of social fragmentation in Italy and Spain makes it possible to take recourse to territorial mediation, in order to compensate for the weaknesses of the state. This approach enables her to criticise Putnam's work on Italy, which, in succumbing to the 'demon' of developmentalism [Putnam, 1993; see the criticism by Lupo, 1993], establishes a too evident link between the institutional performance of different Italian regions and the existence of political subcultures (civic, non-civic) which are supposedly anchored in long-term historical determinants. Ritaine's chapter thus clearly illustrates the methodological need to eschew considering the notion of regional political culture (and political culture in general) as the heritage of history but, on the contrary, as an ongoing process of exchanges and conflicts between social actors [Bagnasco, 1994; Bayart, 1996]. Examining Wright's study on the social consequences of the crisis of the welfare state (rise of individualism, social exclusion) from a political economy perspective, Mick Dunford focuses on the erosion of the institutional structures that regulate modern capitalist societies. In this new environment, according to Dunford, regions and cities have to look for ways to improve their competitiveness and above all, to try to gain a greater share of the market at the expense of others. This chapter, when considering the hypothesis that institutional factors represent critical determinants of the success or economic weakness of regions, invites us to think in a more normative way than the preceding ones about the nature of a new theory of regulation to be applied to post-Fordist regional development.

These transversal analyses were to have been completed by some national studies, especially given the rapid transformations within certain countries. We regret that for material reasons, it was not possible to take into account all the EU countries. National case studies were not intended to be a mere 'summary of the regional question' from a common framework. We asked the authors, on the one hand, to identify a problem which seemed important and, on the other, to deal clearly with a theoretical issue. The analysis and conceptualisation of sub-regional territorial dynamics are open to different types of approach which are sometimes complementary. Thus, in his chapter on Germany, Arthur Benz adopts an intergovernmental relations perspective to show how the process of European integration has triggered strong resistance from the powerful *Länder* that are faced with the forceful emergence of regions within their own area. From a similar perspective, focusing on competition between cities and regions, Theo Toonen demonstrates not the impossible quest of the regional level in The Netherlands, but rather the abundance of institutions at an intermediary level as well as efforts to organise a regional level. Stefaan de Rynck takes on Putnam's hypothesis and methodology to contrast Wallonia and Flanders but rejects historical determinism. William Genieys adopts the perspective of the development of institutions from the point of view of the strategies of intermediary political elites, their dynamism and their competition which sustain the process strengthening the Spanish Autonomous Communities. Arnaldo

Bagnasco and Marco Oberti examine Italian regions from a sociological point of view. They address the question of whether Italian regions (as institutions) play a role in the economic, social and political organisation of Italy. By outlining the changes in the social structure in the three Italies linked to the reorganisation of Italian capitalism, they outline the strengths and limits of the Northern League and the lack of importance of Italian regions. For France, Richard Balme proposes an analysis in terms of public policy and the creation of a public space which underlines the diversity of networks, and the problems which every level of government has to face, and renders the idea of regulation and regional governance problematic. Finally, John Mawson analyses the possible emergence of British regions in terms of public management which well reflects the extraordinary organisational complexity of the British politico-administrative system as well as its centralisation and fragmentation.

The concluding chapter highlights the weakness of European regions, their weak institutionalisation and their relative incapacity to organise the play of economic and social actors. European regions seem to be rather minor political actors in European governance.

Part I

The regions in Europe

1 Is there a regional level of government in Europe?*

Michael Keating

THE IDEA OF REGION

If we take the title of this chapter literally, the answer could be very short. Europe possesses no uniform or homogeneous level of regional government in the judicial, political or administrative sense. On the other hand, if we consider the notion of region or regionalism in a larger sense we find various forms of regions and regional action. The political, economic and cultural meaning of the term is undergoing important changes in Europe today. In some aspects politics, economy and governmental processes are becoming de-territorialised, but at the same time we are witnessing a re-territorialisation of economic, political and social action. New forms of regionalism and regions are emerging. This is the product of the decomposition and the recomposition of the territorial frameworks of public life, of changes in the state, the market and the international context. There is no new territorial hierarchy to replace the old one but there is a wide variety of new forms of territorial action.

The word *region* possesses a wide range of meanings in the various disciplines of social sciences and in the historical tradition of European countries.[1] While there is consensus that the term refers to space, the notion of space itself can have several meanings: territorial space; political space and the space of social interaction; economic space; functional space. A region is the result of the meeting of various concepts of space. It is also an institutional system, either in the form of a regional government or as a group of institutions operating on a territory. In this chapter the idea of region is used in the larger sense not only of the institutional system but also of the system of social and economic interchange underpinned by institutions, and as a system of action. It is in the combination of these various logics

* Translation Uttam Bharthare.

that the phenomenon of regionalism can be understood. To deal with this question we need to recall the historical development of the ideas about regions and regionalism, linked to the process of nation-building, notably the development of the post-war interventionist state. Yet regionalism is also a contemporary phenomenon, moulded by the context of European integration and of the changes which are transforming the West European state.

THE STATE AND THE REGIONS OR TOP-DOWN REGIONALISM

The nineteenth-century nation–state spurned the regions, considering them obstacles in the construction of the national identity and the modern state. Certainly, the German *Kaiserreich* was a federation but, while the federated states had some administrative autonomy, there was no real territorial balance because of the preponderance of Prussia in the federation and the autonomy of the imperial government *vis-à-vis* the territorial powers. In France, Italy and Spain, governments tried with various degrees of success to wipe out regional or provincial particularities, while in the United Kingdom, the historical nations kept some of their distinctive administrative features but without much decisional autonomy.

After the Second World War, and particularly in the 1960s, regions were recognised as an important element for the modernising state. In Germany, federalism was imposed due to the pressure of the Allies and the German desire to avoid the excesses of the national–socialist centralisation. The form of federalism was primarily influenced by the German federal tradition. In the other states regionalisation resulted rather from functional exigencies and the necessities of territorial management. In many states, notably in France, Italy and the United Kingdom, the region emerged in the 1960s as a space of action for the state. Territorial disparities were recognised as a problem (albeit marginal) within the otherwise successful macro-economic policies of the Keynesian era and the region was chosen as the appropriate level at which to address them. From broad brush policies such as industrial investment diversion, states proceeded more or less successfully with more specific interventions in the form of regional planning and development growth poles. States, including the United Kingdom and Belgium, also used a regional framework for concessions to cultural minorities policies, more or less generous (more in the case of the United Kingdom (Wales) than of France let alone Franco's Spain), linked to the cultural and linguistic singularities of the concerned territories. In France successive governments tried to strengthen the co-ordinating power of the prefects. In the United Kingdom even the Conservative Government – hostile to any idea of political decentralisation – has recently set up unified regional offices [Hogwood, 1995].[2]

In their modernisation efforts, states looked for collaborators on the ground in order to implement regional development policies and to harmonise their actions with that of the local communities and the private sector. In some cases, they wanted to renew local political elites either for partisan reasons, as with the arrival of the centre–left in Italy or the consolidation of Gaullism in France; or because they considered the existing territorial elites and their networks as not sufficiently progressive, as in France and the United Kingdom in the 1960s [Biarez, 1989]. In places where the traditional elites were considered too resistant or too attached to the traditional logic of distribution rather than to modernisation and development, states did not hesitate to by-pass them with new regional institutions, especially in southern Europe where it is very difficult to reform the system of local government, for example in France after 1972. In Spain, technocrats like Lopez Rodó, were less successful in their attempts to circumvent the apparatchiks of the *Movimiento*. Although provided for in the constitution of 1947, the establishment of regions in Italy was postponed until 1970, when political circumstances at the national level were more favourable [Pastori, 1980]. Although policies for regional development and setting up regional administrative institutions were pursued in a rather depoliticised and technocratic manner, the political implications of state intervention were soon evident. In Spain the paranoia of the Franco regime with anything to do with regionalism was such that it was impossible even to mount coherent regional policies [Garcia, 1979; Cuadrado, 1981]. In the democratic countries state intervention often destabilised the traditional systems of territorial representation and regions came to be contested by the state, by the traditional elites and the territorial notables; and by the new emerging regional actors, or *forces vives*. Political issues were increasingly seen in a regional perspective, producing a politicisation of regionalism, which was given further momentum by political mobilisation within the territories themselves.

MOBILISATION WITHIN THE REGION OR BOTTOM-UP REGIONALISM

Regionalism as a political movement has taken diverse forms. It has been linked at one time or another to almost all the ideologies, from the extreme left to the extreme right, passing through liberalism, social democracy and christian democracy. We can distinguish six ideal types, whose characteristics are combined in individual cases to produce a complex movement.

First, there is a conservative regionalism rooted in the idea of affective community which resists the modernisation embodied by the homogenising and secular state. In the nineteenth century regionalism, especially in France, was often seen as reactionary and hostile to progress [Mény, 1982b]. In the twentieth century, regionalism was a component of the Christian Democratic thought, a way of reconciling tradition with modernity, as well as an instrument to realise the principle of subsidiarity. Regionalism is not, however, a fundamental principle of Christian Democracy [Durand, 1995]; it was often subordinated to the needs of the parties, as in Italy after 1948 or even in the Sturzo period after the First World War [Zagario, 1981], or exploited for clientelistic aims [Barbera, 1985].

On the right also there is a 'bourgeois regionalism' [Harvie, 1994], associated with industrial and economically advanced regions. In these regions, a dynamic bourgeoisie tries to free itself from the obstacles of an archaic state or seeks modern governing structures to encourage industrial development. An example of this is Catalanism in its 'regionalist' phase of the nineteenth century when it was struggling for the modernisation of Spain [Oltra *et al.*, 1981; Vincens, 1986]. One can also recognise an element of bourgeois regionalism in German *Länder* such as Baden-Württemberg or present-day Catalonia. In Italy, during the 1960s the Confindustria supported the regional reforms [Rotelli, 1973] and one can detect an element of bourgeois regionalism in the present-day *Lega Norte*.

Another type of modernising regionalism is technocratic and depoliticised and less linked to class interests. We have already mentioned the regional policies of the 1960s and 1970s, motivated by a largely depoliticised vision of development and modernisation. There is a corresponding movement by actors on the ground, who see the region as a series of technical questions and favour depoliticised institutions which give a large role to technical experts and professional interests.

On the left, there is a progressive regionalism. Even in the nineteenth century there were some regionalist movements that supported the themes of progress, democracy, reforms of the state and equality, such as the short-lived *Félibrige rouge* in France [Touraine *et al.*, 1981], the progressive movements in Scotland [Keating and Bleiman, 1979] or in Wales [Morgan, 1980], the *Meridionalismo* of Dorso or Salvemini

[Galasso, 1978]. Since the 1960s, regionalism has been linked to the movements of the libertarian Left born of 1968, to ecology movements and to popular struggles against the plant closures [Keating, 1988, 1992b]. This regionalism fed on the notions of unequal development and internal colonialism which served as its ideological base [Lafont, 1967], but it remained quite weak due to the heterogeneity of its constitutive elements, and the difficulties it faced in forming an alternative model of economic development.

Another regionalism, populist and right-wing, is directed against the centralising state, against the fiscal equalisation in favour of poorer regions and against immigrants, whether these are foreigners or incomers from other regions. Examples are the *Lega Norte* [Biorcio, 1991] and the *Vlaams Blok*. Some of the regionalist movements in France have also veered to the populist extreme Right [Keating, 1985b, 1988].

Finally, separatist movements exist in the historic nations within the older European states. The strongest, not counting the case of Northern Ireland – irredentist rather than separatist – are to be found in the Basque Country and Scotland. In Catalonia and in the Belgian regions there are strong nationalist movements, but these generally aim for a new system of power in Europe and within the state, rather than seeking a state for themselves in the classical sense.

It is in the dialectical relations between the regionalisms and the state that we find the dynamics of political regionalism. Each movement contains a particular mixture of elements. Each state provides a distinct range of stimulating elements, of possibilities for action and constraints. Some of these movements can be qualified as integrating, as they aim to integrate themselves fully within the state, removing obstacles which prevent them from participating in the life of the state. Others are disintegrating and demand increased autonomy or even separation from the state. While in general since the 1960s regionalism has veered to the left, there are exceptions such as the Catalan CiU , drawing inspiration from Christian Democracy or the right-wing populism of the *Lega Norte*. Regionalism has given up its affinity with reaction and is generally associated now with democratic maturation [Sharpe, 1993b].

From time to time, states have faced crises of territorial representation. We find examples of this towards the end of the nineteenth century, at the time of the First World War, then briefly after the Second World War and during the 1970s. After each crisis West European states have succeeded in re-establishing the territorial equilibrium, but at the end of the twentieth century, the state is again facing a new regionalist wave which is calling into question the whole tradition of territorial management.

THE NEW REGIONALISM

An important phenomenon of the 1960s and 1970s, regionalism stalled after the economic crisis. The French regions established in 1972 remained weakly institutionalised and had to wait until 1986 to become local authorities elected by universal suffrage. The attempts at devolution (for Scotland and Wales) failed in the United Kingdom and the English Regional Economic Planning Councils were abolished in 1979. The institutional development of the Italian regions after the 1977 law was disappointing. In Belgium and Spain the pressure of the linguistic/nationalist movements ensured a continuous movement towards regionalisation and, indeed, even federalisation of the state. Democratisation in Spain was accompanied by the establishment of Autonomous Communities but the *LOAPA* (*Ley Orgánica de Armonización del Proceso Autonómico*) law of 1981 represented an attempt on the part of the state to recover its powers.

A new impetus was given to regionalism in Europe during the 1980s and the 1990s by economic restructuring, state reform, globalisation and especially by European integration. Economic restructuring follows two complementary logics. On the one hand, the process of transformation responds to international influences, including decisions of transnational enterprises, and capital flows. On the other, it follows a territorial logic. There is a contradiction between the border-free rationality of the transnational enterprise with its numerous branches all over the world, and the area-bound rationality of communities dependent on the investments of the enterprise [Keating, 1991]. The enterprise frees itself from territorial influences while territories become increasingly dependent on the enterprise. In the face of globalisation, the state can no longer maintain the territorial balance by policies of regional development or investment diversion. At the same time it is widely recognised that economic development and the insertion of territories in the world economy today depend on specific territorial characteristics. So development policies now lay more stress on endogenous development or on attracting investments with qualities linked to territory, such as the environment, the quality of life, the labour force, than on state subsidies [Stöhr, 1990; Gore, 1984]. Researchers have rediscovered the idea of the industrial district characterised by networks of territorial interdependence [Dunford and Kafkalas, 1992b; Morgan, 1992].

Some observers have insisted that the international and continental market and the individualisation of social relations can destroy territory as an organising principle [Badie, 1995b]; but it also creates new forms of space [Keating, 1996a; Amin and Thrift, 1994]. The new paradigm of development places emphasis on the building of identities, systems of action and territorial solidarities.

Much has been written on the crisis of the state and the end of sovereignty [Camilleri and Falk, 1992]. One should not exaggerate the decline of the state in Western Europe, in so far as it is still endowed with a formidable arsenal of powers and resources. We must also avoid the error of opposing a mythical state of the past, all powerful, monopolistic and sovereign, to the contemporary state which is weak, pluralist and shares its powers with supranational, sub-national, and private authorities. It is true, none the less, that the state has undergone a major transformation and that the spheres of social, economic, and political action have become dissociated. There exists a hiatus between the system of political representation expressed through state institutions, and decision-making which takes place in territorial and social networks; in other words, there is a divorce between *politics* and *policy*. This fragmentation of the social world can have harmful effects not only on governmental efficiency, but also on democracy and social cohesion [Touraine, 1992a,b]. Yet there is a reaction on the part of those who want to re-establish a public space and realise, however, that it must be constructed at various territorial levels and not simply on that of the state [Keating, 1995].

European integration has had very important effects on regions and regionalism [Bullman, 1994; Jones and Keating, 1995]. Market integration risks widening economic disparities, as well as depriving states of the traditional means of facing disparities, such as tariffs and subsidies [Dunford, 1994]. In the Single Market, regions are in competition to attract investments and to gain market share; this phenomenon is well known in the world's other large capitalist market, the United States. Community policies have had different effects on the various regions of the European Union [Molle and Cappelin, 1988]. At the political and institutional levels, the building of the Community and the European Union (EU) has modified the state–region relationship. First, it has given states an opportunity to centralise policy, using the doctrine that Community affairs are foreign policy, even when they concern matters of regional competence [Keating and Jones, 1985]. Since the Single European Act (1987), there has been a reaction from the regions which insist on being heard by the EU institutions as well as by the national governments when they are preparing negotiations within the EU. The regional policy of the EU, which began in 1970 as an inter-state compensatory fund, grew in the 1980s into a fully-fledged policy [Marks, 1992; Hooghe and Keating, 1994]. The structural funds were increased to become the second most important item in the Community budget, about 25 per cent of the total expenditure. The Commission insisted, more or less successfully, on the principles of additionality and transparency, to ensure that region and not state budgets benefited from them. A planning system was set up, with a partnership between the regions, the states and the Commission, allowing some direct links between the regions and the Commission. Although the states are still in control of the Community's regional policy, Community interventions have none the less encouraged a strong regional mobilisation, together with the emergence of new actors. Some countries have even established regional structures in order to conform more closely to the rules governing the allocation of the Structural Funds, for example, in Ireland [Holmes and Reese, 1995]. In other countries like France and Germany, the exigencies of European competition have put on the agenda the need to strengthen regional institutions and to redraw regional boundaries [Némery, 1993; Benz, 1992b].

In this restructured political space in Western Europe, regions are emerging in two ways. They are political arenas in which various political, social, and economic actors meet and where important issues such as economic development are debated and decisions taken. Simultaneously, they have become actors in the national and Community political arenas, pursuing their own specific interests. The region is not a natural creation but a social construct in a given space [Agnew, 1987; Balme, 1994]. But what is the nature of this regional space, and can one speak of a regional area when the phenomenon is so heterogeneous?

REGIONAL SPACE

We can speak about regional space as a territorial space, a functional space and a political space. Most of the regions appeared rather late on the institutional scene, but wherever there is a space, they can be institutionalised, they can become political forums and eventually constitute themselves as actors.

Territorial space

A region is a territorial entity, but the definition of this territory varies greatly from case to case. One can define regional space negatively as the intermediary level between the state and municipal government, although this definition has to admit exceptions. Where there is a tradition of strong and autonomous municipal government in combination with a unitary state, as in the Netherlands or the Scandinavian countries, there is little room for regions. Elsewhere, regions exist on different territorial levels. There are the metropolitan regions, established around large cities with their hinterland, connected by economic and transport links, and a system of functional interdependence. There are provincial regions resulting from the division of the entire state into large units; other regions were created on the basis of smaller traditional units or are 'leftovers' remaining after the neighbouring regions have been delineated. Within the same state one can see regions on many different levels. In Germany there are the *Flächenstaaten* (ranging in size from North Rhine Westphalia to the Saarland) and the *Stadtstaaten* (Hamburg, Bremen and Berlin). In Spain there are large regions such as Catalonia or Andalusia, and simple provinces which became Autonomous Communities, such as La Rioja or Cantabria. Even on the European scale, there is no single definition of the region. The European Commission uses the NUTS system with three levels but these are mere aggregates of national administrative units for the implementation of its regional policy [Hooghe and Keating, 1994].

Functional space

It is also difficult to generalise about the functions which are specific to the regions. Generally, as a territorial and functional intermediary level, the regions have powers of planning and programming. They are also an important level for economic intervention. The new models of economic development, which stress vocational training, the building of networks, external economies of scale, local small and medium-sized firms, the environment and the quality of life, point to the region rather than the state as the appropriate level for intervention. The necessity of co-ordination in employment catchment areas and the need to avoid mutually harmful competition, call for a level of intervention which goes well beyond the local.[3] Vocational training has been regionalised and localised in several countries including France and the United Kingdom.

Regions play an important cultural role, especially in places where there is an ethnic or linguistic particularity. It is not always easy to link the handling of linguistic and cultural issues to territory because the groups concerned are rarely concentrated within borders corresponding to regions as defined by other functional criteria. Only a minority of people speak Welsh in Wales and Breton in Brittany. In Belgium, regionalisation corresponds only partially with cultural autonomy because the region and the linguistic community coincide only within the Flemish government [Hooghe, 1991].

On the other hand, regions generally do not have much responsibility in matters of social solidarity. The welfare state remains the responsibility of the national state and solidarity at the community level is a matter for municipal government and politics.

Regional governments can position themselves in areas where there is a lacuna in the institutional coverage of the state. When the regions are not strongly institutionalised – due to lack of elected local governments – they can become a *terra incognita* or a no man's land, that is a free area where new groups and social movements can establish themselves on the margins of the power system. It is not a coincidence that new social movements, such as ecologists, feminists and pacifists, have often sided with regionalism. Corporate interests can also establish themselves in regional institutions where there is neither hierarchical bureaucratic control from the state nor horizontal control by the elected government. A notable example is provided by quangos in the United Kingdom (and particularly in England) colonised by the technocracy [Hogwood and Keating, 1982]. In several countries, economic development agencies were insulated from political influence to allow them to respond to the exigencies of the market, although in Italy they were later colonised by the political class and made to serve their clientelistic interests. States may also locate some functions at the regional level to insulate them from political pressures and financial demands, especially in the case of functions like public health where expenditure is hard to control: [Sharpe, 1993b].

At the territorial as well as at the functional level, regions can serve as intermediaries or relays. The *CODER* (*Commission de développement économique régionale*) in France and the REPCs (Regional Economic Planning Councils) in the United Kingdom were used to aggregate regional interests and to encourage a dialogue with the state. The system of regional decentralisation, such as regional prefects in France, regional offices in England, or the system of co-ordination, such as administrative conferences in France or regional economical planning boards in England,[4] were meant to make the state's own action more coherent in the field in these two countries.[5] Unfortunately, this idea of co-ordination was too often understood in the technical sense rather than the political one and failed. The German system of co-operative federalism provides a more politicised and institutionalised model of territorial co-ordination, but which is hard to export to countries which do not have a tradition of political consensus.

Political space

Political space means a space in which political debate takes place, a space recognised by political actors in which decisions are taken and legitimised. This may not necessarily correspond to autonomous government institutions. Scotland, for example, constitutes a political space with internal debates and political issues which are specific to it although it does not have political autonomy.[6] On the other hand, the French and the Italian regions, though they have elected governments, are not political spaces but relays of partisan national systems or federations of local units. The German *Länder*, the Belgian regions and the Spanish Autonomous Communities, especially the historic nations of Catalonia, Galicia and the Basque Country, are at the same time political spaces and autonomous institutional systems.

The constitution of a political space depends on several factors. One of the fundamental elements is the feeling of identity which may be the result of ethnic or linguistic solidarity, or which may be based on institutions and an organic solidarity. This feeling of identity is not a historical given which persists independently of institutions. In historic nations such as Catalonia or Scotland, a process of nation-building is under way to adapt their historical identities to the exigencies of the modern world [Keating, 1996b]. In other regions such as Brittany, there is a rich historical tradition which is adapting itself with more difficulty [Guillorel, 1991]. On the other hand, in the German *Länder*, which were mostly created artificially after the Second World War, the feeling of identity was developed by the political institutions. In Italy, although there exists a strong local identity, identification with the administrative regions is weaker, even among supporters of the *Lega Lombarda* [Woods, 1995].

The party system plays an important role in the building of a political space. In places where distinct parties exist or state parties adapt themselves to the local situation, such as Catalonia, the Basque Country, Scotland and Corsica, political issues can more easily be regionalised. In France, with the exception of Corsica, the party system is not regionalised. In Italy of the *Partitocrazia*, regional party structures were quite weak compared to the provincial level [Dente, 1985]. The *Lega Lombarda/Lega Nord* explicitly introduced regionalist themes into Italian political discourse; but these themes were transposed later into a more general populism [Schmidtke, 1993] and a pronounced anti-statism [Savelli, 1992]. On the other hand, in Spain the regional personalities are gaining influence within the national parties and a real regional political class is emerging. The regional electoral system is also important. The French system makes it difficult to forge coherent majorities in the regional councils and favours interests based in the constituent *départements*. The existence of distinct media is another element which helps the building of a political space, while the existence of distinct political questions fosters a regionally focused debate.

Regions do not exist only as structures of government, but also as a principle of organisation in civil society. Some studies show that regional government works better when civil society is well developed, has a sense of identity, civic traditions, community life, and relations of confidence and interchange [Putnam *et al.*, 1985; Putnam, 1993). The origins of this civil society are less clear. It is only in France that a serious effort has been made to trace out the continuities and the discontinuities of social and political behaviour in the territories through history. Even if the conditions of institutionalisation are indeed more favourable in certain regions than in others, politics still has some room left to manoeuvre in the shaping of a civil society. Piattoni [1996] shows how changes were achieved in certain regions of the Mezzogiorno through political action. We have already mentioned the case of Catalonia and Scotland where the elites are refashioning an identity or as Jordi Pujol puts it, *fer país*. In Wales a new identity is replacing the old one; it is concerned more with economic development and the insertion of the region in the new Europe, than with old cultural and historical questions [Jones, 1996].

The region is both a functional and a political system. It is a place for taking decisions and it is also an actor in the state, European and international systems. The way these two dimensions are articulated and their connection in practice depends on the institutionalisation of the region.

REGIONS AS INSTITUTIONS

To the variety of regionalisms correspond different modes of regional government. In certain cases, regional institutions are simply decentralised arms of the state. In the United Kingdom, the administrations of Scotland, Wales and Northern Ireland are parts of the central government and are governed by national ministers. In France a system of state administration coexists with the administration of regional councils in the regions. Regional administration can also be constituted of *ad hoc* agencies whose directors are named by the state, the unions and the employers, and the local communities, as is often the case in the United Kingdom.

If we are talking of regional *government*, however, we should restrict ourselves to autonomous institutions elected by universal suffrage. Here, too, there are different models. The most advanced model is federalism which is to be found in Germany, Austria, Belgium and Switzerland. It is also possible that Spain is evolving towards a federal system. In federal states, the regions have constitutionally guaranteed powers and the right to participate in national politics through territorially based second legislative chambers or through a system of institutional co-operation. Then there are systems with strong regionalism such as Spain. During the Second Republic, Spanish governments, seeking to reconcile unity with their desire to avoid the federalisation of the country and the weakening of the central power, developed the idea of the *Estado Integral* [Hernandez, 1980]. The same compromise between unity and diversity is implied in the Spanish Constitution of 1978, through the *Estado de las Autonomías*. In France and Italy there are regions with limited powers and without great autonomy. There is also the formula of asymmetric regionalisation adopted by certain states as a response to specific territorial demands, while maintaining a unitary constitution. Italy and France have regions with particular status (Sicily, Sardinia, Valle d'Aosta, Trentino-Alto Adige, Friuli–Venezia–Giulia, Corsica). Similarly, in the United Kingdom, from 1922 to 1972 Northern Ireland had its own parliament while the Labour Party is currently proposing a special status for Scotland and Wales. The institutionalisation of the regions does not depend solely on their constitutional status. Where municipal government is strong, it represents an institutional rival to the regions. Thus in France the regions compete with the *départements* and the large cities, who have benefited the most from decentralisation, while the *Generalitat* of Catalonia rivals the city of Barcelona. In Italy, the regions often find it difficult to find their place between communes, provinces and the state [Cassese and Torchia, 1993]. Despite the Europeanisation of the regions, state traditions continue to be very influential. In France, Italy, Spain and the United Kingdom, the traditions of centralisation are deeply rooted in political practices and the state bureaucracy. In the French administrative tradition public policies are often shared between the state and the regions, which forces the regions to accept national priorities and subsidise activities, such as universities and railways, which are the responsibility of the central government. The intertwining of state and regional action continues all through the process of implementation. Only the peculiarly French form of personalised power linked to national power networks can counter this institutional weakness. In Italy, central government also possesses parallel responsibilities and continues to legislate on matters of regional competence [Ministro per gli affari regionali, 1982]. The relations between the state and the regions are sectoralised and there is often detailed intervention on the part of the central ministries [Merloni, 1985].

In Germany, on the other hand, the federal government does not have its own territorial administration, except in some clearly defined spheres such as military matters, and depends on the *Länder* for the implementation of its policies. In Spain and Italy, the territorial administration of the central states acts as a brake on the autonomous action of the regions, a factor which motivated Manuel Fraga's recommendation for a single regional administration, according to the German model.

AUTONOMY

The institutionalisation of the regions is accompanied with more or less a large degree of autonomy. Traditionally, regional autonomy was considered a matter of bilateral relations between the regions and the state, a zero-sum game. Nowadays matters are more complex. First, with the EU there is a 'third level' of politics [Bullman, 1994] and a pattern of triangular relationships between the regions, the states and the European authorities [Jones and Keating, 1995; Petschen, 1993]. The regions try to influence the EU policies through various means: pressure on their own governments, inter-regional lobbies, and partnerships established by the Commission to implement its regional policy [Keating and Hooghe, 1995; Engel, 1994]. At one time some regions thought that it was possible for them to compensate their exclusion from national politics by establishing direct ties with the Commission. In practice, it turns out that regions which are well connected with the national circuits of influence are the ones who exercise the greatest influence in Brussels. The resources of influence are cumulative and the regions cannot easily substitute one for another. Nevertheless the EU has opened territorial politics to new influences. So regional politics is increasingly Europeanised, while national politics is both Europeanised and regionalised. Public policies at the regional level are now rarely discussed without taking into account the influence of Community policies and of the Single Market.

A second influence which has favoured the opening of regional politics is the increase in cross-border relations between regions of different states. With the Single Market, regions are subject to contradictory logics. On the one hand, they compete for market share, investments and technology; on the other, they seek opportunities for co-operation. Regions seek ties with foreign partners for a number of reasons. The main ones are economic: regions seek investment, technology transfers, and markets for their exports. In some cases there are also cultural motivations linked to the recognition or the widespread use of minority languages. Finally, there are political motivations. Regional leaders use their external projection as a means of building up a strong identity at home, by postulating a strong general interest for the region in contrast with the outside world – of course, this can also serve the prestige and promotional interests of the leaders themselves. Even though there is no real prospect of regions replacing the states or even competing with them as actors on the international scene, their actions are nowadays modifying the traditional roles [Hocking, 1996].

The third element to be taken into account is the relation between the region and the market. In an open economy, regions depend on the continental or even world markets for investments, for the sale of their products, and for the resources necessary to meet their other priorities. The paradox of decentralisation is that the more autonomy regions gain from the state, the less the state protects them from market forces and so they become increasingly dependent on the market. This shows once again that there is no independence in the present-day world, but only strategies for managing dependencies. The relation with the market varies a lot from region to region, depending on resources, on the capacity to attract investments, the level of economic development, the technological assets and the labour force.

There are also large differences in the will to establish an autonomous regional power, especially between the rich and the poor regions. The latter often prefer centralisation because it allows their regional actors to have access to the central government. So in Spain, the poorer regions of Andalucia and Extremadura had privileged relations with the Socialist government of Spain between 1982 and 1996. Rich regions, when they dominate the state, may also support centralisation, as in

France and the United Kingdom. On the other hand, rich regions which have no privileged links with the central government, such as Catalonia and Lombardy, are likely to seek autonomy.

Instead of talking about regional autonomy, it would be preferable to introduce the notion of governing capacity [Keating, 1991], that is to say the capacity to plan and execute a development project. The nature of the project differs from region to region depending on the balance of social forces. Sometimes we find a project oriented towards the international market, sometimes a project with a larger social content tries to adapt the market's impact on the region. The project sometimes lays stress on the cultural development as an instrument for collective action. In regions with strong regional governments, political forces may lead the development project. In other cases leadership is determined by the combination of internal pressure, from firms, unions, social movements and political forces, and external circumstances. In some cases, the external circumstances are decisive and the region then has no capacity to impose its priorities.

REGIONAL POWER

The power of regions can be analysed through seven dimensions:

1 institutions;
2 policy-making capacity;
3 powers;
4 the power of integration;
5 financial resources;
6 the intergovernmental system;
7 relations with the market.

Institutions

Institutions include not only political or administrative institutions, but also those belonging to the civil society and economy. Amin and Thrift [1994] use the concept of *institutional thickness* to describe the density of institutions and their interaction.

Policy-making capacity

There are some regions which have a political system, a decision-making capability and which can legitimately establish a 'regional interest'. There are others which lack this unity of action and are reduced to being simple relays of other systems of action.

Powers

It is obvious that the powers attributed to the regions are an important factor, especially in cases where they have a real decisional autonomy. When these powers are divided or shared with the central government instead of being largely given to them, the role of the regions often becomes secondary and subordinate to the state, as in France and Italy.

The power of integration

Regions are territorially and functionally intermediary institutions. Their power depends mainly on the capacity for integration which ensues from their knowledge and control of political and policy-making networks. Regions can strategically position themselves within the networks or can be marginalised. The power of integration also depends on the existence of partners in civil society. Where capital and labour organisations exist at the regional level, some type of harmonised action is possible although, given their overall weakness, it would be an exaggeration to talk of a regional corporatism [Anderson, 1992].

Financial resources

To implement public policies, regions need resources but also a degree of freedom in their allocation. The power to levy tax allows the regions a greater freedom if they dispose of a substantial tax base. Otherwise tax freedom strengthens the dependence *vis-à-vis* the market because they are obliged to maintain their tax base by attracting investment and this requires concessions to the owners of capital. It is not necessary for the region to dispose of large financial sums. Large budgets can even become a source of weakness if they bring with them administrative burdens and subject the regions to pressures from service providers and clients. The power of integration depends on the degree of freedom in the allocation of resources which allows the regions to intervene in a strategic manner. In the absence of their own tax base, they are forced to play along with the intergovernmental system.

The intergovernmental system

This refers to the relations between the regions and the state and the EU authorities. In some cases this is a relation of dependence, while in others the regions can influence national and European policies. There are institutional relations (in Germany), personal relations (in southern Europe), partisan relations (in Spain, the United Kingdom, Belgium), and also networks of personal power found notably in France, the product of a complex process of legitimisation composed of territorial, personal, institutional and partisan elements [Abélès, 1989].

Relations with the market

For economic development, which is one of their main tasks, the regions depend on the market. They cannot control the market, but they can sometimes manage the specific conditions of their insertion in national, European or world markets. Of course, some regions, being in a favourable market position, find this easier than others.

CONCLUSION

There is no level of regional government in Europe because such a level is not conceivable in a world where the link between the territory and the political power has been so attenuated. Power is dispersed in networks and multiple spheres of authority [Badie, 1995b; Keating, 1996a; Camilleri and Falk, 1992; Lenoir and Lesourne, 1992]. In this context there are some regions which can impose a territorial order and intervene as actors in these complex new systems. In other cases, large cities will take the upper hand. Elsewhere strong states will maintain their power, albeit challenged by new territorial and sectoral power centres. Finally, there are territories which do not have the capacity to impose their own logic and will be forced into dependence on the state or on the international market. Regionalism is a complex phenomenon which cannot be reduced to the notion of a 'level' in the new territorial hierarchy.

NOTES

1 As Perry Anderson [1994, p. 6] puts it, 'From the outset, the term was highly indeterminate – floating between the specifically territorial and the generically sectoral, and lending itself to any number of metaphorical applications or extensions'.

2 In Scotland and Wales, a single administration already exists in the Scottish Office and the Welsh Office.
3 Experience suggests that small investment premiums can influence decisions on the location of investments within a region but are less effective in attracting investments from other regions. So in fragmented urban areas, local governments are tempted to attract investment by incentives and bonuses which benefit the shareholders and are at the expense of the taxpayer but do not have any impact on employment.
4 In Scotland and Wales, the system was a little different, because of the existence of territorial ministries of central government.
5 For example, see Braudel [1986] and Le Bras [1995]. On Europe, see Todd [1990].
6 This chapter was written before the referendums of September 1997 in Scotland. Hence the crisis of government legitimacy in Scotland [Keating, 1996a].

2 The region as the new imagined community? *[1]

Marie-Claude Smouts

In times when the principle of territorial sovereignty is being damaged both from the top by transnational modernism and from the bottom by the new definition of old identities [Badie, 1995b], the upswing in favour of the idea of the region is not purely fortuitous. In the imagination of the actors and observers, regionalisation is seen as the ultimate means of safeguarding the regulatory functions of the territory; it is a political process with which some very precise powers are associated to guarantee a certain internal and international order. The region would allow the principle of territoriality to adapt itself to new economic, cultural, sub-national and transnational logics which are now calling it into question. With the regional parameter, the famous distinction between 'spatial distribution' (*area is a social concept*) and 'territorial strategy' (*territory is a political construct*) would lose its relevance [Sack, 1986]. With its mobilising virtues coupled with a great flexibility, the region would simultaneously reconcile modernisation and tradition, the territory and the soil, mastery of the future and the rewriting of history.

Does a construction, so heavily charged with meaning, have any reality or is it but a discursive representation? Will the regional construction/development bring forth new substitute models in the domestic and the international order?

AN INDEFINABLE CATEGORY

It is a characteristic of the region to have neither a definition nor an outline. The empirical criteria which allow the socio-economic entity to be recognised as sufficiently homogeneous and distinct, are vague and mixed. The 'region' category regroups disparate aggregates and

*Translation Uttam Bharthare and Claire O'Neal.

the same term serves to denote sub-national formations, intermediaries between the local and the national levels within the state (Bavaria, Catalonia, Lombardy, Aquitaine), various co-operation zones including states, indeed, entire subcontinents (the South-American cone, North America, the Pacific region), and trans-border areas between several sub-national regions belonging to different states (Neisse,[2] the new economic development zones in East Asia[3]).

In order to clarify things, five levels of 'regionness' have been distinguished [Hettne, 1994].

1 The region as a geographical and ecological unit delimited by natural barriers (but when the author gives as examples 'Europe from the Atlantic to the Urals' or the Indian sub-continent one may be a little confused).
2 The region as a more or less conflictual social system of cultural, political and economic interaction.
3 The region as an organised co-operation in cultural, economic, and political or military fields, institutionalised by the multilateral regional organisations.
4 The region as a civil society emerging from a culture, social communication and the convergence of values.
5 The region as a historical formation of a distinct identity acting as a political actor and endowed with a certain level of legitimacy (the European Union).

Curiously, this list does not take into account the administrative partitioning carried out by the central government in order to manage the national territory: the 'region', for example, in the French, Italian or Spanish sense.

When such carved-out areas come into existence, after difficult bargaining between the state and the regional entities concerned, the definition of the region is given by the national administrations. At first sight it seems quite certain: a well-traced out geographical framework, the attribution of specific powers, often the structures of regional government and elected representatives (with certain notable exceptions such as the United Kingdom). However, even in the European framework where the region has for a long time been recognised as an object of national and Community public action, this mode of territorial determination remains problematic [Botella, 1994]. Thus, as Richard Balme points out [1994, p. 240], to frame the regional policy of the European Union, the Commission bases itself on types of statistical measures which vary according to the case. The Community area is sometimes divided into 64 major regions (the 16

German *Länder*, the 7 French economic developmental zones), sometimes into 824 units (the 96 French *départements*, the 65 counties and local regional authorities of the United Kingdom), sometimes according to the definitions of regions chosen by the national administrations (26 French regions, 17 Autonomous Communities of Spain, 20 Italian regions).

When the Maastricht Treaty mentions the regions, it refers to vaguely defined areas, 'zones' ('The Community shall aim at reducing disparities between the levels of development of the various regions and the backwardness of the least favoured regions, including rural areas', art. 130 A). When it set up a Committee of Regions (art. 198 A) or plans to develop the trans-European networks (art. 129 B), it did not make a distinction between the local and the regional.

Any partitioning does pose problems. Within the same country the regions may have different status (in Spain and Italy, for example), they are always a response to specific histories (what do Corsica and the rural areas of the Loire, Andalusia and Catalonia, the eastern *Länder* and Baden-Württemberg have in common?). Between states the policies of regional construction vary and states pursue their own different logics: what is the common denominator between Germany's absorption of five new *Länder*, the decentralisation policy adopted by the French state since 1982, and the regional policies of Greece or Portugal where the regions do not exist as administrative units?

The impossibility of viewing the region both as a concept and a perimeter of real interacting groups at the same time indicates the substantial difficulty involved in understanding a continually changing process which, in the absence of a well-defined typology with precise criteria, escapes generalisation. Isolating the sub-national regions of the European Union, for the purposes of analysis, from other expressions of regionalisation in other parts of the world, is a temptation and certainly a necessity when we come to the indispensable comparisons and case studies. However, an *a priori* approach of this kind would be reductionist. First, because a number of regions want to participate in international competition by accepting the challenge of globalisation of production and the networks. They are not insensitive to the various modes of regionalisation elsewhere in the world. Second, German reunification has plunged the European Union in the maelstrom of territorial reorganisation in Central Europe and the prospect of an eastward enlargement will only emphasise the need to understand the general mechanisms of trans-border exchanges and the forging of new territorial stakes. Finally, the problems raised by regionalisation all over the world can help to fine-tune a mode of questioning specific to the European regions.

THE SEARCH FOR A RELEVANT AREA

The transformation of the international system has set all the actors – political forces and bureaucratic machineries, economic operators and private networks, citizens and identity groups – off in frantic pursuit of a relevant area for action. Everywhere in the world dynamic forces are at work, tracing out new borders within the states, cutting across existing multinational wholes and creating new areas of exchange, if not of solidarity. New competing forms of regionalisation are coming up, sometimes intentionally, sometimes accidentally, sometimes real, sometimes imaginary.

The officially designed region

The challenges of the Westphalian division of international territory were first analysed from the viewpoint of political economy within the 'regionalisation vs globalisation' scenario. Those claiming that distances were abolished, geography was definitely outdated and globalisation was triumphant [O'Brien, 1992], were opposed by those who saw proximity as a key determinant in international exchanges.[4] Gradually the representation of a new 'regionalisation of the world' imposed itself with the making of three major commercial blocs (the famous 'Triad') superimposing itself on the classical inter-state system. The new vision of 'the regionalisation from the top' replaced the geopolitics of the cold war with a new geo-economy. A 'co-operative' regionalism with a liberal external policy conforming to multilateral rules [Sapir, 1993], appeared to be the best means to manage globalisation and obtain the gradual opening up of fiercely competing national economies. But above all regionalism offered an ordering principle. The picture of a world divided in three sub-groups around the United States, Europe and Japan replaced the picture of a world divided in two by the East–West cleavage. As in the time of rigid bi-polarity, the existence of two blocs limited the possibilities of non-alignment and forced all the regrouping tendencies into one or the other camp, in the same way the proliferation of sub-regional agreements has first to be considered in relation to the dominant zones: MERCOSUR in relation to NAFTA, ASEAN in relation to APEC, the Visegrad group in relation to the European Union, etc. On this view, regionalisation was a deliberate strategy by the states, supported by multinational firms. Its instruments were borrowed from the classic panoply of institutions and regional agreements: free trade agreements, customs unions and the development of common markets.

Such a sketchy presentation could not explain the deep differences between the integration process taking place in the three major regions under consideration: Europe, America and the Asian–Pacific region. It put on the same level the project of political unification pursued in the European Union, the judicial and institutional garb provided to the American domination by the NAFTA agreements (more than 2,000 pages), with its heavy treading on the sovereignty of Mexico and Canada, particularly in matters regarding the environment and the right to work, and the very flexible economic integration in Asia moving ahead with a minimum of texts, without any constraining institution, with the shared concern of all to avoid the creation of a 'bloc'. In addition, this representation did not understand the intensity of reorganisations between the sub-regions within as well as outside the three mega-regions, and the novel character of the dynamics in operation.

Jean Coussy has clearly shown the limits of this 'economic fantasy of regionalisation' put together by the analysts and the political actors. By underlining the phenomenon of 'de-regionalisation' by the 'erosion of existing zones', he aptly remarks: 'instead of regionalisation, it would be more appropriate to talk of the reorganisation of regions' [Coussy, 1995].

Thus, regionalisation 'from the top' did not have the expected, or dreaded, outcome. On the economic level its reality is contested. The battle of indicators continues to be keen about 'globalisation/regionalisation' in the commercial exchanges between the members of the 'Triad'. The effects of regional construction on the well-being of the populations involved are still being debated.

At the socio-political level, the phenomenon is still too recent for final conclusions to be drawn but one can already see the phenomenon of polarisation which has such profoundly devastating effects: the example of Mexico or China is quite telling in this regard. Investments, technology, jobs flood into these transnationalised areas. Growth becomes concentrated in the adjoining areas. This type of regionalisation accentuates the developmental inequalities on the national territory and widens the disparities.

On the other hand, regionalisation 'from the top' works only if it is understood 'at the bottom' by entrepreneurs, tradesmen, workmen, consumers, etc. The increase in the transnational flows is accompanied and fed by the development of private networks. In return, these private networks ensure increased social regulatory functions with increasingly larger groups [Bach, 1994]. The attitude of the state *vis-à-vis* the logic of private actors and this movement of territorial expansion and contraction is ambiguous. It dreads them while at the same time encouraging them. It uses them without controlling them. Often it abandons its responsibility of supervising large sections of the territory. In extreme cases it ends up securing its survival only by its break-up and its 'de-territorialisation': this paradox is expressed in the excellent formula of Roland Pourtier as 'the archipelago State'.[5] The state then hinges around the relays dominated by the local political bosses controlling vast regions placed in the circuits of trans-national economy, either legally or illegally [Pourtier, 1987; Bach, 1995b].

The spontaneous region

These new forms of regionalisations have nothing to do with the notion of 'integration' which developed during the 1960–70 decade, from the European experience. That idea stressed the will of co-operation between the elites and national bureaucracies. The emergence of a supranational entity through the fusion of states was to be its final accomplishment. This form of regionalisation develops without the formal will of inter-governmental co-operation, beyond political and ideological co-operation. It is the result of transnational flows generated by thousands of daily decisions made by the local actors, businessmen, consumers, migrant workers, small traders, etc. This is what we call 'neo-regionalism' [De Melo, 1993; Badie, 1995b]. New areas of exchange with fairly large geographical dimensions are drawn up and they come to form spontaneous regions on the margins of existing areas. The case of Asia is exemplary in this regard, the zone of the Sea of Japan,[6] and especially the 'triangles' within the zone of the South China Sea (see note 2). New growth zones are being chalked out and are forming distinct regional areas, although still timidly defined, within larger groupings such as ASEAN or APEC. Some of them are largely de-territorialised: the state there no longer has a monopoly on legitimate violence and taxes. Kidnappings, ransoms, crime, racketeering, private justice are accompanying the phenomenal expansion of special economic zones in South China. Guangdong has become one of the most dangerous regions in the world for businessmen.

In Africa, the border phenomena have been known and studied for a long time [Igue, 1988]. Sometimes they are the result of the changeover of entire populations into the informal economy

[Mbembe, 1994]. They do not wipe out the borders between the states, in fact, they benefit from them. Daniel Bach has shown for Western Africa how parallel economies benefit from the monetary disparities on both sides of the frontiers which were inherited from the colonial times and how the economic knitting of adjoining areas is all the closer when the borders are strongly traced out [Bach, 1995a].

The whole question is whether the increase in and fact of making exchange areas autonomous, responding solely to a business logic, can create long-lasting and institutionalised political configurations. The transnational dynamics active in these zones weigh on the organisation of the production, the financial movements, the wage returns and the workings of the market. They structure dominant relationships, generate particular forms of accumulation and call into question the material basis of political power. In this sense, neo-regionalism is an area of political action although the actors may not always be aware of it. But does it give rise to new modes of regulation with the setting up of common rules on the basis of shared satisfaction? One can doubt this. Neo-regionalism traces out vague, moving borders which cross pre-existing state and regional areas and keep on changing on the whims of the market. But it does not generate an identity-related awareness.[7]

The chosen region

The links woven by history and geography create 'natural' areas of exchange of which the recent examples in Africa, the Caucasus or the Balkans remind us that they do not necessarily form areas of solidarity, still less 'security communities'. Different communities (or those perceiving themselves as such), totally interlocked, find it difficult to perceive of themselves as a distinct 'region'. The choice is too difficult (the case of Moldova is interesting in this regard: which region to choose?). They waver between the identity of the soil, belonging to a community, faithfulness to a state as defined at a given moment. In places where the populations do not perceive themselves as a group, the 'region' cannot fulfil its outlining function. Conversely, neither homogeneity nor proximity are required to produce the phenomenon of regional identification: resumption of nuclear tests by France was enough for the coastal populations of the Pacific, thousands of kilometres apart and totally separated by culture, history, and level of development, to turn the Pacific into a region.

The chosen region by definition is a subjective space. It is constructed out of symbolic representations which operate a synthesis between the current data, a reinvented past and a coveted future. It defines a new area to be mobilised for action: it offers resources, legitimises practices, and structures strategies. It establishes a stake, all the more valuable, as the symbolic creation is driven by the real ambitions of some to secure material and non-material resources.

THE EUROPEAN CASE IN PARTICULAR

The phenomenon of the region in Europe has enough diversity for us to find a scattering of some traits borrowed from these three forms of regionalisations but they share one undeniable particularity: the building of the European Community has decisively marked the relations of its members to territoriality.

The continuous extension of Community policies, both in the fields covered by them and the range of powers pooled by the states have progressively made the European countries accustomed to what Bertrand Badie calls 'multiple territoriality'. Different levels of authority operate on the same territory. Public policies, sometimes national ones, sometimes Community ones, are implemented depending on the nature of questions. The competing actors have long since learned how to structure their strategies through a complex mesh of distinct areas, local, national, and those controlled by Brussels. With its inherent vagueness, the notion of 'subsidiarity' illustrates quite clearly the flexibility of the European area. There no longer is an *a priori* defined principle of territoriality. All depends on the nature, on the objectives, on 'the dimensions or the effects of the envisaged action' (art. 3B).

The encouragement given to the regional fact by the Community policy has produced an unprecedented dialectic in other parts of the world. Community regional policy is participating in the fashioning of a European territory. It aims to 'promote a harmonious development of the whole Community' by reducing the gap between levels of development not of the Member States but of the 'different regions' (art. 130 A). It turns the development of Euro-regions and the increase in trans-border co-operation networks into an integration laboratory. By putting the regional question on the agenda and giving it important subsidies, it has created effects, giving rise to 'objective' regional areas in places where they did not exist. In return, a number of interested actors – national governments, notably local administrations, regional lobbies – have been mobilised to join the European networks and access the Community funds (a mechanism very well described by Balme *et al.*, 1995).

There is nothing to show that by doing this the region will be led to introduce a new territoriality which will have priority and will marginalise other areas of political action. Of course, it is introducing new structures, new stakes, new action repertoires, new political transactions. It is modifying the distribution of resources, and the relations between the actors at all levels, whether they are local, national, or international. But it is only one among other areas for mobilisation. It is part of a flexible functional regulatory mode which is now becoming common throughout the world.

NOTES

1 This chapter is part of a reflection on the subject of regionalisation in the world and particularly in Asia, conducted at the Centre d'Etudes et de Recherches Internationales (CERI). It owes much to Bertrand Badie, Jean Coussy and Denis Martin as well as to Jean-Luc Domenach, David Cameroux and Jean Marie Bouissou and I am grateful to them.
2 The 'Euroregion' which links Saxony, North Bohemia and the Polish Sudetenland and which plays a leading role in the process of the territorial recomposition of the German, Polish and Czech states [Bafoil, 1995].
3 Hong Kong and the Guangdong, Taiwan and the Fujian province, the triangle of growth between Singapore and a part of Indonesia and Malaysia, etc. [Gipouloux, 1994].
4 [Gemdev, 1994].
5 The expression was coined to describe some of the African states such as Zaire or the Cameroon. Is Italy's case completely different?
6 It covers Far Eastern Siberia, the North-East of China, West of Japan and the Korean Peninsula. See the thesis by Karoline Postel-Vinay, *Japanese Actors and Transnational Relations in the Zone of the Sea of Japan* [1996].
7 For a reflection on the essence of politics compared to popular modes of social action, see Bayart *et al.*,1992, pp. 27-52.

3 Intergovernmental relations and regional government in Europe

A sceptical view

Vincent Wright

Over the last twenty years throughout Europe we have been witnessing great changes both in the structure of intergovernmental relations and in regional government. In France, the slow process of decentralisation, begun by the Socialists in 1982, has established its own dynamic and has created new power configurations, some of which are centred on the regional layer of government. In Italy, the regionalisation of the state progresses by fits and starts, and has become embroiled in debates about reshaping the Italian state – debates by constitutional reformers as well as fuelled by Northern Italian resentment against financial transfers to the South. Federalism is now firmly on the political agenda. Portugal and Greece are taking the first hesitant steps on the regional path. Germany has seen the absorption of the Eastern *Länder* after the traumatic process of reunification and is experiencing some problems in managing that absorption process. But even before reunification the traditional federal system was experiencing several tensions, notably over regional disparities and financial transfers. Spain has been caught up in a continuing process of asymmetric regionalisation – a process which is totally bewildering to the foreigner, because intergovernmental relations are so intimately linked to the political conjunction and seem to change every day. In Belgium we witness a radical federalisation of the state and even signs of the very disintegration of that state. And, of course, in Central and Eastern Europe post-communist states are restructuring intergovernmental relations and local government – often in appallingly difficult economic, political and social circumstances.

The one exception to the general trend towards decentralisation is the United Kingdom which has experienced an unprecedented attempt to push towards the centralisation of certain aspects of intergovernmental relations, although, at a high cost, not always successfully, and with unintended and unwelcome consequences.

Many of the changes taking place are described in detail by the contributors to this volume so there is little point in summarising them here. Suffice to say that, first, the broad trend in Europe is towards decentralisation, often to the regional level, that the pressures and motives for change differ from country to country, that the nature of the regional decentralisation process differs sharply, that the timing and pace of the process also differ. In other words, general convergence masks great specificities. And, second, the process is fluid, is dynamic: just as centralisation fed centralisation, so decentralisation appears to be pushing towards further decentralisation: the genie appears to be out of the bottle.

This brief chapter will deal with two issues: first, the pressures which are reshaping the politico-administrative environment of both intergovernmental relations and of regional government, and, second, some of the paradoxical consequences of the current regionalisation trends.

The factors reshaping the general politico-administrative environment may be seen at three levels:

1 At the level of the state, broadly defined.
2 At the level of the market.
3 At the level of society.

All three are undergoing transformation and all are interconnected. The last ten to fifteen years have witnessed a reshaping of the state as a result of a wide variety of factors. Three major ones, which are again interrelated, may be identified. In the first place, there has been an ideological shift against the state in favour of the market on the one hand, and on the other, in favour of the individual: the neo-liberal assault against the state has led to a serious questioning of the axioms of yesterday. While we should not exaggerate the extent of the withdrawal of the state – a point I shall come to later – there has been an unquestionable shift in thinking and priorities: budgetary prudence and not expansion; scepticism about state macro-economic interventionism of the Keynesian demand-led type; efficiency rather than redistributionalism; a dislike of universal welfare provision for citizens and a preference for targeting the needs of particular groups or clients or customers; privatisation and deregulation instead of nationalisation and regulation; a preference for private goods and service delivery; a move from direct provision to contracting out. To the impact of the anti-state ideology must be added that of the school of public choice, with its animosity towards public bureaucracy which allegedly harbours intrinsic tendencies towards budget maximisation, bureau-expansion, and collusion with producer groups – tendencies which, it is argued, lead to the over-production of public goods.

The second factor at the level of the state is, of course, budgetary restriction or squeeze – an attempt by all governments to at least contain costs if not reduce them. Domestic as well as European Union pressures have combined to pressurise most governments into policies of financial rectitude. Factor number three which is dislocating the traditional state picture is one which is internal to the state machine: it is broadly organisational or managerial. There have been systematic attempts to reduce the number of permanent, full-time, tenured public officials; a reduction in real terms of their salaries; an increasing emphasis on their efficiency, on management by agencies, on performance indicators, on frugality, on transparency, on private provision through sub-contracting or transfer to the so-called third sector (charitable institutions, voluntary organisations), on evaluation and monitoring. Again, the pattern differs from country to country, but there is clear evidence of the spread of at least some of these practices across European frontiers.

Now, why is this process of state reshaping significant in terms of intergovernmental relations? The answer is that it is so in several ways, and largely because the three pressures – ideological, budgetary and organisational – have not been absorbed at mass or electoral level. People grumble about paying state interventionism and taxes but they remain firmly attached to high welfare spending: health, education, pensions, unemployment and sickness benefits are seen as rights to be universally available and rooted in social citizenship. In spite of many efforts, state budgets remain high – and are likely to remain high. The ageing of the population, high and stable rates of unemployment, new technology in health, the electoral demand for better standards accessible to all – all these continue to exert upward pressures on the state budget – whether national or local. What better strategy, then, for the central state to transfer responsibilities for costly services to local government, particularly at a time of budgetary squeeze and fiscal resistance? But there is a further point. The electorate is attached not only to the welfare state: it also continues to believe that public goods encompass the utilities – gas, water, electricity, basic telecoms – even if they are in private hands: this means that, privatisation or not, certain goods will be perceived not as ordinary commodities but as politicised and as part of the general welfare package. Public authorities, national or local, are therefore inevitably drawn into the complex game of regulation and that requires time, personnel, expertise, i.e., costs.

A further impact of state restructuring is the increasing

fragmentation of public delivery, whether at the national or local level: many more institutions are involved, often of a private or mixed public–private character, and linked to politics by contracts. This fragmentation raises acute problems of duplication, of control, and of political accountability.

If we turn to the second area of turbulence – society – we witness equally important changes. We note, first of all, the emergence of a new political agenda compared with ten to fifteen years ago. This agenda has been reshaped by a number of issues, including:

- unemployment at persistently record levels, the rise in the number of the long-term unemployed, of the 'new poor', of homelessness;
- law and order issues, with apparently insoluble problems of rising crime rates and drugs problems;
- immigration;
- environmentalism – the so-called 'greening of politics';
- feminism and gender-related issues;
- consumerism.

At the social level, we see, second, demands related not only to output but also to input– how decisions are made: so there are increased demands of a conflicting nature for decision-making which is quicker, more participative, more transparent, more representative. Third, at the social level, we note the decline in the stabilising quality of the traditional mechanisms of governance:

- the Church;
- the family;
- trade unions;
- political parties.

These institutions, which provide ballast to political society, which articulate but also aggregate demands, are now in decline and are incapable of containing the increasing demands of single-issue groups: small groups that pursue, often outside traditional political channels, one issue only.

Fourth, at social level, we see the increasing disrepute with which established elites are held and, indeed, a certain disenchantment with politics. And, finally, at the level of political society, we witness the persistence and even accentuation of conflicts related to territorial identity. It would be much too easy to illustrate this particular point.

If we analyse the impact of these social changes on intergovernmental relations we have to conclude that they are, again, highly problematic, since they confront decision-makers at both levels – state and local – with acute problems. Thus, the new political agenda involves issues which probably cannot be solved by political action alone (drugs and crime), are very costly (environment and unemployment), may require international co-operation (immigration, environment and crime), or involve increased public intervention and regulation (gender issues, environment and consumerism). The disrepute of many established political elites raises the crucial question of legitimacy. And territorial tensions and conflicts clearly singularly complicate intergovernmental relations. In other words, the redefining of intergovernmental relations in Europe is taking place within the context of a reshaping of the state which itself is taking place in an unstable and unpropitious social environment. The instability of the politico-social environment is compounded by changes in a third area, that of the market. That market is much more complex and difficult to control or regulate. We have only to mention the big financial frauds of the BCCI bank, the Metallgesellschaft scandal, the Baring Bank affair, and the great scandals of the Daiwa banking group and the Sumitomo group where millions of dollars were lost as the result of inadequate or absent regulation. Some markets – the futures markets and certain financial derivatives – are extraordinarily difficult, even impossible to regulate.

The contemporary market is also:

- more liberalised, particularly in the financial sphere: money is footloose and restless;
- more service-based;
- more metropolitanised, with a continuing drain of population and resources to the major cities;
- more privatised;
- more globalised (and that has several dimensions);
- more rationalised in some sectors, with fewer firms controlling increasing shares of a sector;
- and, of course, more Europeanised.

Each of these changes in the economy impact upon the central state and upon localities and upon their relationship, and some of the consequences have been explored in this book. One or two examples perfectly illustrate the point. We need not dwell upon the impact of metropolitanisation which is too obvious. Rather, let us take the case of globalisation which, as noted, has many dimensions. One of these dimensions is the multinationalisation of the activities of major groups and their rationalisation across national boundaries – a trend we begin to see in the utility section: water, gas, electricity, waste disposal and street cleaning. So far, many of these large utilities have remained protected behind national barriers. But several factors – the strategic and capital needs of the firms, liberalisation, membership of the European Union, new technology, privatisation – are combining to dismantle the old protective barriers. The result is the arrival into the national and local political environment of major foreign-owned utilities. Britain has taken this process the furthest: the privatised water, gas and electricity companies have been the object of successful predatory raids by the Americans and – even worse! – the French. This is a phenomenon that all European states will come to experience: and it involves the removal of some economic decision-making power away from the locality and even from the state. Increased inward foreign investment produces a similar effect. This investment also, of course, triggers increased competition not only amongst states but also amongst localities: localities in the same country or even in the same region.

But it is perhaps the Europeanisation of the market that is having the most profound dislocatory impact on traditional intergovernmental relations. I do not wish to repeat what has been written in this volume, but it is worth pointing out that the consequences of membership of the EU are very far-reaching, both in a direct and indirect way:

- it has displaced the arenas of some policy-making, has increased the number of relevant decision-makers from outside the nation–state, and has rendered policy outcomes more unpredictable;
- it has become a rallying political slogan for some localities;
- it has provoked a range of institutional reforms, particularly at the regional level;
- it has severely hampered traditional state regional policies, or has provided central elites with the pretext not to pursue such policies;
- it has created new networks linking Brussels, the nation–state and regions, or even Brussels directly with certain regions;
- it has strengthened central banks and finance ministries – the bastions of financial orthodoxy – as well as the major industrial and financial groups which are becoming increasingly important political actors;
- it has imposed new tasks on regions in areas such as the implementation of environmental directives;
- it establishes pressures for competition and emulation (particularly for those much sought after regional and Structural Funds);
- it has reinforced some regions (generally those that are well equipped with the necessary resources), and weakened others, many of which are already weak.

In other words, membership of the European Union has reconfigured the traditional map of intergovernmental relations, and it has done so in asymmetrical fashion.

Changes in the state, in society and in the economy each have distinct impacts upon local government and upon intergovernmental relations, but they also interact in dynamic fashion: they feed upon one another in a highly destabilising and unpredictable manner.

But what conclusions may we draw from this brief account, apart from the fact that intergovernmental relations are unstable, more competitive, tension-ridden, problematic, and characterised by institutional innovation, the emergence of few actors and reconfigured networks and, above all, by decentralisation often of a regional nature?

Several conclusions emerge, and they may be presented in the form of a set of provocative paradoxes.

Paradox no. 1

Regional decentralisation is often presented as a symptom of and as an instrument for the weakening of the central state. However, one does not have to be a cynic to suggest that transferring intractable problems or costly welfare obligations down the territorial chain may be a perfect way for central elites to strengthen the centre. It is clearly far more convenient for the centre to stabilise its own tax demands while denouncing the increases in local taxes which are frequently necessitated by the transfer of those obligations.

Paradox no. 2

Regional decentralisation is seen as a means of respecting the territorial diversity of the nation. But there is no necessary correlation between decentralisation and heterogeneity in the policies pursued. Indeed, we witness the paradox that increasing decentralisation appears to be accompanied by increasing policy convergence. And this is because the pressures of homogenisation are so great: in economic and industrial policy, for example, localities, under the combined pressures of the budget, of competition and of emulation, pursue broadly similar supply side programmes. Also, the impact of evaluation – one of the current management crazes driven by budgetary considerations – tends to be very homogenising because it reveals disparities in policy performance and output which become unacceptable to those identified as being the relatively badly treated. Thus, it creates political pressures for remedial action (with the paradoxical consequence that evaluation designed to cut costs may have the long-term consequence of increasing them). In the area of culture and leisure there may be greater scope for diversity, but even here the omens are not promising. To be really mischievous one might argue that in Belgium the cultural identity of the Flemish is threatened less by the French, but by American films and fast food and by the English language. The same might be said of Catalonia and the Basque Country in Spain.

Paradox no. 3

This paradox concerns democracy, and here several arguments may be deployed. Regional decentralisation brings government closer to the people: true, but if the political decision unit at regional level goes beyond a certain size, this advantage can be weakened or even annulled. Studies in the USA suggest that citizens in the state of New York make little distinction between the state capital and Washington in terms of perceived distance. When decentralisation moves power to large regional units, problems inevitably arise over regional centralisation, with the regional capital replacing the centre as the object of local dislike. Regionalisation raises, too, the delicate issue of minorities in regions which have a strong and distinctive ethnic or linguistic identity. It raises, finally, the issue of technocracy, since the bigger the unit to be administered, the greater is the power of the bureaucrats and of the technocrats. This problem of technocracy at regional level is aggravated by the emergence in the European Union of sectorally structured networks which link technocrats at European, national and regional level.

Paradox no. 4

This concerns clarification through rationalisation. Regionalisation has often been presented as a means of clarifying the relationship between the centre and the regions by a clearer definition of powers or by a legalisation of existing practices. However, in no country in Europe has regionalisation resolved disputes over respective competencies, over overlapping jurisdictions and over institutional mismatches. Indeed, the destabilising impact of regionalisation tends to increase the number of such disputes. Moreover, many problems which were centre–local in character have also been displaced to the local level; regional capital versus other towns in the region: conflicts between municipalities within metropolitan areas within a region because externalities have to be managed; conflicts between the various territorial layers – regions, provinces, towns – which are almost inevitable, because regionalisation has rarely been accompanied by true rationalisation and the abolition of 'lower' territorial entities. Regions, provinces and towns now jostle for position in an increasingly complex picture. And this picture has been further complicated by membership of the European Union. It is tempting to see territorial politics as a multi-level game embracing Brussels, states, and localities, particularly regions. My own view is that we are increasingly confronted with a mosaic, almost a kaleidoscope: differentiated and shifting games are taking place. In some, parts of the central state are the critical actors, in others, regional political barons. And the game is very sectorally specific. So territorial politics is characterised less by clarification than by heightened complexity and obfuscation. And these twin problems of complexity and obfuscation are aggravated by the new modes of service delivery and of regulation.

Paradox no. 5

This paradox may be stated simply: regionalisation underlines the limits to regionalisation. We may be witnessing a constitutional, juridical or political transfer of powers to regions, but major actors – firms, banks, employers' organisations, trades unions, professional organisations such as doctors, teachers, architects and engineers generally remain stubbornly national or even international in organisation or culture. Belgium remains the exception to this rule.

Paradox no. 6

This has already been stated but may be reiterated: regionalisation is intended to satisfy local territorial demands. In fact, it tends to feed them: *l'appétit s'accroît en mangeant*: one's appetite grows with eating. Regionalisation establishes a process which pushes for further regionalisation, because it creates interests or coalitions which favour it. It is intrinsically destabilising. As a result, we perceive a growing gulf between the push towards political or constitutional regionalisation and the metropolitanising, centralising, Europeanising or internationalising logic of economic, professional and judicial networks.

Paradox no. 7

Regionalisation is intended to strengthen local government, but it highlights the weakness of some regions and their difficulties in adjusting to many of the changes outlined above. In some cases, there is a clear need for regions to continue to lean on the central state for salvation. More importantly, regionalisation, by transferring powers and responsibility to local authorities at a time of rising demands and of budgetary squeeze renders them more vulnerable to popular hostility: responsibility has a price. It is worth emphasising that adapting to the new social, state and market environment requires a wide range of resources: good physical location, leadership which is durable and legitimate, financial resources, expertise of a budgetary and technical nature, knowledge of key networks, local entrepreneurship, and skilled and adaptable labour markets, high social capital (education, hospitals, leisure), decent public infrastructure, a culture of partnership state–locality, public–private. What is clear is that too many regions lack some of these key features.

Paradox no. 8

Finally, regionalisation is intended to make the processes of decision-making more democratic. In practice, however, it has often involved the transfer of increased power to powerful barons entrenched in one-party regions. The critical issues of citizen participation and of legitimacy are not necessarily resolved by regional decentralisation.

The broad trend towards regionalisation, which have been described in this book, has been inspired by several, often contradictory factors, and encouraged by very different groups. In some senses it is inevitable and even desirable, but it is clearly problematic and paradoxical. The paradoxes may be explained by three factors. The first is the very nature of regional government which has to fulfil several conflicting requirements, since it is concerned with functional efficiency, democratic accountability, equity and distributionalism, identity and participation. In other words, with both input and output. Now, regional government, because it is more politically and functionally important, is increasingly locked into the traditional demands of the nation–state: balancing contradictions and constructing legitimate forms of governance. And governance requires co-ordinating, in complex settings, multiple layers of mutual interdependencies, and it encompasses not only official politico-administrative actors but also includes that vast range of social and economic actors, of both a public and private character, who guide, control or manage fragile societies, who interrelate in networks many of which effectively transcend official political boundaries. This leads to the second reason for the paradoxical and problematic nature of regionalisation: territory constantly intersects with sector, and territorial boundaries may overlap with, but they rarely coincide with, sectoral networks. There is, therefore, a frequent mismatch between regional and sectoral institutions and logics. Attempts to 'rationalise' territory, through the creation or consolidation of regions are doomed to fail, because they fail to recognise that different activities require different, if overlapping, spatial units, that externalities have to be managed, and that interdependencies have to be co-ordinated at different territorial levels.

Finally, problems and paradoxes arise because intergovernmental relations are embedded in the wider context of the state, the market and society and in the relationship between these three. And all three, as I have briefly argued, are increasingly unstable.

Perhaps the major lesson of recent years is that centralisation and regionalisation are both problem-ridden, since each sets up conflicting pressures both for its own furtherance but also its own dismantlement. This dynamic, combined with the increasingly contradictory requirements of regional government and the constantly evolving political, social and economic context, mean that intergovernmental relations are inherently fluid, and that the attempt to create stable optimal territorial units in the form of regions is likely to prove as much an illusion as the search for the Holy Grail.

4 The sub-regional level*

Key battleground for the Structural Funds?

Andy Smith

Almost all the most common versions of the history of Community Structural Funds underline the fact that until their reform in 1988 these interventions have mostly strengthened the grip of national governments on the development of the so-called 'disadvantaged' territories. Such analysis, largely based on research carried out in the 1980s [Martins *et al.*, 1985; Mény, 1982b], minimises the degree of autonomy given to the European Commission and infra-national actors for the elaboration and implementation of actions financed by these funds.

Today, with the benefit of hindsight, a richer story emerges which helps us better understand the political impact of the Structural Funds since their reform in 1988, and this on two levels. First, the discovery of the actors' strategies and resources outside the national governments allows us to approach the complexity of the political transactions involved in the process. More fundamentally, returning to this development compels us to think about the correctness of the implicit and explicit analytical grids which were adopted to explain the complexity which was created, at regional as well as national levels. Paradoxically, so far the impact of the Structural Funds on the political capacity of the regions has often been handled through a prism of an adjusted version of intergovernmental analysis which favoured the study of international changes rather than deepening the analysis of hierarchies emerging around the Structural Funds in a given territory.

We have attempted to fill this gap in empirical research and theoretical reflection with our work centred on the Structural Funds in the rural environment of three Member States: France, Spain and the United Kingdom [Smith 1995, 1996]. It will be argued that analysis of the role of national governments is indispensable but insufficient. New

* Translation Uttam Bharthare.

configurations of actors fed by the Structural Funds also needs integrating into such studies.

Indeed, although some authors want to jump to the conclusion that 'Structural Funds = regionalisation' [Sidjanski, 1990], it is more productive to try to define the models of public action which have been produced by adopting less determinist working hypotheses. If the Structural Funds–regionalisation relationship is verified in some cases, research on the impact of these funds more often tends to underline the importance of political activity *within* each region.

FINISHING OFF THE INTERGOVERNMENTAL APPROACH

In an article published in 1992, Jeffrey Anderson underlined the importance of state actors in the planning and implementation of actions financed and orientated by the Structural Funds. Using a key term from international relations, according to him, national governments played the role of 'gatekeepers', a more or less open interface between the Commission and the national non-state actors. Analysis in terms of gatekeepers basically supposes the predominance of bilateral relationships between national governments and the European Commission. Our research concerning the implementation of the Structural Funds, since their reform in 1988, leads us to propose a quite different analysis. Contrary to Anderson, we did not find in the three state bureaucracies we studied actors who possess all resources enabling them to act as check posts between sub-national actors and the Commission. Neither the idea of total control nor that of a blocking power stands the test of empirical study. However, some parts of every state make the most of the new rules of the game.

The inter-state dimension: an ever-present but partial explanation

A large body of literature already exists on the impact of Community integration on the internal composition of governments of the Member States [Lequesne, 1993]. If these studies have brought to light the interlocking nature of the national governments of the Twelve, they have tended to ignore both the state actors working outside national capitals and the nature of their main counterpart in Brussels, namely the European Commission.

In the case of structural policies, the ignorance of these factors constitutes a serious deficiency. The blurring of borders between the national government and the Community's administration is intensified by the distance which separates these framework-type policies from the

Council of Ministers and the COREPER. Once the rules have been formally fixed by the latter, planning, implementation and evaluation of the Structural Funds are dealt with between actors of another type. However, multilateral modes of action (Council of Ministers–Commission) do not simply become bilateral (national government–Commission). Two series of relations make this description of reality inapplicable.

First, it is necessary to take into account the political transactions which take place prior to the adoption of rules at the Community level. The framing of Community public policies implies a continuous process of setting up more or less stable coalitions. As such, the example of coalitions necessary to get through the two Structural Funds reforms under the 'Delors packages I and II' is very telling. These reforms in the beginning involved the president of the Commission, his entourage, the commissioners and the relevant Directorates General (DGS). But they were also guided by national governments and to a lesser extent by the European Parliament. Of course, there is nothing automatic about the emergence of alliances between these different types of actors. They are the result of ceaseless consultations, proposals, counter-proposals and mobilisation of support at appropriate moments [Wallace, 1985]. Consequently, the involvement of sub-national territories prior to the decisions of the Council deserves closer attention. In 1993, the participation of representatives of the concerned territories, in the renewal of the Council's commitment to industrial reconversion zones (Objective 2), provide an interesting case in point [McAleavey, 1994b].

The second challenge to the intergovernmental analysis of the Structural Funds arises from the procedures and the methods which are used to translate these Community interventions into actions. At first sight the interpretation in terms of the state as gatekeeper still seems to apply to the United Kingdom. The centralisation of the British political system adopted by successive governments since the mid-1970s is continuing, and, according to many officials interviewed, *has to* continue. In some respects, the strategy adopted by British officials with regard to the Structural Funds has been successful. The use of the ESF by the Department of Employment is a good example. However, the use of the ERDF by coalitions of local actors tends instead to reduce the capacity of central government to impose its priorities.

In contrast, one of the main peculiarities of the Spanish case is the relatively discreet position taken by state actors *vis-à-vis* the Community Structural Funds. This positioning is partly a result of the 'autonomisation process'. It is relayed at the local levels by the fact that the state no longer possesses a developed network of decentralised representatives. The strategy of the state actors is also explained by their quest for new sources of legitimacy. In fact, the relative discretion of state actors concerning territorial development does not necessarily mean that they find themselves marginalised within the network of actors gathered around the Structural Funds. As the main negotiating partners with the European Union, and participating directly in the meetings of the Council of Ministers and of the COREPER, the Madrid-based officials have important resources at their disposal. The example of the implementation of the LEADER programme, where their alliance with local development actors turned out to be beneficial to both parties, underlines the importance of a strategic margin of liberty for the Spanish state in the framework of the 'State of Autonomies'. In fact the quasi-federal nature of the Spanish political system does not produce only *one* unique model for regulating the stakes of territorial development. On the contrary, quasi-federalism should be considered as *one* of the variables determining the type of actor favoured by Community intervention. Spanish institutions are characterised by their favourable attitude *vis-à-vis* the Commission's actions, an attitude not to be dissociated from widespread awareness that in the Community political context, everything is far from being decided by the Council of Ministers.

The nature of the interaction between national governments, infranational administrations and the Commission invalidates the 'gatekeeper' hypothesis. The margins of uncertainty of the Community political system are such that the level of control described by Anderson seems illusory. However, this situation necessitates intense political activity on the part of regional and sub-regional actors, an opportunity which they have often been quick to seize. Studying this, however, requires more complex approaches. One step in this direction is to deconstruct the state to show the differences which may be present between its representatives at the centre and those present elsewhere in the country.

The state is dead. Long live the state. A new direction for state action

State actors have far from disappeared from the network of actors involved in the Structural Funds. If the financial sums corresponding to the contributions of the three states provide one reason, their presence is more often consolidated by the involvement of their agents in the implementation of the Structural Funds. In order to understand this situation what needs to be grasped is that the legitimacy of the state actors is no longer the same as it was before the early 1980s. Consequently, they can no longer act with the same long-term effects as before. Similarly, the internal hierarchy of the state has also declined. As a result, its capacity for action has largely to be built up by civil servants in the field. If the Structural Funds are certainly not the only factor responsible for this modification, analysis of their deployment highlights five series of reasons which enable state actors to 'salvage' something. These dimensions are of the following orders: institutional, informational, intellectual, relational and symbolic.

The first asset which the state actors enjoy is direct access to the institutional forums of the European Union. Infra-national communities have a very weak formal representation in the Community political system. Although the Maastricht Treaty has established a Committee of the Regions, the status and the powers of this authority remain unclear. However, in the case of the Structural Funds it is important to relativise the importance of the institutional advantages of state actors. The framework rules for these funds are negotiated by the Council of Ministers every three, four or, indeed, six years. Meanwhile local actors and agents of the Commission enjoy a considerable level of autonomy.

The second asset of the state actors is a direct result of the institutional position we have described above, namely the quality of their information sources. As the main formal negotiating partners of the Commission, state actors draw from three sources reliable information about the instruments developed by the Commission. First, the civil servants of national capitals responsible for the Structural Funds are in direct contact with the persons in charge of the Directorates General. The Permanent Representations at Brussels constitute a second source of information. Finally, this information circuit is completed by the link set up between the Commission and the representatives of the decentralised state. Of course this multiplicity of information sources can lead to competition and contradictions. The agents of the Commission may take advantage of the situation to favour an actor from outside the process, such as a *Conseil Régional* or a County Council. Generally, however, state actors admit the value of being the first informed about all that happens in the Commission. On the strength of controlling such information they can subsequently win acceptance of two other dimensions of public action: the intellectual and the mediation functions.

The instruments of current territorial development are extremely complex. Between the Community measures of all kinds of local and national actions, the number of actors who know how to move from one policy instrument to another is limited. Therein lies the third asset of the state actors. In the three countries under study, the selection and training of civil servants favour the mastering of the diversity of data. This intellectual capacity is very much solicited by the Structural Funds and facilitates a slight modification of the role of the state. Without claiming that disadvantaged territories actually need this quality, it is certain that the planning and implementation of the action co-financed by the European Commission definitely require a capacity to deal with complex situations. The decentralised services of the Spanish state lack this. On the other hand, in France and the United Kingdom, state actors at regional and the sub-regional levels seem to possess the required intellectual capacities. In both cases this type of civil servant serves as a kingpin around which other actors can get to know of available Community aid, plan out action, redefine it according to the formal rules and collect the money.

Obviously, the intellectual capacities of the state actors are almost worthless if they cannot be mobilised through *mediation* [Jobert and Muller, 1987]. To allow the state actors to find their place in the network of actors involved in the deployment of the Structural Funds, it is necessary that they manage to combine their forces in terms of the mastery of information with its relational work which transforms one-way relationships into mutual exchange. This is not just a matter of simply changing the mastery and interpretation of information into an element structuring a new form of hierarchy with regard to actors of the concerned territories (*decoding*). In a context where the state ceases to manage most of the financing, 'imposition' becomes out of place. On the other hand, state actors can facilitate the task of other territorial actors by acquiring the Structural Funds and engaging in localised public policies with them (a *recoding* task).

Finally, any analysis of the role of state actors in the working out and implementation of the Structural Funds cannot neglect the presence of the social representations attached to the state as a historical public authority: the symbolic dimension. The respective histories of the three member countries are accompanied with the emergence of an important range of symbols which later become the underlying components of national identity. It is obvious that these symbols have to be mobilised to influence the dynamics of the network of actors engaged in public policies. In the case of the Structural Funds, notably in France and the United Kingdom but also in Spain, state actors can at suitable moments invoke the 'national interest' as a means to get their priorities through. As the mobilisation of symbols, however, is difficult to control, the notion of national interest can become an object of controversy and negotiations.

The agents of contemporary states work within political systems whose structures and dynamics have greatly evolved. The existence of actor networks, already important in the past, has now become a key element of each actor's working environment. At the national level, this development has produced and accompanied change in the logic governing the state's action [Metcalfe, 1993]. In the case of the Structural Funds, the increasing importance of the Community context tends to hasten such progress. The state is certainly not dead, but it has undeniably become different.

A SEARCH FOR NEW PARTNERS

From the European Commission's point of view, there has never been any question of blindly supporting the regional authorities through the Structural Funds [Smith and Smyrl, 1995]. For most of the agents of the Commission, the aim has rather been to 'open up' public action models by introducing new actors. Ultimately, however, the type of actors favoured by the Structural Funds in each territory reveals the power configurations which are to be found therein.

The regional level: a possibility, not a probability

The Structural Funds feed the regionalisation of actor networks on two levels: the regions considered as territorial communities and the regionalisation of the state itself. Together, in some cases, these two processes contribute to the emergence of what some authors define as 'meso-government' [Pérez-Diaz, 1990a].

As regards regions as territorial communities, it is especially in Spain that the Structural Funds accompany the evolution of the national political system which some people call regionalisation, but which corresponds more to a *federalisation*. Although in 1988, this process was already under way in 'historical' Autonomous Communities such as Catalonia, the Structural Funds supplied the embryonic regional governments with vital resources. The case of the *Junta* of Extramadura is an almost perfect example of the impact of financial resources, but also of the political endorsement which accompanies the responsibility of deploying the Structural Funds. The actors within the *Junta* have not only become the keys to all Spanish public financing for rural development, but now they are also the main negotiating partners of the state and the Commission. For example, during the selection of the LEADER projects, the actors of the *Junta* defined the eligibility criteria for the Community funds. In the Spanish case, one can thus conclude that the Structural Funds figure as catalysts in the federalisation of the political system.

While in Spain the borders of the Autonomous Communities tend to contribute significantly in the setting up of specific actors' networks, the territorial aspect contributed by the political system in France does not play the same role. Any diagnosis in terms of the impact of the Structural Funds on the *conseils régionaux* has to be more detailed than in the Spanish case. In certain regions this politico-administrative level is very active in the planning and implementation of Structural Funds, whereas in others the *conseils régionaux* do not fully control these processes. These differences are partly due to the balance maintained between the *conseil régional* and the state services present in the region. This will be discussed later. They are explained also in terms of endogenous factors of every region which cause the regional level often to be considered not as a place of strategic political regulation (a government), but as a simple crossroads where the *département*-level preferences come together [Darviche, Genieys and Joana 1995]. The relation here, between the regional authority and the *conseils généraux*, is clearly fundamental. One of the reasons why the regional council of Rhône-Alpes has become weak with regard to the Structural Funds is because of the strength of the *conseils généraux* (notably those of the Drôme and Ardèche) and the political clout of the *Conseillers généraux* within the regional council.

Other factors such as the shortcomings of the administrative organisation of the regional council have also to be taken into account. In sum, given the range of variables determining a regional council's worth as a negotiating partner of the Commission, in France it is difficult to establish a linear relationship between the Structural Funds and the emergence of a level of regional government. It is true that quite a few regional councils have opened up offices in Brussels. However, this does not in any way reflect the regional councils' capacity to modify the guidelines fixed for Community interventions concerning territorial development [Balme and Jouve, 1996]. In fact, the power of a regional council depends on its relations with the state and the nature of the sub-regional balance of power. In both cases the Structural Funds are far from being a natural asset for the regional actor.

From an institutional point of view, talking about regional government in the United Kingdom clearly makes no sense [Sharpe in Mény, 1982a]. In fact the British case raises the following question: in a country where there are no regions, can there be meso-government? Paradoxically, our study of the implementation of the Structural Funds tends to suggest that without there being elected assemblies at the regional level, in certain parts of the country there are regions capable of organising themselves and using the Structural Funds to consolidate a regional power centre. Scotland and Wales are the most obvious cases in point. In both situations, particularly dense actors' networks exist which include powerful regional development agencies. Drawing support from a strong *national* identity, not only political actors but also economic and social ones have been able to create a partially autonomous area, away from the central government in London. The case of some parts of the United Kingdom therefore conforms more to a situation of *meso-governance* than to that of a meso-government because the absence of formal institutions does not rule out politics being dominated by sub-regional coalitions of public, para-public and private actors. Of course, the degree of independence of these coalitions should not be exaggerated. The Department of Trade and Industry (DTI) and the Department of Environment (DoE) still enjoy relatively favourable positions. Nevertheless, the Structural Funds have furnished resources to actors who are now better equipped than in 1988 to act as a counter power facing central government.

The regionalisation of the state apparatus constitutes the second aspect of the impact of the Structural Funds on the emergence of the meso-government. In fact, it is not possible to understand the British and the French cases without recognising the importance of the type of state organisation in the region. In the United Kingdom, state civil servants working in the regions are at the very heart of the process of formulating and implementing the Structural Funds. In Wales, and in Devon and Cornwall, a number of civil servants are identifying themselves more and more with the territories they are working in. A large number of these agents are actively adopting a more flexible approach to London-based interpretations of Community norms. For this reason it seems to us that a phenomenon of *peripheral power*, similar to the one which existed in France before decentralisation, is emerging in certain parts of the United Kingdom. The case of Scotland is a good example here, notably in the region of Strathclyde where the secretariat of the Operational Programme has been transferred from the Scottish Office to an independent authority (the programme manager) [McAleavey, 1994a]. In Wales the Welsh Office is trying to distance itself from Whitehall, without, however, getting any closer to the local authorities. On the other hand the government office in Bristol in charge of the Devon–Cornwall Operational Programme remains attached to the logic of centralised power. Without claiming that this phenomenon can be generalised to the whole country, or that it is solely a product of the Structural Funds, it may be said that the financing, the norms and the procedures involved in these mechanisms are a force in favour of the spread of 'periphery power' relationships.

Compared to the United Kingdom, it is clear that in France the power of the state actors in the regions is strengthened by their role in the implementation of the Structural Funds [Balme and Jouve, 1996]. This situation is explained by the constant presence of the state in the French actors' imagination and also by the endogenous weakness of the regional authorities mentioned earlier. In the absence of strong development guidelines coming from the territorial communities, very often the services of the state in the regions have been able to regain, and in a way, *have had to* regain control of the Structural Funds.

Finally, only in Spain have representatives of the decentralised state failed to use the processes accompanying the Structural Funds to their own ends. In a country on its way to federalisation, the state actors outside Madrid are still marginalised. In fact, in the Spanish case, it is rather the state actors at the centre who can utilise the Structural Funds to cover up the lost ground *vis-à-vis* the political and administrative importance which the governments of the Autonomous Communities have assumed.

The powerful rise of the regional authorities constitutes a key factor in the withering of conceptions of sovereignty linked to nation–states. However, this is not restricted to the regional level alone. The Structural Funds have also destabilised relations between the sub-regional actors, the state and conceptions of sovereignty.

The sub-regional actors: varying poles of power

Our empirical research has enabled us to show that Community Structural Funds have clearly contributed to the reorganisation of politics in the territories concerned. If the Community initiatives, notably the LEADER programme, have allowed the European Commission to reach sub-regional negotiating partners one should not neglect the involvement of authorities such as the French *départements* and the British counties in the Operational Programmes. Far from confirming the hypothesis that the Structural Funds are fashioning a Europe of the regions, these instruments are instead encouraging new configurations *in the heart* of every region.

Given the relative importance of the Autonomous Communities in Spain, it is difficult to make out the impact of the Structural Funds on sub-regional authorities. As the driving force behind the process of greater autonomy, these Autonomous Communities have been able to play a dominant role in the negotiations which took place around the Structural Funds in 1988. However, it is noteworthy that some of the political actors within these regions managed to get hold of the Structural Funds and use them for their own ends. In the case of Extramadura, the *Junta*, however, did not damage the legitimacy of the representatives of the two provincial *Diputaciones*. Taking support from the local employers' organisation, the *Diputaciones* continued to participate indirectly in the negotiations which command the use of Community grants. Concerning the regrouping of actors involved in the LEADER projects in this Autonomous Community, the Junta actors have also had to maintain a delicate position. For its part, the Catalan *Generalitat* is constrained not by the *Diputaciones*, but by the need to work out an inter-territorial and inter-party balance at the level of Catalonia. Having revived the *Comarcal* (intercommunal) echelon of local government, the actors of the *Generalitat* now have to manage the inter-actor relations which correspond to a rural/urban opposition. It would be wrong to consider the *comarcas* as simple relays of the *Generalitat*. On the strength of their local legitimacy, the *comarcas* leaders are now developing political capacities, independent of the *Generalitat*. For the moment the relations between the local action groups and the *Generalitat* have mellowed due to the adhesion of all the actors to the CiU. What will happen when the balance between the political parties changes, remains to be seen.

In the case of these two Autonomous Communities, it is difficult to say that in Spain the Structural Funds have favoured one type of sub-national negotiating partner. On the contrary, a twofold strategy is dominant in the approach of the Commission's agents in Spain: reach a maximum number of negotiating partners in every territory, creating thus a direct link between the locals and the Commission; and inculcate a negotiation-based method of public action to combat any kind of regional hegemony.

In France, the strengthening of sub-regional actors is even more explicit. The peculiarities of the *départements* and of *intercommunalité* are two of the factors which explain this. By mobilising, more or less skilfully, the departmental level which is historically the strongest, a large number of actors within the *conseils généraux* have been able to take advantage of the Structural Funds in order to position themselves *vis-à-vis* the regional authorities. In several cases (Morbihan, Ardèche,

Drôme), the *conseils généraux* also had the advantage of having been associated with Community programmes before the 1988 reform. Benefiting from close links with the state services at the departmental level (particularly the DDA and DDE), certain departmental councils managed to use the Operational programmes as resources, providing finance and legitimacy, and allowing them to strengthen their formal powers in matters of rural development.

As regards 'intercommunal' authorities, it is through the Community Initiatives that the Structural Funds have managed to become objects in the reorganisation of actor networks. The LEADER programme of centre-west Brittany is the perfect example of this kind because it regroups *communes* from three different *départements*. More often the intercommunal authorities in place take up the LEADER programme to continue pre-existing initiatives. Ultimately, however, the local action groups have not been able to do anything about the weakness of *intercommunalité* as a component of the French political system. When the state had the resources and the legitimacy to support local actors on the basis of the contents of their projects, the 'outsiders' from *département* political networks could avail themselves of much support. Today the French state does not have that autonomy and this development underscores the importance of relations between intercommunal authority and the departmental and regional councils.

French–Spanish comparisons allow us to emphasise the fact that, in France, the Community Structural Funds are not necessarily advantageous to the regional authorities. That is why in other studies we have extended the notion of 'concentric power' developed by Marc Abélès to describe the models of actors' configuration which surround the president of the *conseil général* [1989].[1] This model of authority is not simply a matter of politicians' networks. It is also a product, as well as the creator, of a whole series of relations existing between the services of the departmental councils, employers, interest groups and the deconcentrated services of the state. Consequently there is no natural link between specific actor networks working out and implementing Structural Funds and the setting up of a concentric power configuration. In a political system, subject to so many centrifugal forces, the constitution of this type of power model depends on the existence of two types of actors' networks.

At the level of elected representatives, it seems essential that the leaders of the territories concerned become actively involved in the circuits connecting the local grouping to national and the Community levels. Thanks to the practice of *cumul des mandats*, the French political system is equipped with a channel well suited for transmitting information and political support. More recently, authorities such as the Association of Presidents of the *conseils départementaux* have begun providing another means for this kind of political activity. This action is more visible when the zones eligible for Community funds are being defined.

On the level of local authority officials, the act of linking up to national and Community network is also indispensable.[2] These networks are not only sources of information but also provide contacts with potential partners in other member countries. In a context where transnational relations are becoming one of the key criteria of attributing Community Initiative Programmes, officials possessing an international address book are a considerable asset for local authorities.

It follows that there is no concentric organisation (concentrism) without a strong local level organisation. At the same time there is little power available unless a part of this local organisation is geared to seeking resources outside the territory.

As regards sub-regional institutions in the United Kingdom, the deployment of the Structural Funds has given rise to situations which are midway between those found in Spain and France. Whereas the Operational Programmes have been objects seized by actors at the level of an *ad hoc* regrouping of two or three counties (in this case, deconcentrated state officials, developmental agencies and certain county councils), the impact of Community Initiatives on the sub-regional actors has sometimes been more powerful than in Spain. The actors of the District Councils quickly understood that this form of Community aid could help them set themselves up as leaders in charge of local economic development [Pickvance, 1990, p. 35]. Thus they tried to gain support both from Community norms, but also from the preference of central government for a form of public action closer to enterprises than to the County Councils.

Despite the centralising will of the actors of central government, other aspects of the deployment of the Structural Funds in the United Kingdom show that centralisation has serious limits. In fact, despite the centre's activity against them for over fifteen years, local actors have often been able to use the Community interventions to increase their own margin of autonomy within specific actor networks. This destabilisation of the local–national relationship has occurred at the financial, institutional and conceptual levels.

In a context where the funds allocated to the national policy of regional development are fast declining, for local actors the

Commission has become a considerable source of finance. Even though the funds allotted to the less favoured rural territories are not large, they nonetheless have the effect of maintaining a budgetary commitment in a domain of public action which the central government would like to limit or indeed to abolish altogether.

Second, local actors have been able to take advantage of the norms defined by the 1988 reform of the Structural Funds to re-legitimise their institutional position within the British political system. In fact, the Community obligation to channel the structural policies through territorialised partnerships constitutes an unhoped-for occasion for the local actors to recover their legitimacy after years of attacks on their legal powers. Thus the Structural Funds are proving to be objects of negotiations around which certain actors, marginalised within actor networks, were able to develop a more central place within coalitions of actors regrouping public, para-public, and private bodies.

Finally, these institutional developments have been accompanied and driven by the modifications underlying approaches to political action in favour of territorial development. The Commission's demand to involve a greater number of actors in public development policies was interpreted in a manner which is favourable to them, notably about all that concerns the Community Initiative Programmes. Most of these programmes seek primarily the involvement of associations for *community development* and of the local authorities (LEADER, NOW), but others are centred more on regrouping of private companies (BIC). This diversity in the Commission's interventions tends to emphasise the differences of approach of officials from different ministries. If the DTI officials continue to decry all the PIC as superfluous interventionism, those from the DoE and the Ministry of Agriculture have adopted a different attitude. In fact, a good number of agents from these ministries have joined the camp of those who would like to diminish the weight of sectoral interventions in favour of a more territory-based approach to social and economic development. The case of the Ministry of Agriculture in the face of the Common Agricultural Policy is very revealing here. The ministry's growing divisions due to the multiplication of agencies, but also in the face of the competition put up by the Rural Development Commission, constitute strategic reasons which complete earlier analysis of the CAP as a mechanism opposed to market principles.

In the face of the growing centralisation of the British political system over the 1980s [Duncan and Goodwin, 1988], the progressive entry of the components of this system in a Community policy area has contributed to the emergence of less uni-directional tendencies. If in France and Spain local actors were able to take support from important institutional changes, in the United Kingdom, on the other hand, such actors had to achieve a somewhat endogenous conversion. Given the situation described above it will be doubly interesting to observe the politico-administrative impact of the important increase in Objective 5b zones which has been fixed for the period 1994–99. A liberation of the local authorities encouraged by Community interventions seems unlikely. Some fields of public action continue to be real preserves for state actors from London. However, today a certain number of indicators suggest that the clear opposition between the central and the local governments, so characteristic in the 1980s is now giving way to another mode of regulation.

In the three national cases studied, the different models of translating the structural policies confirm that, since 1988, the Community level has significantly contributed to strengthening a more horizontal logic of action than in the past. If the implementation of LEADER is enlightening in a number of regions, the implementation of the Operational Programmes has also hastened the disintegration of obsolete hierarchies. However, this is not a natural trend. If the local relays do not manage to profit from this situation, as in Devon and Cornwall, state actors are ready to rush in to fill the breach. In any case the reorganisation of actors networks is closely linked to the compatibility of the logics of their members which are necessarily different. In places where the criteria for enrolling in a partnership sponsored by the Structural Funds are not the same as those of a well-knit actor network (confidence, discretion, capacity to anticipate), the politico-administrative impact of the Commission is limited. Instead of pacts where the same representations of objectives are shared, and where negotiations and bargaining are carried out to attain a common stand, partnerships decompose into multiple actors who move from one compromise to another, thus strengthening pre-existing contradictions and rivalries.

CONCLUSION

In the three countries which have been studied, the political impact of the Structural Funds does not necessarily increase the power of regional authorities. For such a trend to become apparent, it is necessary that the actors of each region be in a position to translate the funds and the norms which these European funds incorporate into forms which are compatible with their own modes of work and conceptions of territorial development. Having made this observation, however, the existing research gives us little information about the manner in which the local actors have adapted their habitual methods to use the Structural Funds, or how they could have adopted the Structural Funds to reconcile them with their methods. Such studies using a 'bottom-up' approach applied to a region, to a *département*, or to an intercommunal body will enable us to know more about the strategies of the actors concerned and the behavioural changes induced by Community interventions. In this way they will help nourish approaches centred on the notion of local governance [Stoker, 1995].

The opening up of these paths is interesting but we may ask whether we should content ourselves with the study of 'local orders', [Friedberg, 1993], sustained by the Structural Funds. Such approaches tend to overlook the fact that the Structural Funds are parts of a larger political game involving questions about the very nature of European integration? It is for this reason that we are pleading for the development of a second, more abstract, concomitant approach, concerning 'legitimate order of powers' in the European context.[3] The insufficiency of existing studies on the relationship between Community intervention and the reorganisation of local–national relationships translates the overall deficiencies of the study of Community integration as a phenomenon extending to the local level. With the notion of sovereignty gradually disappearing, some authors, taking up the notion of local governance, are probably right in pointing out that a major challenge to contemporary political systems is to 'develop institutions which continue to reproduce the social contract between the individual and society' [Sorenson, 1995, p. 15]. However, the revitalising of the local as a source of democracy and public participation merits being considered as a hypothesis rather than as an affirmation.[4] Indeed, only methodical studies will allow us to answer the question whether Community interventions like the Structural Funds positively contribute to a fundamental challenge: 'local governance in an age of internationalism cannot limit itself to a democratic localism . . . local collective action needs to incorporate a transnational dimension' [Humold, 1995, p.21].

NOTES

1 We have extended the scope of this term to take into account the exchange networks which have developed between the actors of the *conseils généraux* (or *régionaux*), their partners in the economic and social domains and their counterparts in the deconcentrated state. Thus, concentric power becomes a phenomenon exceeding the elected representatives while integrating at the

same time the importance of the links among them and the representatives of the state [Smith, 1995].

2 It is interesting to note that in a recent paper, Jean-Claude Thoenig observes the same thing about the officials who surround the mayors of large cities. He talks about the '*cumul des mandats* which appear to be more technical' [1994, p.15].

3 As Edith Brenac shows in the case of telecommunication policies, every political system whether national or local has till now favoured a 'legitimate order of powers'.

> Comparative analysis shows that this politicisation of the sectoral policies, in fact is supported by the actors and involves political authorities who differ from country to country in a configuration which is indicative of a legitimate order of powers and of forms of democracy specific to each of them.
>
> [1994, p. 318]

4 C. Humold, for example prefers to affirm that 'whereas internationalisation reduces the sovereignty of nation–states, it does not necessarily reduce the autonomy and the legitimacy of local states whose action capacity was never dependent on the notion of sovereignty' [1995, p.20].

5 The political capacity of southern European regions*

Evelyne Ritaine

What is the relationship between territories and political mediations, on the one hand, and politico-administrative institutions (in this case the regional institution) on the other? If seen from the institutional point of view, one could talk of institutional performance[1] as Putnam does. Seen from the point of view of civil society [Pérez-Diaz, 1993], one would speak of political capacity as do M. Keating [1992b] and C. Trigilia [1989]. Some new lessons can be learnt from these changes of perspective, notably thanks to a comparative analysis concerning the area covering the South European [2] countries [Ritaine, 1994].[3]

The theme 'political territory' refers to the idea of territorialised socio-political formations built, more or less, on the historical or socio-political level [Balligand and Maquart, 1990]. In the segmented societies of Southern Europe, it is always a question of an easily available political capacity, even if there is no ethnological basis of political subcultures, or a political heritage of regionalist protest. In societies based on the polycentric principle, the mere competition between zones, or between territory-based political entities, if they exist, can 'produce political territories'.

The concept of territory can be put forward to identify the existence of socio-political areas with different regulation modes, with different types of political mobilisations, in relation to a territorialised state: this is how C. Trigilia studies territorialised political subcultures in Italy [Trigilia, 1986]. The meaning of this term is more sociological than that of the functionalist–diffusionist paradigm of the centre and the periphery, which supposes 'a progressive disappearance of the regional differences within the nation–state, as a result of the centre–periphery interaction in the development dynamics of the unitary European States in the XVIIIth and the XIXth centuries'

* Translation Uttam Bharthare and Claire O'Neal.

[Giner and Moreno, 1990, p.172]. This definition is also much more political and interactionist than the one which has been implemented in the studies carried out on the process of nation-building and on nationalistic demands: being less essentialist, it refers much more to different modes of political organisation. In this sense, socio-political territories are defined by research as 'the product of a historical dialectic of cumulative differentiation' [Bourdieu, 1980], and are capable of showing different political capacities.

If this concept seems to work specifically for the South European countries, it is because the largely varying modes of regional development have been counter-balanced, only to a small extent, by the old and powerful processes of national integration. These 'cumulative imbalances' on the contrary were at the root of the growth of state structures. The states with little legitimacy or little efficiency used the local structures to mediate their political control: clientelism in Italy, Spain and Portugal was at first an expression of territory-based political control. The later economical and political developments have maintained the disparity between the types of territory-based developments: these are regular resurges of regionalist and nationalistic protests, the protests rooted in various territories, quests for more or less federal types of political solutions. The interest of the analysis is here more historical and sociological than economic. The debate on relative economic development and on the dependence of the development is complex, as has been demonstrated by discussions on post-Fordism [Piore and Sabel, 1984]. For a political science approach, questioning the various modes of socio-political regulation seems more promising: the historical evolution which has fossilised these differences, does it still today play on the differentiated, social formations [Bagnasco, 1977]? Depending on the answer to this, two interesting questions, among several others, arise; that of the mediations between these social formations, between them and the state, between them and the European Union, and that of the perverse effects of public policies defined on the national or the European level (cf., for example, [Trigilia, 1992]), and the difficulty of setting up a redistributive principle between social formations with diverse and sometimes competing dynamics.

The highly segmented character of southern societies raises the interesting question of 'virtue' and 'vice' of the effects of mesogovernment, understood in the functional as well as territorial sense. V. Pérez-Diaz, in a chapter entitled 'Region, Economy, and the Scale of Governance: Mesogovernments in Spain' [1993], rightly points out that in a situation of segmentation, neo-corporatists practice or regional government practices can have negative as well as positive effects [cf. also Schmitter, 1983].

CRITIQUE OF THE INSTITUTIONAL PERFORMANCE OF REGIONS

A socio-historical approach applied to southern areas requires us to take a stand on R. Putnam's approach in *Making Democracy Work: Civic Traditions in Modern Italy* [1993]. The debates going on about this work provide an excellent opportunity to show to what extent the study of institutions and civil society are complementary, unless one admits a lot of approximations.[4]

Indeed, this long-term observation has produced a comparative analysis of the dynamics and ecology of institutional performance of the ordinary Italian regions [Putnam *et al.*, 1985; Putnam *et al.*, 1981]. The regions of the centre and the north-east appear to be highly efficient; on the contrary, Calabria, Molise, Campania and Puglia turn out to be less so. How can we explain these differences in institutional success? At first, the correlation between the performance and the level of economic development was analysed. A high degree of economic development only increases the potentiality of institutional performance: the correlation is strong for the less developed and less performing regions, but becomes insignificant for others. Particularly Piedmont, Liguria and Latium which are relatively rich do not perform as well as would be expected of them. The institutional performance was also correlated with sociological stability, measured by demographic indicators. This correlation is significant only if controlled by the degree of development: the regions which have undergone very strong demographical and social changes, surprising in comparison to their level of development, are in reality Piedmont, Liguria and Latium whose institutional performances are abnormally low. On the contrary, Emilia-Romagna draws an additional resource from the fact that it has remained relatively unaffected by the demographical changes which the regions of the north have undergone [Leonardi and Nanetti, 1990]. Finally, a correlation was established between institutional success and political culture. The regions with a more developed 'civic culture' (understood as a greater political and social participation) are also those which have a greater institutional performance. The correlation is much stronger for the economically developed regions, whereas for the underdeveloped regions it is the level of development which remains the most significant explanatory variable. In this sense, the regions with a strong 'civic culture' and with a good institutional performance (Emilia-Romagna, Lombardy, Tuscany, Umbria, Veneto) are opposed to the poorer regions which have a clientelistic political culture and a weak institutional performance (Calabria, Molise, Campania, Puglia). From this measure of institutional performance emerges an attractive working hypothesis: 'The traditions of social activism and civic solidarity explain the socio-economic development and not the reverse. The political culture, and not the socio-economic structure, is the main determinant of institutional performance' [Putnam, 1988b].

Unfortunately the consequence of this hypothesis gave rise to a questionable demonstration, especially in the eyes of the Italian researchers, in the latest publication of the group [Putnam, 1993]. In this study, the author in fact supports the thesis of a long-term historical determination of Italian political cultures which are the foundations of institutional success: one in the centre–north (civic is cautiously translated as *più civico!* in Italian) rooted in the tradition of medieval communes, the other in the south (non-civic, cautiously translated in Italian by *meno civico!*) rooted in the heritage of the feudal and monarchic delegation. This work, published at a time when Italy was in the midst of a political crisis, and with much publicity, supplying arguments to the anti-south discourse of the Leagues, gave rise to many controversies. The more moderate critics point out that if this study has the merit of underlining the importance for institutional innovation or resources and reciprocity and trust (thus following the line of the writings of J.S. Colman, 1990), it suffers from an important lacuna: it does not take sufficient account of contemporary factors as important as the influence of local political subcultures, the partisan specificity of the local governments, the type of urbanisation, etc. [Bagnasco, 1994]. In doing this, it neglects the process of actualisation of the political cultures through conflict: take Emilia-Romagna, for example, is it not based on the co-operative gains of the violent socialist and communist struggles in the beginnings of the century rather than on the communal tradition? This criticism can be extended to the fact that the analysis is embedded within the global comprehension of the Italian political system and ignores the perverse effects of the recurring blockade of the mode of government, of the financial and political delegation, of the collapse of the system of control. Also, it cannot see that Italian regionalisation was a new form of occupation of the civil society by a largely corrupt political class, thus resulting in more destructive effects in the south than in the north [Lupo, 1993]. The harshest criticisms are about the use of history which is considered to be abusive and little informed, and possessing dualist bias: one has even gone to the extent of talking about 'politological Taylorism', evoking thus the return in disguise of the developmentalist demons [ibid., 1993].

In this passionate and complex debate, it is interesting to underline two points. First, from the methodological point of view, it seems worrying that the notion of institutional performance is so vaguely defined. In the earlier works, devoted to the institutionalisation of the Italian regional reform, the notion of performance is assimilated with a vague notion of institutional success:

> The attempts to create new political institutions are not rare. What is rare that such attempts result in success; that is to say that the created institutions are able to attain their objectives efficiently and conclusively, and thus satisfy the various interests. How is it that certain new institutions are successful and others fail? . . . The central question is: which are the favourable and unfavourable contextual circumstances for the creation of an efficient representative institution?
>
> [1985, pp. 127–8]

As A. Bagnasco [1994] writes in a review of Putnam's 1993 book, institutional performance is understood as the possibility of rendering the political choices effective, which seems to be an excessively inductive conception, and, to use a popular French expression, a way of 'retreating in order to make a greater leap': because, when all is said and done, how are these political choices made? In this first version it was still a matter of designing a method to measure performance.

It is in the introduction of this last book [1993] that the presuppositions of this analysis are clearly revealed.

> What do we mean by 'institutional performance'? Some theoreticians view political institutions primarily as 'the rules of the game', as procedures that govern collective decision-making, as arenas within which the conflicts are expressed and (sometimes) resolved . . . 'Success' for this kind of institution means enabling actors to resolve their differences as efficiently as possible, given their divergent preferences. Such a conception of political institutions is pertinent, but it does not exhaust the role of institutions in public life.
>
> Institutions are devices for achieving *purposes*, not just for achieving *agreement*. We want government to *do* things, not just *decide* about things – We do not agree on which of these things is most urgent, nor how they should be accomplished, nor even

> whether they are all worthwhile. All but the anarchists among us, however, agree that at least some of the time on at least some issues, action is required of governmental institutions. This fact must inform the way we think about institutional success and failure.
>
> The conception of institutional performance in this study rests on a very simple model of governance: societal demands —> political interaction —> government —> political choice —> implementation. Government institutions receive inputs from their social environment and produce outputs to respond to that environment. A high performance democratic institution must be both responsive and effective: sensitive to the demands of its constituents and effective in using limited resources to address those demands.
>
> (Putnam, 1993, pp.8–9, underlined in the text)

This is a somewhat surprising conception as it reminds us of the famous theory of the 'black box' system: in fact it seems to be circular logic to consider that, despite all the criticism about decision-making and institutional anthropology, institutional functioning could solely be evaluated along the explicit aims which were assigned to it. In brief, one does not see how with these suppositions, the institutions of the zones most dependent on the economic level and culturally furthest from the rational legal norms would not be less 'capable of performing well' than the richer zones or those closer to these norms; how Lombardy or Emilia-Romagna would not be more 'capable of performing well' than Puglia or Calabria. This is the old developmentalist refrain which led, for example, to the diagnosis of the failure of the democratic state in non-Western societies, rather than analysing the impact which its importation produced, and the local logic of its 'anamorphosis', rather than asking questions about the 'paradoxical invention of modernity' [Pallida, 1992; Leguil-Bayart, 1994].

The second remark concerns the strange status given to social and cultural processes which in the beginning are considered as contextual variables but later go on to become the main explanatory factors. Under the term *civic culture*, the connection with the works of G. Almond and S. Verba or with those so contested of E.C. Banfield, is evident. Incidentally it should be noted, for the sociology of knowledge, that the American critique of the work considers it as rather a novel and decisive step in the studies of civic culture [Laitin, 1995]. One can say that this conception is explicitly on the side of the most classic and dualistic developmentalism: of the social formations of the north and the centre of Italy, characterised by the relations of trust and reciprocity as opposed to the southern social formations characterised by the relations of subordination and exploitation.[5]

Again, recent critical research on the southern zones seems to have been useless. It is based on the historical production of norms and radically different political practices, centred on networks and clientelism, on particular kinds of solidarities and on the existence of political mediators [Gribaudi, 1991]. The Mezzogiorno is conceived as a group of historical subjects and not as a social group defined solely by the dearth of bourgeoisie, proletariat, collective action, sense of collective interest, etc. [Lupo, 1993], as a social space subject to the perverse effects (in the exact sense of effects of composition) caused by the forms of state intrusion in a different political dynamics. We know in fact that a number of vicious circles in which some of the territories of southern European countries have fallen, are the product of 'forced' nation- and state-building and the states have often used territorial break up as a resource for their own building process:

> Predating the formation of these states or having little to do with it, these hierarchies organized space in a way that did not coincide with political frontiers but was located in spaces that were larger or smaller . . . But at the same time, they offered the states a framework that was immediately available and operational, within which to act. What could have been more tempting for them than, in the very name of their own rhetoric, to have the cost of the modernization of the state structures and the economy borne by those sectors that were already inferior and dependent, locally and internationally? These were choices that aggravated internal tensions and stimulated a debate that took the form of an accusation against the state and its model of development. This debate occupied a central place in the culture of the countries in question and tended to unify the discourse of the social sciences into a critical analysis of a century of contemporary history.
>
> [Aymard, in Arrighi, 1985]

Now it is the same tendency which is at work today which makes G. Gribaudi, for example, write today:

> the overwhelming and centralising presence of the public institutions, and their monopoly on the quasi-totality of the (southern) economy provokes the perversion of the mechanisms of accumulation, turn aside the intelligence and the enterprising spirit,

> consolidate these networks of mediation and parasitism which bring in inefficiency and corruption.
>
> [Gribaudi, 1990]

Cf. also the work by C. Trigilia eloquently titled *Sviluppo senza autonomia. Effetti perversi delle politiche nel Mezzogiorno* [Trigilia, 1992]. We can see to what extent this kind of research takes us far away from the quasi-moralising reasoning of civic and non-civic.

It seems, indeed, that the habitual developmentalist value judgement comes out here in all its splendour: for proof, what would be put forward is the uncontrolled 'gliding' of the notions of vicious and virtuous circles, the vicious effect becoming synonymous with bad government and producing by opposition, the idea of virtue as equivalent to the legal rational model. 'Without the possibility of gradation, virtue is defined in opposition to vice, the north against Mezzogiorno, in a mental diagram dominated by the most crude and elementary dichotomous opposition: A vs. Non-A' [Lupo, 1993]. To this dualistic thinking we may prefer those which worry about nuances of anamorphosis, the forms of rational–legal, state when they are applied to societies with different socio-political regulations, as S. Pallida defines for Italy:

> the continuous and uncontrolled passage, in both directions, of the norm, proper to the rule of law, to the informal rules, indeed illegal (and even criminal), proper to the specific belongings to each segment, group or social entity; hence the passage or the coexistence of the legal and the illegal, from democracy to authoritarianism, from tolerance to intolerance . . . This is translated in the fact that the power-broker can be considered the central figure of the political organisation of society. In practical reality it manages the local society, translating, according to its rules and its methods, the norms and functions of the state. The central power is not in a position to penetrate the local society which is closed up in its specific rules which are cleverly manipulated by the power-broker. In this manner the heterogeneous segmentation of Italian society and the multiplicity of sovereignties or authorities and the forms of social discipline are perpetuated . . . The anamorphosis of the legal state, as a consequence, established itself as the possibility to govern a society whose rational political organisation henceforth seems impossible, because there are no forces capable of designing and realising a project aimed at the primacy of the collective interests over the individual interests. The anamorphosis is the end result of the adaptation of the traditional political categories to the effec-

> tive reality of economic relations, social and political, internal and external of the different actors dominating the Italian space.
> [Pallida, 1992, pp.270, 272, 289]

Or, as V. Pérez-Diaz put it in another way, about Spain:

> To the extent that these formal, universalistic rules do not apply fully to the institutions of a given policy and society, we may observe that the rules of the game of democratic pluralism and the due process of law, open markets, and meritocratic competition may be systematically distorted. They are made to coexist with, and are subverted by, other, very different rules, such as those on the model of patron-client relationships . . . Such distorted arrangements can be observed in all modern societies. But the point is whether they are contained within certain areas of life or are all-pervasive, whether such arrangements actually condition the greatest part (or a substantial part) of social life or are of only marginal importance.
> [Pérez-Diaz, 1993, pp.51]

PERSPECTIVE: THE POLITICAL CAPACITY OF REGIONAL INSTITUTIONS

That is why, if the problem of institution is posed instead from the point of view of civil society, we are better equipped to analyse political capacity. Let us note that in most European languages this term derives from the Latin term *capax*, and refers to the idea of capacity and the power to act: hence, here it is conceived of as denoting the processes by which civil society, its organisations and its values permeate the institutional structures. Michael Keating develops the idea of political capacity linked to territory. Invoking the change in the nature of the demand in regional autonomy in a new international order marked by the stress laid on economic interdependence and by the proliferation of co-operating institutions between states, he remarks:

> Only certain territories have the capacity to take advantage of this. This capacity does not depend solely on the constitutional structures but also on the nature of territorial civil societies, economic resources, the capacity for political mobilisation, and the capacity to project the territory into the international, particularly in the institutions of co-operation between the states . . . In the new context the nature of the stakes has changed. Autonomy implies a dexterity in handling complex political stakes, of placing them at the appropriate

> level (region, national or international) and exercising influence at that level. Influence and power in their turn are a function not only of the governmental powers but also of the territorial capacity.
>
> [Keating, 1992b, pp. 44, 55]

He analyses it according to economic capacity (structure of the local economy, links with the national and international markets), and capacity of social mobilisation on a territorial base (structure of the civil society).

We shall willingly follow him when he evokes the notion of 'the social construction of territory', founder of the 'secularised' forms of nationalism and regionalism, compared to the extreme and rarer forms of interpretation in ethnic terms (Lebanon, the Balkans and partially Ireland). The idea of social construction allows us in fact to escape the risks of cultural essentialism more frequent in these subjects, and also to integrate the fundamental variable of time. If a territory politically constructs (or deconstructs) itself in time, analysis can reveal its different moments: militant reconstruction then institutionalisation as in the Catalan case between nineteenth and the twentieth century; the appearance of political territorialisation under the game of political competition as within the 'non-historical' Spanish Autonomous Communities, for example, Andalusia; the wiping out of political territories under the influence of demographic and economic changes, as was the case with the wine-producing and rebellious Languedoc in France from the 1960s onwards [Ritaine, 1991]; the quasi-inexistence of territorial roots as is the case in a number of French regions, etc. Territory is always a potential resource, and a potential political work: the conditions of affirmation or failure of this resource and this work seem to be important dimensions of this analysis. On this reasoning the fact that there exists a descriptive ethnological substratum is only one of the possible conditions, neither necessary, nor sufficient, neither necessarily 'virtuous' nor 'vicious'. Who could say, for example, if the strong Basque cultural substratum is today only a positive factor (foundation of a nationalistic affirmation), or also a negative factor (the historical characteristics of the nationalistic movement having created an atmosphere of withdrawal, violence, and difficulty of actualisation, in the face of contemporary challenges) [Heiberg, in Rokkan and Urwin, 1982; Pérez-Agote, 1992]?

It is in this sense possible to write:

> Southern Europe is an ideal terrain to put forward two meanings of the notion of territory-based political cultures. The first one, illustrated by the Italian case, is a research construct, an

> anthropological and historical analysis proves the strong sociological foundation of the territorial basis of political traditions; it is possible to qualify them as political cultures rooted in territory, meaning by that, that their dynamics are basically neither linguistic nor cultural but political (the Italians talk of local political subcultures, thus denoting their inclusion in a much larger system of reference). In this case it is the observation which delimits the territory and not the claims of the actors. Contrary to what happens in the second type, which is more important in Spain, where the construction processes are revealed by the work of political cultures with nationalistic dimensions.
>
> [Ritaine, 1994b]

> The regionalist discourse is performative discourse aiming to impose as legitimate a new definition of frontiers and to make known and recognised the regions thus outlined against the dominant definition and unknown as such, hence recognised and legitimate, which ignores it. The act of categorisation, when it manages to get itself recognised or when it is exercised by a recognised authority, exerts power by itself: 'ethnic' or 'regional' categories, like the categories of kinship, establish a reality by using the power of revelation and construction exercised by objectivisation through discourse.
>
> [Bourdieu, 1980]

It would be fair to add an additional dimension of political competition, between political actors [Genieys, 1994] and between territories, which seems to be a process of producing political resources with an increasingly important political base, notably in relations between the Spanish Autonomous Communities, and between them and the state. The very pragmatic principle which has been behind the creation of these Autonomous Communities has in fact triggered off a dialectic of competition which harms the principle of national solidarity and the implementation of redistributive policies. Two examples illustrate this process. The first one is that of tax resources, for which the richer and more nationalistic Communities, Catalonia and the Basque Country, continue to demand greater autonomy whereas the poorer Communities, specially from the south, refuse to give up the principle of state redistribution. The second one is that of hydraulic resources, for which there is a national plan for compensating between zones running a surplus and those in deficit, which presents the same problems of competition. The progress in the balance of power between political party organisations, notably the fact that no possibility of governing exists without more or less tacit support, depending on the case, of nationalistic organisations, evidently increases the force of this process, drawing Spanish political life into a spiral of territory-based and contradictory overbidding. Therefore, it is very important to know whether the evolution of this political and institutional development represents a resource or acts as a drawback in the face of the vital challenge which economic crisis presents in Spain: will the balance of territorial powers lean towards co-operation or towards competition?: will the rules of the game be solidarity with poorer zones or an outrageous differentiation?

With the notion of political capacity applied to the existence of political territories, an inversion of the studies on institutional performance and performance takes place. The social and cultural processes are considered neither as contextual variables, nor as a univocal, explanatory factor. In a medium-term perspective they are constructed as potential resources for political action. As in the case of previous studies, we are back to social capital [Coleman, 1990], networks and relations of trust [Gambetta, 1988], mediators [Gribaudi, 1991]. However this construction increases the interest taken in processes of socialisation and mobilisation, in political exchange and in representations of interests, in political work. In this manner we would agree with the fundamental criticism which G. Pasquino directs against Putnam's work:

> I would rather go and look at conflicts and struggles, at the modalities of the organisation of the political life and in the modalities of government, of the political community the roots of the affirmation of the pair 'reciprocity/trust' or of the pair 'subordination/exploitation' . . . Good government is a result, on the one hand, of organisations with a strong political content (leagues, unions, parties), and on the other of conflicts and struggles, tensions and confrontations which, in their manner of appearance and unfolding, create, model, redefine the civic traditions . . . The conscious political organisations have internalised struggles and conflicts in their attitudes and have incorporated them in their behaviour of the government and the opposition. Civic traditions are important, but the civic behaviour and the behaviour of the government are even more important.
>
> [Pasquino, 1994, pp.312–13]

The analysis of struggles and recent political practices is in fact a more modern and more modest means than recourse to long-term explanations to try to understand local political trajectories. For example, much has been written about the political success of Emilia-Romagna, that it is better to take an interest in the violent political and trade union struggles of the century than the medieval traditions of communalism. It is also a better method of analysing the distinct resistance to the establishment of Leagues in all the 'civic' regions [Caciagli, 1995]. This is yet another way of approaching the position of southern researchers in Italy who instead of calling for a legal–rational transformation of behaviour, end up calling for a 'modernising twist of the clientelistic relationship':

> a clientelistic relationship with a minimum of stability between public machinery (central and peripheral) and social actors (individual and collective) which does not fade away in distributive policies but allows the planning and the implementation of regulatory and redistributive and innovative policies could constitute for the South a passageway to modernity more accessible than purely and simply bypassing the traditional form of clientelistic political participation. The modernising sections of the political parties and of the state machinery linking themselves with the innovating social groups in a clientelistic mode could produce a kind of political exchange (internal to the South and in the centre–periphery relations) capable of stimulating the economic and politico-institutional modernisation. It should succeed in producing this strategic autonomy and this bureaucratic capacity of the public power, which are being considered more and more indispensable for the development of late-comers and which seem to be particularly lacking in the Mezzogiorno. This would also constitute a prior condition for an effective struggle against crime.
>
> [Mutti, in Cesare, 1992, pp. 25–6]

Because, despite its provoking aspect, this proposal has the merit, instead of excluding it in Manichean terms, of asking the fundamental question of the possible function of the clientelistic structures in modernisation, as do other studies [Roniger and Günes-Ayata, 1994].

That is why V. Pérez-Diaz wrote:

> However, in the Basque region the potential for the segmentation of society seems to be a much more critical problem, and one which is directly related to the role of violence in that region. A double phenomenon may be observed there. On the one hand, an enormous potential for linking up the community is being invested in the operation of regional, provincial, and local self-government, and in the dramatic self-assertion of identity and culture. This

> argues well for a process of learning and moral development, but there has been an erosion of trust between communities and a breakdown in the social fabric. People have become accustomed to exasperation and violence, to the emotional evaluation of their own interests, and to the rejection of possible reasons on the part of their adversaries. All of this of course delights militant and billigerent groups, but makes it ever more difficult to sustain a policy of economic recovery, and paves the way for all kinds of demagogy. It suggests a process of increasing chaos and tension where only violence itself can be established.
>
> [Pérez-Diaz, 1993, p. 214]

FOCUS: POLITICAL EXCHANGE AROUND REGIONAL INSTITUTIONS

This way of redefining the debate on civil society implies an approach organised around the paradigm of political exchange which is understood as a widespread exchange between complex organisations of the political and social spheres. The idea of 'collective actions constructs' shows how the rules of the game, which make 'conflicting co-operation' between organisations possible, are produced (Friedberg, in Marin, 1990). The ultimate development of this paradigm tries to accommodate the pluralistic and neo-corporatist conceptions of the political exchange by considering them as degrees of complexity of a conceptualised meta-game, as 'the politically induced and politically ordered interdependence of a multiplicity of markets and their interpenetration with the politician's spaces' as 'generalised political exchange' [Marin, in Marin, 1990]. For the regional object, it implies particularly taking into account the exchange of the institution with the organisations of interests [Trigilia, 1989], and this, depending on its intensity, can reveal itself as a highly distinctive resource among European regions. This is why certain analysts of neo-corporatism think that European Union-building is a factor of deregulation for neo-corporatist tendencies, and will give rise to the generalisation of pluralistic exchanges, on the level of the European Union and that of the states, and in this manner will subject the regional and the local governments to severe adaptations subject to open competition and permanent political bargaining [Streeck and Schmitter, 1992].

Italian neo-localism is an example of the form of modern regulation which a negotiation capacity rooted in territory can bring about. Within the subcultures of the north and the north-east of Italy, present conditions of political exchange were analysed. All the indicators envisaged since the unification of Italy (intensity and type of strikes in the agricultural and later in the industrial environment, the rate of union memberships, the ideological leanings of the unions, the existence of Catholic or socialist networks, the electoral trends) attest the continuity of these 'red' and 'white' political subcultures. The question was by what process this investment was realised, how the stability and the reproduction of these phenomena are secured. Thinking on this matter consequently has taken on an anthropological dimension by questioning the role of the social processes as the mode of production, work organisation, the type of family, or the religious orientation; but it also has a sociological dimension by taking an interest in the processes of socialisation, mobilisation, or organisation of interests; but in fact, this has a political dimension by imagining the historical consequences of a distinct access to the state centre. This very detailed contemporary genealogy, mainly due to C. Trigilia, 1986, can also give the measure of the extent to which the precise analysis of the processes of reproduction is far richer than a long-term historical explanation.

It is in connection with these circumstances with very strong local socio-political regulation that the notion of *neolocalismo* has sprung up, to render the updating of this heritage explicit in the current stakes of diffuse industrialisation which these territories had to face.

> We want to draw attention to two points [about the presence of political subcultures rooted in territories]: the existence of a pool of resources for the organisation of interests and the influence on a mode of representation largely conditioned by economic and local politics links.
>
> [Trigilia, 1985]

Faced with social destabilisation and the uncertainty produced by this mode of development based on flexibility and the co-operation of numerous economic actors, the homogeneity of local political circumstances, their intensely networked organisation has allowed the emergence of locally based mediation of interests. The neo-localist regulation can be analysed as a model of locally organised permanent negotiation, which

> finds expression in a combination of functional structures (trade unions, organisations of certain categories and entrepreneurs) which interact among themselves and with the local government within specific zones, and by territorial structures of representations (party, commune) which help regulation with their interventions

> and the actions effected at regional and central levels. This process is influenced by the subcultural context, which furnishes resources for the organisation of interests, but also conditions the modalities of interaction of the different actors of the local political system.
>
> (ibid.)

Thus with particular attention paid to the representations of interests, it is defined as

> the specific division of work between the market, the social structures, and increasingly, the political structures, which allows a greater flexibility of economy and permits an adaptability to deal with the variations of the market, but also enables a redistribution of social costs and the advantages of development within the local society.
>
> (ibid.)

However, this localised regulation expresses itself only at the municipal level, indeed, at the provincial level which is but its natural relay because of the provincial organisation of political party and trade-union structures. The Italian regions, on the contrary, only rarely manage to organise the political exchange at their level. The representations of interests are focus on local and national levels. The territory-based regulation in Italy remains for the moment essentially centred on a social dynamics and localised politics, and the evaluation of the capacities of mobilisation around the regional institution is much more variable than what R. Putnam's team showed it to be [Trigilia, 1989]. Only a few regions with particularly vigorous bargaining policy seem to escape this weakness: for example, Lombardy which has managed interesting programme planning performances partially because it has powerful and mobilised entrepreneurs associations for its partners; in contrast, Emilia-Romagna, an exemplary region for its social and environmental policies, has not succeeded in weaving stable relations with the representations of economic interests at the regional level [Leonardi and Nanetti, 1990].

In the Spanish case, the evaluation of the relationship between territory and political capacity is as yet little developed and little theorising. Anyway, it is impossible to approach it without keeping in mind the consolidating function of pluralistic democracy which the creation of Autonomous Communities has played, caught between the twofold transition from authoritarianism to democracy and from centralism to decentralisation [Linz and Montero, 1986]. In this respect S. Giner goes to the extent of talking of an 'ethnic legitimisation of democracy' [Giner, in Hernandez and Mercade, 1986]. J. Botella more quietly considers that

> in the 'historical' regions the creation of Autonomous Communities embodies (or at least tries to embody) profound nationalistic and regionalist sentiments. In the 'new' regions, where these sentiments are absent or almost absent, it seems that the stake is more the political pluralism rather than territory.
>
> [Botella, 1989]

However, the fact remains that the Autonomous Communities draw a very strong political legitimacy from historical origins and is attested by all the opinion polls [Morata, 1992, 1994]. The question of the political capacity of the Autonomous Communities is rendered particularly complex by the famous 'variable geometry' of their institutionalisation. Let us bear in mind that in the Spanish Constitution they have neither the same status (historical Communities in the Basque Country, Catalonia, Galicia; Communities with *fueros* in the Basque Country and Navarra; ordinary Communities) nor the same means for gaining autonomy, nor do they enjoy the same levels of political and financial autonomy [Rodriguez-Pose, 1997]. This last point is particularly important for the future of the Spanish system because certain Communities have a financial capacity comparable to that of federated states, whereas most of the others have limited resources and financial possibilities:

> despite the increase in the budget of the regions, the gap between the regions with large financial capacities (Charter and art. 151) and those with weak budgetary prerogatives (art. 143) has remained more or less constant since the 1980s and the beginning of the 1990s. Five regions represent 80 per cent of the total regional budget. Since 1984 Andalusia has received about a quarter of the total regional financing; Catalonia about 20 per cent whereas three other regions (Valence, Basque Country, Galicia) receive about 10 per cent of the budget devolved to the regions. The other regions are far behind, never exceeding 5 per cent (Ministry of Economy, 1994).
>
> [Rodriguez-Pose, 1997]

Even within this very diversified system, 'the development of the State of Autonomies has configured distinct political arenas according to cultural, political and socio-economic characteristics and political traditions of every territory' [Morata, 1994]. The classic works of J. Linz already showed in 1966 that Spanish heterogeneity is not limited to regional differences alone but rests on different sociological dynamics, and these differences are less clearly rooted in territory than in Italy. Socio-economic differences apart, the different social zones vary as regards recruitment of the elites, modes of social mobilisation, and weight of the religious factor and these therefore vary widely in electoral terms. In this sociologically fragmented context, it is necessary that specific groups of mediators between the state and the diverse social formations appear [Linz, 1966]. Since then, and despite economic and political changes, deep-rooted difficulties of integration, notably territorial, remain:

> In Spain, as in other territories having profound territorial differences . . . , only the practice of solidarity in an organised manner between different regions and nationalities could provide an alternative to the perverse effects, notably of the economic development . . . A federalist co-operative type of philosophy has to be joined by a consociational type of political attitude.
>
> [Giner and Moreno, 1990, p. 194]

It is by comparing the political capacities of the Autonomous Communities which are most studied (because as far as revelations go, our information on the different Autonomies is very irregular, reproducing more or less the hierarchy of the principle of autonomy) that some major lessons are learned, notably the importance of the type of political work accomplished by the nationalistic movements, also the fundamental role of the capacity of mobilising interests.

The nationalistic substratum, consisting of the political construction of language, culture and history, is mobilised in diversified nationalistic movements depending on the social interests, ideological tendencies, and current political stakes [Garraud, in Balme *et al.*, 1994]. Let us recall the struggles, often occurring at different times, of the bourgeoisie and the Catalan workers' movements, as well as the capacity of throwing up interclass solutions in Catalonia: the *Lliga catalana* of the beginning of the century, the *Esquerra Republicana* of Catalunya during the Second Republic, and *Convergència i Unio* today. By contrast, in the Basque Country the rivalry between a moderate autonomy-seeking current (today the 'statutory' of the *Partito Nacional Vasco* and the *Euskadico Eskerra*) and a nationalistic current (the 'rupturists' of *Eusko Alkartasuna* and of *Herri Batasuna*), with an armed branch (ETA), never died out completely. The history of political cultures in this fashion endowed them with very different characters; although both of them had been suggested beforehand by the Carlist oppositions to the Spanish state, and the position of their elites in these struggles made all the difference.

In Catalonia, the elites had opted for economical and political separation, and within this framework, nationalistic political organisations with all kinds of allegiance developed. What resulted from that was a more pragmatic nationalistic movement, more open to negotiation (illustrated among other things by the creation of the Catalan Assembly in 1971 which co-ordinated the different opposition efforts against Francoism) and more capable of managing the present-day stakes. This is how the *Generalitat* of Catalonia keeps as one of its major political objectives the strengthening of its political potential *vis-à-vis* the central government, on the one hand, and *vis-à-vis* the sub-regional political powers on the other (notably in the face of the municipality of Barcelona held by the socialists whereas the *Generalitat* is in the hands of the centrist nationalists). To do this it has at its disposal considerable legislative power. In particular it can reform its territorial organisation and it has not hesitated in doing that. By drawing to it the representations of interest with a view to politically control them, it has thus dissolved the metropolitan institution of Barcelona which tended to bring together the more dynamic economic interests and put to sleep the provinces, for the benefit of intermediary institutions of the *comarca*, responsible for intercommunal co-operation. In a renewed framework, it favoured the creation of regional levels of representation of interests when these did not exist; then it assured the integration of the representation of interests in the process of political decision-making by multiplying, notably in matters of economic policy, mixed participation authorities. Thus, on the political level, it has strengthened the ancient tradition of association of the Catalan socio-economic milieux. These regional representations often joined the national representations to confront the demands of negotiation within the European Union where they acted as engines [Tornos-Mass, 1990; Coleman and Jacek, 1989; Sidjanski and Ayberg, 1990]. By this 'institutionalised political exchange' [Cazzola, 1983], based on an inherited substratum of regional socio-political integration, the Catalan Autonomous Community is working to secure for itself a strategic political importance in a complex system of political exchange.

In the Basque Country the leaders had not broken off their links with the Spanish nation. Hence Basque nationalism developed in the middle classes under the aegis of the Basque clergy. As a consequence it remained socially more isolated and more radicalised at the political level. The direct connection with Catholic traditionalism in fact inspired a conservative nationalism often challenged by new nationalist groups, more radical and more ready to switch over to armed struggle. The cycle of violence and repression further strengthened this tendency. Today the nationalistic Basque movement is more complex, very much fragmented in different political options, also much less able to face the contemporary challenges, notably in the face of the economic decline of the Basque regions:

> when the situation is characterised by a tension with the centre there is certain nationalistic unanimity, whereas in cases which correspond to situations (more and more frequent in view of the present situation of autonomy) where the internal problems of the Basque Country can be politically resolved, deep-level conflicts result from it within the very heart of the nationalist movements.
>
> [Pérez-Agote, 1992]

Also, the Basque Country seems to be showing a lesser capacity to adapt to present-day challenges, notably the capacity of economic reconversion, partially because its recent history deprives it of a *habitus* of negotiations and compromise.

These historically shaped characters have important effects on the political potential of these Communities. For example, the ability to face the challenge of assimilating immigrants coming from the other Spanish regions, or the ability to support the national language policy [Barbosa, 1995]. They also affect the ability to join in with European integration. Confronted with the risk of the diminution of powers of the Autonomous Communities in the European Union, the *Generalitat* of Catalonia initially started off a very voluntarist European policy, which makes it one of the most active European regions in the eyes of the European Union and in the European inter-regional relations. In this strategy it uses its economic potential as well as its abilities to mobilise interests: in relation to the national centre, the European stakes, and in the movement of internal political competitions. The aim of political construction of the territory is in a way permanently at work.

OVERTURE

Regions need to be considered as opening themselves up to current political challenges in southern Europe: these challenges henceforth are instability and unemployment, increasing crime and uncontrolled migrations. To do this, we imagine, on the one hand, that the weakness of the state in the face of the most serious societal problems is to blame for the present origin of the South European challenges; on the other hand, the most important societal problems are linked to the social and territorial fragmentation produced by the history of these countries.

To study this dialectic between the weakness of the national and/or state construction and sociological and territorial fragmentation, research can take inspiration from two major currents of analysis. The first one of comparatist and micro-historical inspiration devotes itself to the political trajectory of these countries, characterised by a contradictory national state construction, by a recent passage through the dictator sequence – democratic transition – democratic consolidation, by the populist and regionalist protests. It traces out a kind of genealogy of political polycentrism. The second of a more sociological and ethnological order, more characterised by research in the field and sociological construction, criticises classical developmentalism and favours keener analysis of the market/reciprocity relations in the south of Europe. If it clearly shows the social production of segmentation, it also reveals the unseen social resources of these societies which we can call 'hybrid', combining norms and legal–rational practices and network norms and practices. If the challenge of linking these two types of analysis can be taken up, it is only through the intermediary of the paradigm of political exchange, and therefore a consideration of civil society. We may then advance the hypothesis that confronted with the weakness of state regulation, these societies have produced other forms of political regulation, of which the most important ones appear in the form of territory and regulation.

These modes of political regulation determine the way in which current problems are tackled and have become major issues. In the south of Europe, the historical construction of territorial and social segmentation has in fact been one of territory-based mediations. These sometimes constitute resources of adaptation, sometimes they turn out also to be a blocking factor. Regional institutions are sometimes taken in, in a circle sometimes virtuous, sometimes vicious, whose institutional analysis alone does not exhaust all the dynamism involved.

NOTES

1 Term used by the author in his latest publication [1993] or 'institutional productivity' (a term used more frequently in the previous works of the same team).
2 Limited to Spain and Italy for the convenience of the present chapter.
3 This research was carried out during a Jean Monnet fellowship at the European University Institute (Florence) in 1995, at the R. Schuman Centre headed by Y. Mény.

4 Still it has to be made clear that this position, although inevitably critical given the scientific designing of the object is not without respect for a research project involving some twenty years of analysis of fifteen regions, an intensity of work few researchers could put forward and which brings a host of empirical and analytical elements as well as a lesson in research organisation. Notably with the creation of a productivity index with some twelve indicators (stability of the *junta*; punctuality in the presentation of the budget; information services and statistics; legislative reforms; innovative character of the regional legislation; crèche development policy; policy of centres for family counselling; tools of industrial policy; expenditure on agriculture; expenditure on local sanitation units; policy of housing construction and urbanism; availability of the bureaucratic machinery) coupled with the degree of satisfaction expressed by the citizens and their leaders.

5 Cf. the astonishing description on page 115 [Putnam, 1993].

6 Regions and economic development

Mick Dunford

INTRODUCTION: COMPARATIVE REGIONAL ECONOMIC DEVELOPMENT

At present critical ideas and progressive values seem to be on the defensive in the face of a new liberal consensus. Yet the performance of the Western economies falls far short of that the mixed economies achieved in the 'Trente Glorieuses' In that era capitalism managed to achieve macro-economic stability but at cost of a de-skilling of work and its meaning. Stability and growth were the result of a series of reforms which temporarily regulated the two main sets of contradictions of capitalist societies: the anarchy of the market and the horizontal conflicts between economic subjects in market societies, and the contested organisation of work and division of value added rooted in the wage relation.

From the middle of the 1970s a productivity slowdown and the globalisation of economic life led, however, to a crisis of nationally organised models of development and an erosion of solidaristic national modes of regulation. One consequence of this was a significant change in the structure of economic life and in the organisation and strategies of the state. At a political level these changes included a deconcentration or decentralisation of the State with in many cases a significant role for regions in the shaping of economic development, market liberalisation, sale of public assets and a switch to supply-side economic measures.

What is interesting is the fact that much of the literature on the decentralisation of economic initiatives to the regions is concerned with the ways in which regional institutions can provide collective resources and can foster trust and localised learning and innovation to overcome some of the contradictions of market society. At the same time, however, it is important to recognise that the switch to supply-side measures was in part a consequence of the inability of national governments to implement voluntaristic Keynesian policies. Deconcentration and decentralisation have occurred therefore in a wider macro-economic environment in which competition has intensified, the contradictions of market societies are expressed in less mediated ways and overall economic performance has deteriorated.

The aim of this chapter is to explore some of these dilemmas. More specifically, in the first section it explores some data on comparative economic performance showing in particular that there are strong tendencies towards greater social and territorial inequality in the European Union. In most Member States strong regions have achieved faster rates of growth than weaker regions. Throughout the EU restructuring has occurred without a reintegration of the displaced workforce in the world of work. Greater inequality and unemployment raise the question as to whether the current rules of the game are such that every region can win. In the second section this chapter aims to identify some of the ways in which local regulation can overcome some of the contradictions of market-led development. The thesis that the degree of organisation of a regional economy is a critical determinant of its competitiveness is one that is widely discussed in the literature and so it receives relatively little attention in this chapter. The reason why is that I wish to ask the question as to whether or not supply-side measures are sufficient. In the third section this question is addressed in more detail, identifying some of the reasons why resources released as a result of regional restructuring may not be re-employed, short of the construction of a new regulatory order. Anyone concerned with regional economic development must consider, I will argue, not just the micro-level or supply-side determinants of regional performance but also the wider rules of the game which condition regional development strategies.

THE STARTING-POINT: DIFFERENTIAL REGIONAL DEVELOPMENT AND ECONOMIC PERFORMANCE

The starting-point for much contemporary regional economic research is a recognition of the existence of significant disparities in the trajectories and development of different nations and of the mosaics of cities and regions that make them up.

Differences in the level of development

If economic potential is measured not in terms of the size of economies but in the value of the goods and services produced per inhabitant, clear hierarchies emerge as Figures 6.1 and 6.2 show. International inequalities in national and regional GDP can be measured in several ways.[1]

There are two further qualifications that need to be made before indicators of income and GDP are used. First, GDP is a measure of the output of the market and the public sectors. It excludes all forms of self-provisioning, informal work and most voluntary work. Second, GDP and income are indicators not of welfare but of the resources which can be used to meet human needs. Welfare depends on how these resources are used. Accordingly, the United Nations Development Programme has constructed a Human Development Index (HDI) which includes not just income (adjusted to reflect diminishing utility or well-being derived from income) but also life expectancy and educational attainment. (A modified index also allows for differences in the distribution of income.) The former communist countries have very high scores on the HDI due to the substantial

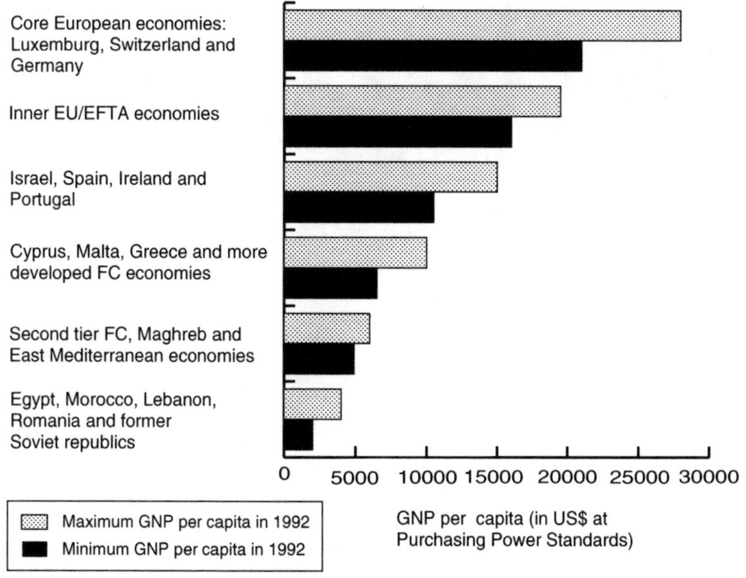

Figure 6.1 Inequalities in development in Europe and its neighbouring countries

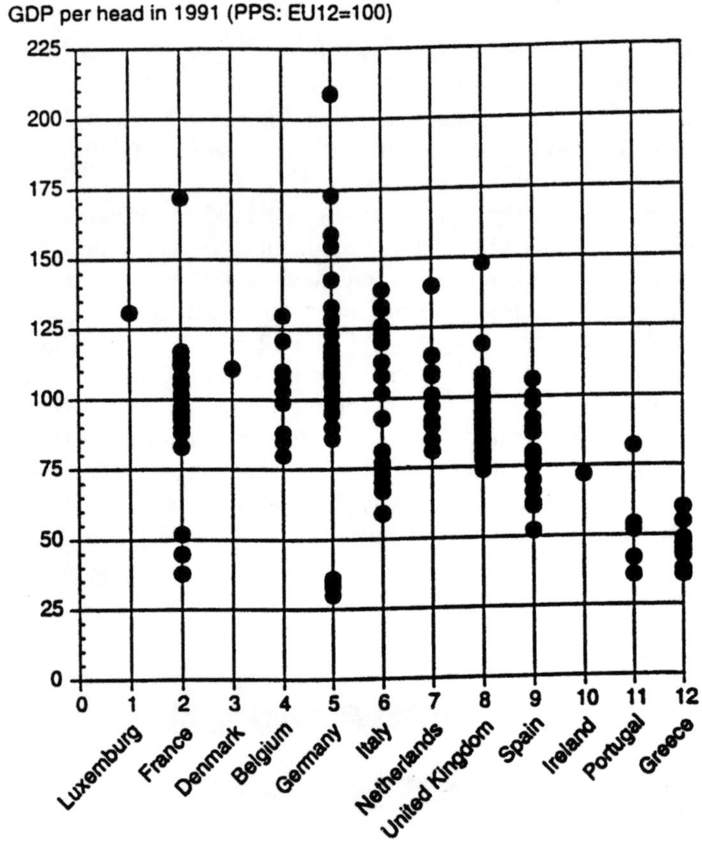

Figure 6.2 Gross Domestic Product per head (in PPS) by NUTS II regions in 1991

investments they made in health and education (UNDP 1993). Figure 6.1 which records the Gross National Product (GNP) per head of the national economies of Europe and the Mediterranean indicates that there are wide disparities in the levels of national development, while Figure 6.2 which records Gross Domestic Product (GDP) of NUTS II regions in the European Union is indicative of the magnitude of regional development disparities. These data on GDP per head which measure the per capita value of all the market and collective sector goods and services produced in an area or produced by those inhabitants of an area who are 'employed', or the capacity of the economic activities in an area to create or appropriate wealth, provide a relief map of economic development. GDP measures of wealth differ from measures of the income of residents. Differences in the two result from the inclusion in the income measure of incomes paid to economically inactive individuals such as pensioners and the unemployed and from the inclusion of profits in GDP and investment income in household income. In this chapter I shall not consider these transfers and the redistribution of wealth that stems from them.

Differential regional dynamics and trends in inequality

Differences in the level of development themselves reflect variations in the timing, speed and quality of development. Two sets of mechanisms seem to be at work. First, there is a set of forces which seems to lead to constant differentiation of the conditions of production and exchange and a reproduction or even an amplification of inequalities. Second, there seems to be a set of forces which lead to an equalisation differentiation of rates of development, relatively faster growth in some less developed areas and a reduction in disparities. The relative weight of these forces varies over time and space. At a global level, for example, national disparities declined until the mid-1970s as many countries gained ground on the United States. After the mid-1970s, however, the situation was much more differentiated with some countries falling back quite sharply while others continued to gain ground.

Within European countries there are also wide variations in the economic dynamism and success of regional and urban economies. In the United Kingdom, for example, there was a turnaround in trends in spatial inequality in the mid-1970s. In the years up to 1976 regional variations in Gross Domestic Product per inhabitant decreased. In 1976–89 there was a dramatic increase in spatial inequalities. Divergence was a result of the relative growth of the South East, South West and East Anglia and the relative decline of much of the rest of the country. With the onset of the recession in the early 1990s the divide declined. In 1977–91 as a whole there was nevertheless a very substantial relative growth of GDP per head in a cluster of counties in the Greater South East (Surrey 25.9 per cent, Buckinghamshire 24.1, Wiltshire 12.4, Berkshire 11.0, Oxfordshire 10.9 and West Sussex 10.6), though similar cumulative increases were recorded in a number of other counties (Warwickshire 27.6 per cent, Grampian 21.1, Clywd 18, Cumbria 16 and North Yorkshire 10.6). At the other end of the spectrum there were very sharp drops in GDP per head in a number of northern industrial cities (Merseyside −23.4 per cent, Cleveland −21.1 and South Yorkshire −20.0).[2]

Determinants of inequality

Differences in GDP per inhabitant can be divided into two elements: first, differences in productivity which themselves reflect differences in physical productivity, prices and earnings; and second, differences in the share of the active population in employment. In the case of international data, differences in the prices an area's output commands on international markets (and therefore the inequalities in prices and exchange rates built into regional trade structures) should be added.

This disaggregation produces a number of insights into the determinants of geographical disparities in development. As a simple illustrative example consider the case of the United Kingdom in 1981 and 1991. In 1981 the dominance of Greater London and to a lesser extent of the South East rested on above-average productivity levels and employment rates. In Wales and the Northern region the major determinant of less than average GDP per head was low employment rates, whereas in most other areas a productivity divide predominated. In the ten years from 1981 to 1991 several changes occurred. First, the employment rates deteriorated quite sharply in a number of areas: included were Greater London, Yorkshire and Humberside, the North West, the Northern region and Wales. The position of Greater London which was eroded over this period depended to a much greater extent than in the past on its productivity lead. This productivity lead increased in the 1980s due presumably to changes in the structure of employment and in the earnings of those employed in high status jobs in the capital. A number of areas around the capital saw a relative improvement in their employment rates but their productivity differentials declined indicating their dependence on the expansion of relatively low productivity jobs: included in this group were the South East, East Anglia, the South West and the East Midlands

MARKET FAILURE, INSTITUTIONAL CAPACITIES AND THE SUPPLY-SIDE REGULATION OF REGIONAL ECONOMIC DEVELOPMENT

In economic geography and economics there are important debates about the determinants of the structure, dynamics and strength of regional economies. Traditionally, an area's specialisation was seen as depending on its resource endowment, though more recently economists have given much greater emphasis to the role of increasing returns. According to Krugman, for example, economic activities emerge as a result of historical accidents but their subsequent development acquires a self-perpetuating momentum: suppliers develop around original manufacturers; local research and educational institutions specialise in related research and training; purchasers flock to the area creating returns to scale that are so important that no producer can afford to locate elsewhere. This increasing returns argument is, however, very close to the one put forward by Kaldor [1970] and earlier by Myrdal [1957] and it is quite consistent with a view that resource endowments matter except that resources are interpreted to include created resources, skills, know-how, and so on. An area's resource endowment creates certain possibilities for development. What determines its dynamism is in part its capacity to mobilise savings and invest in ways that mobilise these resources and achieve high levels of productivity and rates of productivity growth, while productivity growth offers possibilities of increasing real wages, raising living standards and improving the quality of life. The main reasons for the character, level and quality of development are:

1 The character, level and quality of development depend on an area's resource endowments: natural resources, infrastructures, population and its skills and level of development of the forces of production. An area's endowment of natural and created resources/assets is a cause of development, specialisation and the division of labour.
2 The character, level and quality of development also depend on the effectiveness and the degree of mobilisation of an area's resources/assets and its human potential which itself depends on institutional structures and capacities, systems of regulation, and social relations of production.
3 As resources are created, conserved and reproduced in and through development resource endowments are also a consequence of development: many of the resources on which development depends are endogenous rather than exogenous, are a result of growth and investment and are greatest in areas that are already developed. Development processes are therefore potentially cumulative.

These statements require qualification. First, as Colletis and Pecqueur [1993] have argued, a distinction should be made between resources (latent and potential conditions of development) and assets (activated conditions of development) and generic (found in a number of places at different costs) and specific resources/assets. The most sensible aim of local development strategies is, they argue, the creation of specific assets, though differences in development also depend on differences in the quantity and quality of generic assets (communications and telecommunications infrastructures, generic skills, and so on). Second, at any point in time development does not just depend on already given regional resource endowments but also on the scale of the new resources regions receive to finance programmes of development. Third, the economic strength of an area may not simply reflect its productive strength but also the fact that its inhabitants can command and control the resources of others: an example is the transfers of wealth that stem from unequal exchange.

At any point in time, however, the performance of a regional economy will depend in part on its resource/asset endowment. The effectiveness with which resources are used will depend in turn on a complex array of institutional, social and cultural factors: the organisation of productive activities, and the structure of the industrial relations system; the character of inter-firm relationships and networking strategies and of structures for the mobilisation of finance for economic development; the character of regional systems of innovation, of strategies for the development of skills and of systems of interest representation along with the roles of partnership, reciprocity and trust; and the character of government–industry relations, the significance of partnership relationships between regions, the structure of governance and the scale, character and articulation of policies at local, regional, national and supranational levels.

What this claim leaves unanswered is the question of the relative importance of these different elements. The first questions that need to be answered concern the relative significance of (1) the initial resource endowment of a region, its location and degree of remoteness, (2) external resources whether from national or supranational institutions and companies and (3) institutional capacities and structures in determining the scale of resources deployed to develop regional economies and the efficiency and the effectiveness with which resources are used and the timeliness of action to redeploy resources released as economic activities are restructured.

A regulation theoretic approach to the supply-side dynamics of regional economies would normally be seen as implying that institutional capacities and social relations play an important role. Certainly at a societal level it embodies the claim that dynamic and stable growth occurs when a regulatory order is in place which temporarily regulates the contradictions of capitalist societies. These regulatory orders are a reflection of specific structural, cyclical and conjunctural conditions, are not intended but are the outcome of struggle and are an expression of power relations.

At the centre of this approach is a claim that there are two critical sets of contradictions: first, there is a set of horizontal contradictions captured in the concept of the 'anarchy of the market' which itself reflects the conflicts beween the interests of subjects in market societies, the co-ordination losses associated with excessive competition and more generally the contradiction between private and social interests; second, there is a set of vertical contradictions and conflicts associated with the organisation of work and division of value added which themselves are rooted in the character of the wage relation (and perhaps also with centre–periphery relations).

The regulation theoretic approach is clearly distinct from the methodological individualism of conventionalist approaches in its insistence on the existence of relations of wealth, power, parenthood and of other structural confrontations that underlie contingent social interaction. Conventionalists reduce all relations to horizontal interactions, reduce the despotism of capitalist co-operation to a problem of transactional co-ordination, reduce institutionalised compromise to cognitive rules (this is a return to intentionalism: conventionalism minimises transaction costs and perverse effects). For regulationists regulatory orders do not necessarily serve to regulate contradictions as they are compromises in a struggle that leads to phases of precarious and transitory stability [see Lipietz, 1995].

Of the horizontal contradictions, most are associated with the existence of externalities and market failure. Two examples will suffice. First there is analytical evidence which suggests that market economies suffer from widespread co-ordination failures which can result in situations in which savings and investment get locked into an equilibrium of low investment and low growth. In most market situations the pay-off for any one player depends on the actions of others so that if, for example, all firms raise their investment, returns rise rather than fall as overall demand rises. If, therefore, all firms raised their investment, there would be mutual benefits, yet any firm acting alone would not gain. Market prices are, however, unable to signal the value of such a general increase in investment. As there is no market incentive for any firm to change its existing strategy the mutual gains from an all-round change can never be captured and there is a co-ordination failure.

As some recent studies of the Korean and Taiwanese economies have shown, co-ordination failures of this kind do hold back economic development. Investment returns were held down due to the cost and difficulty of finding reliable subcontractors in a partially industrialised economy and the risk that if investment in new capacity did take place, demand would be insufficient. To overcome these difficulties, the costs of finance were reduced, public investment was increased and measures were adopted to persuade private firms to raise investment through the construction of chains of subcontractors or the development of vertically integrated conglomerates. With the consequent growth of investment, productivity increased as did exports: investment rather than export growth was the motor of development [see Hutton, 1995].

A second example of co-ordination failure lies in the creation of skills. As Streeck [1987] has shown, however, the provision of skills is subject to a prisoners' dilemma problem where the optimal outcome for all requires co-operative, co-ordinated behaviour of all but where, for individuals, co-operation is too risky and the potential rewards of non-co-operation are too great. The prisoners' dilemma is a classic example of a two-person non-constant sum game. The pay-off matrix adapted to a consideration of a situation in which firms are deciding whether to train or not instead of the classic situation in which two prisoners must decide whether to confess or not to a crime where there is insufficient evidence for a conviction unless one of the prisoners turns state's evidence as set out in Table 6.1. The first figure in each cell is the financial gain for firm 1 and the second is the pay-off for firm 2. In this game there is a unique equilibrium where each firm chooses not to train and receives a pay-off of two units each. Neither of the other strategies is an equilibrium, for if one firm trains or is expected to train, it is in the interest of the other not to train and to poach its rival's workers, while if one firm does not train, the optimal strategy for the other is not to train either lest it lose the workers it trains to its competitor. The critical feature of this game is that the equilibrium outcome is worse for both players than a joint strategy in which both agree to train. The optimal solution is to agree on and enforce a joint strategy as co-operation increases the welfare of all players. The need for enforcement is, however, critical if the two players play the game independently, and even if they agree on a joint strategy it is still in their individual interests to break the agreement.

As a result, therefore, of the existence of a free contract, job market firms invest less in training than is in their own interest. The reason why is that skills are a collective resource. A firm's investment adds therefore to a pool of skills on which others, including its competitors, can draw. Various factors qualify this situation, but in general firms tend to provide firm-specific skills. Transferable and non-transferable skills are, however, interdependent, and so a firm that confines itself to the creation of non-transferable skills will under-develop them. Knowledge also, on which a more active involvement of workers depends, is kept from them in part for similar reasons. A market-oriented approach which is weak in creating dedicated skills will,

Table 6.1 The skills dilemma

		Firm 2	
		Not-train	Train
Firm 1	Not-train	(2,2)	(10,1)
	Train	(1,10)	(5,5)

concludes Streeck, fall far short if it is asked to create skills as cultural resources which will appear to rational decision-makers as excessive qualifications. Yet the central role of generalised and polyvalent skills and the need for skills that can be used in as yet unknown ways transform skills into cultural resources of central importance.

The self-interest of firms on which market models rest cannot therefore be relied upon to achieve the desired results. Nor will the self-interest of individuals lead them to choose to acquire the required skills not just because of the inappropriateness of financial rewards but because of market failure [see Barr, 1987]. The reason why is that individuals acquire fundamental skills when they are young and when they are least able to accept the long deferral of gratification that is the essence of an investment, since it presupposes certainty about what one will value in the years to come, and this certainty is itself a product of an individual's social and personal identity which in young people is still in the process of being formed. Young people whose personal identity has not yet been formed lack 'the crucial properties and capacities needed for rational decision-making of a neoclassical kind' [Streeck, 1987].

The alternative approach that Streeck favours involves a re-integration of learning and work, a treatment of learning as socialisation and as an obligation, and the social regulation of firms. In Streeck's opinion, enterprises in the West as in the East should be places of learning as well as places of production. But if the acquisition and development of skills can only occur in conjunction with work within the firm, and if the firm does not have the rational motivation to fulfil this role of its own accord, regulation, of the kind embodied in the West German vocational training system, is required.

As the position of a region in wider divisions of labour, its development potential and its distribution of income depend on its skills and human resources and on the rate of investment, institutional factors that qualitatively improve these conditions of development should reinforce an area's self-reliance and its performance in export markets.

MACRO-REGULATION AND REGIONAL ECONOMIC PERFORMANCE

All of the factors identified in the last section relate to the supply-side dynamics of regional economies and their comparative competitiveness. The factors identified are independent of the structure of a regional economy. A few years ago it was common to argue that the future lay not with large corporations and spatially fragmented divisions of labour but with a craft-related model of flexible specialisation, small firms and industrial districts, but the reinforcement of metropolitan areas and the re-emergence of large firms have placed a question mark over the extent to which that thesis is valid. Accordingly, it is better to identify factors that shape the competitiveness of large as well as small firms and of services as well as industry. In that section I suggested that local regulatory mechanisms that overcame co-ordination failures would reinforce the position of particular cities and regions. In the wider world, however, the same dilemmas that confront individual firms confront wider regions: a course of action that raises investment may only be advantageous if it occurs in a number of regions at the same time. In any case, even if there were gains in the areas that overcame co-ordination failures, gains on external markets may simply occur at the expense of other areas which lose market shares. Indeed, if all regions raised their levels of competitiveness and all modelled themselves on successful regions, would contemporary problems of unemployment, inequality and slow growth be resolved? As I shall argue, the answer to this question depends on the dominant rules of the game.

There are three essential points I wish to make. First, resources released as a result of the dynamic restructuring of urban and regional economies are not re-employed. Second, non-re-employment is a consequence not of job market rigidities but of the mediating role of money in market societies. Third, I shall argue that a recognition of the essential role of state intervention in any strategy for full employment is no longer in itself sufficient and that if cities and regions are not to engage in a process of competition that will in the end prove self-defeating, new supranational rules of the game and a new regulatory order are required.

The non-re-employment of human resources and the dynamics of unemployment and non-employment

In the first section I argued that the degree of mobilisation of the human potential of a society is an important determinant of its economic dynamism and of economic performance and that disparities in the rate of employment are important determinants of regional and urban imbalances. In Britain, as in other advanced countries, the recent increase in disparities has gone hand in hand with increases and greater regional differentials in unemployment and in male non-employment.

In the case of data on unemployment two features warrant particular attention. First, unemployment varies with the economic cycle. The point around which unemployment revolves has increased after each of the major shocks since the end of the post-war 'golden age' of full employment and comparatively high growth. Market societies do not automatically restore full employment. Instead unemployment tends to oscillate around an 'attraction point' which reflects the institutional characteristics and the nature of the social compromise in each society. Second, in Great Britain there is a much greater degree of instability than in other European countries, as is suggested by the comparative data on trends in unemployment. The volatility of economic cycles is a consequence and a cause of the greater emphasis on market-led models of adjustment: in the job market insecurity of employment, short notice periods and comparatively small redundancy payments as well as short-term profit pressures extend employment and unemployment cycles as in recessions comparatively large numbers of workers are laid off. The costs of reproduction of a part of the workforce are transferred to the state though the consequent loss of disposable income amplifies the drop in demand, as do the tax increases or reductions in public expenditure required to offset increases in the size of the public sector deficit, as a result of lost tax revenues and increased social security payments. In other European countries firms are slower in shedding employees in a recession and slower in recruiting unemployed workers in the subsequent upturn as fewer were laid off in the recession. In Germany for example the *Kurzarbeit* system financed out of a 2.5 per cent levy on gross wages allows employees to be put on short-time at full wages for up to 2 years. (This system was put in place as a result of the devastating consequences of the instability of a market-led model in the inter-war period.) German firms therefore suffer less from the loss of skilled staff, gain from less volatile demand and can expand output more quickly in an upturn [Bischof, 1994].

Market adjustment and full employment

The change in direction of the early 1970s was a response to the breakdown of the post-war model of development. The years since the early 1970s were, however, years in which rates of output and productivity growth in advanced countries remained on average much lower than in the post-war golden age, and in which an earlier tendency for inequalities to diminish was thrown into reverse gear. With this deterioration in economic performance, mass unemployment and widespread social exclusion returned, insecurity and inequality increased and the performance of regional economies diverged. Clearly, some places were comparatively successful – increasing their competitive advantage and increasing their market shares in the 1980s and 1990s – and much effort has gone into the identification of the determinants of success and the possibilities of transferring experiences from one region to another. Most attention has been paid to supply-side factors – the transformation of the productive system, the creation of a framework for co-operative industrial relations, the development of transport and telecommunications infrastructures, the establishment of synergies between public research and industry and of strategies for technology transfer and investment in education and skills. A preoccupation with supply-side adjustments is understandable: each organisation and each area wants to do as much as it can for itself. Supply-side approaches are also consistent with the view that the crisis of the golden age model essentially involved a set of supply-side difficulties associated with the crisis of its characteristic (Fordist) productive order and the saturation of solvent markets. This interpretation is in part correct. There is, however, a second side to the problem: globalisation added a set of demand-side problems as a result of the destruction of regulatory orders put in place to manage the contradictions of market societies. The implication of this view is that it is in fact questionable whether the current development model crisis would end if all regions modelled themselves on regions that were successful: a productive system change is not enough to end a crisis of accumulation. An emphasis on the transformation of the supply-side of successful regions is also problematic for a second reason: much of this work underemphasises the extent to which the growth in employment in the 1980s was dependent on services and in particular the extent to which expansion was unsustainable due to the predominance of rent-seeking and speculative motives [see Palloix, 1993]. The significance of an innovation-oriented and needs-determined productivist logic is conversely exaggerated.

Greater uncertainty and increased volatility in the volume and composition of demand also played a major role in the transformation of the productive system. Widespread use was made of new information and communications technologies and the organisation of productive work was transformed to allow the mass production of quality goods at low cost. At the centre of this transformation was an attempt to increase the ease and speed of reaction to firms to changes in their external environment. First, in the face of the saturation of markets and the absence of new products capable of renewing the consumption norm, strategies were developed to accelerate obsolescence and to follow shifts in fashion in order to speed up replacement. Second, attempts were made to increase the variety of goods and services offered to consumers, to improve the quality, price and performance of normalised products and to improve the responsiveness of manufacture and assembly to variations in the volume of demand in order to gain market share at the expense of rivals. These two solutions require more production flexibility which was achieved in a variety of ways: greater co-ordination/integration of Research and Development and product manufacture; integration of marketing, design, manufacture and management; creation of networks and integration of activities in 'extended firms'; and an increase in the skills, learning capabilities, functional flexibility and involvement of the workforce in the struggle for improved productivity and quality. With this restructuring of production, however, human resources were often not re-employed.

Almost all regional economists assume that markets will lead to a full employment of resources, and if full employment does not occur the reasons why lie in the existence of monopolies, minimum wage legislation or other institutional constraints which prevent the adjustment of prices. If structural change releases resources that do not find alternative employment, the policy recommendation is a removal of restrictions and in particular reductions in real wage rates. (In a neo-classical world what exists are two hypothetical vectors of non-negative prices and interest rates which, if established, would result in full employment, while movement from one to another simply involves changes in relative prices and a reallocation of factors of production from one activity/region to another.)

The curious fact is that the endurance of unemployment in the inter-war years led Keynes to reject neo-classical concepts of market adjustment and to advocate wage rigidity as a policy to combat unemployment. What Keynes argued was that the initial response to a decline in demand was not a price adjustment but a quantity adjustment. Keynes did not deny the existence of a hypothetical vector of non-negative prices and interest rates which, if established, would result in full resource utilisation. What concerned Keynes were the difficulties of reaching the market clearing vector in economies in which: (1) all the information needed to ensure the perfect co-ordination of all the current and future activities of all traders does not exist and is not provided free of charge by an all-knowing Walrasian auctioneer; and (2) money is the medium of exchange. If a resource is made unemployed due to a change in demand, traders do not have perfect information about the new market clearing price. The seller will set a reservation price in the light of past experience and a knowledge of the current price of comparable services and search for the highest bidder, adapting the reservation price as the search unfolds. Adjustment is not therefore instantaneous, and in this state of disequilibrium trading occurs while the resource itself remains unemployed.

To this argument it is necessary to add another. In this state of disequilibrium the loss of income from the services of the unemployed resource will impose a constraint on the owner's effective demand for other goods and services. This constraint on money expenditure and on effective demand provides the rationale of the multiplier analysis of competitive markets. What is more, this constraint is, as Marx and Keynes demonstrated, a defining characteristic of a money economy. As Clower [1969a; 1969b] has pointed out, in a money economy it is essential to make a clear distinction between activities that are often conflated. First, it is essential to make a distinction between offers to exchange money for goods (purchase offers) and offers to sell goods for money (sale offers). Second, it is important to make a related distinction between planned transactions (what an economic agent intends to do) and realised transactions (what an economic agent actually does). According to Say's Law, no economic agent plans to spend money on the purchase of goods and services without at the same time planning to earn the money to pay for them, whether from profit receipts or the proceeds of the sale of other commodities. If resources are unemployed, however, realised current receipts will fall short of planned receipts. In these circumstances actual consumption expenditure as expressed in effective market offers to purchase goods and services will fall short of desired consumption expenditure. As Keynes showed, therefore, current income constrains current expenditure: an individual who is forced by a lack of buyers to sell less of a factor than he or she wishes to sell is also forced by a lack of money income to spend less than he or she wants to spend. To make sense of the mode of functioning of a decentralised money economy the Walrasian *tâtonnement* process which lies at the heart of neo-classical conceptions of price adjustment should at the very least be redefined to ensure that no purchase order is accepted unless the purchaser already has sufficient income to pay for the transaction as a result of the completion of a previous sale order. (This analysis abstracts from the fact that an economic agent may be able to borrow money.)

The implications of this conception of market adjustment are profound. In orthodox general equilibrium theory it is assumed that the sum of excess demands – the difference between the quantity demanded and the quantity supplied of each good and service – is zero. A consequence of this proposition, which is called Walras' Law, is that the existence of excess supply of any factors of production necessarily implies the simultaneous existence of excess demand for some goods and services. In the Walrasian universe the co-existence, in any disequilibrium situation, of an excess supply of some goods with excess demand for others will lead to movements in the structure of relative prices that will cause the economic system to converge on an equilibrium. If, however, allowance is made for the mediation of money in all exchanges, it is clear that Walras' Law is valid only in situations of full employment. If full employment does not prevail, there will be an excess supply of some factors of production yet this situation of excess supply will not correspond to an effective excess demand for other goods and services. Wherever goods can be exchanged for money and money for goods but goods cannot be exchanged directly for other goods, realised current income is in short an independent constraint on effective demand. Excess supply in the labour market – involuntary unemployment – diminishes effective excess demand elsewhere. As Clower shows, with unemployed resources there is an excess supply of factors of production and there is a notional excess demand for goods but adjustment will not occur as the effective excess demand for goods is zero due to the fact that the demand for goods is constrained by the lack of money income that stems from unemployment.

What this account of market adjustment shows is that unregulated market economies do not tend towards full employment and that involuntary unemployment is a result not of market imperfections but of the mediating role of money and the costs and time involved in the acquisition of information. As soon as this point is understood, it is possible to understand why the neo-liberal agenda has had such devastating deflationary consequences. What this argument also emphasises is that the regulatory order established after the Second World War was a response to fundamental contradictions in market societies. To restore market adjustment is to allow these contradictions to resurface.

Full employment in a post-Fordist order

The implication of the arguments in the last section is that a re-regulation of the economic order at a supra-national scale is a precondition for creating a set of rules which will allow all regions to win. International Keynesianism is, however, not sufficient. In advanced countries there are of course great social needs to be satisfied and an investment of resources to meet these needs would significantly reduce unemployment and non-employment. A sustained renewal of growth would depend, however, on a renewal of the consumption norm. Yet the new information and communications technologies have not yet led to the creation of new products and new needs of sufficient value to relaunch the virtuous spiral of mass consumption and mass production. Nor have information technologies yet led to major increases in the productivity of unproductive labour. There is therefore a contradiction between the renewal of productivity growth and the non-renewal of consumption norms. The implications are twofold. First, within the western half of Europe the choice is between slow growth in a divided society, on the one hand, and slow growth, a reduction of labour time organised at a European scale and the creation of a more cohesive society in which work is shared, everyone has more free time and extra-economic activities expand, on the other. Second, on the wider global scale a renewal of consumer-led growth – whose merits are questionable on environmental grounds – will depend on increases in income and consumption in less developed countries.

CONCLUSION

The essential argument of this chapter is simple. The neo-liberal turn has resulted in the creation of a divided society with growing insecurity and social exclusion and has achieved rates of economic growth that are worse than those in the post-war golden age. Deregulation has reinforced speculation and eroded the institutional structure put in place to regulate the contradictions of market societies. In this new environment the competitive struggle is intensified: all cities and regions must seek to improve their competitiveness and secure greater market share at the expense of others. Institutional factors are critical determinants of success as the experience of a number of strong regions suggests. This game is, however, one in which not everyone can win. In this article I have suggested that new rules may make it possible to create a situation in which everyone can play a role and everyone can win. The essence of regulation theoretic approaches to the Fordist era is the demonstration that an institutional order could regulate social contradictions and create the foundations for generalised increases in prosperity. A challenge for the present is to see whether economic geographers contribute to the design of a new set of rules for the recreation of a cohesive and sustainable model of regional and urban development. A cohesive and sustainable model of development would of course have other consequences. A decline in uncertainty would leave less scope for speculation and encourage more socially responsible long-term investment. A reduction in unemployment would ease the fiscal crisis of the state and remove the need for privatisations that have resulted in massive transfers of resources to a comparatively small elite. A change in this direction would involve finally an emphasis on a wider conception of regional economies in which the productive order is connected with the domestic and political spheres.

NOTES

1 Measurements in European Currency Units (ECU) or US dollars ($) involve the use of exchange rates to convert nominal GDP in national currencies into ECU or $. Indicators of this kind do not reflect the different relative purchasing powers of national currencies and apply variable measures of value to the quantities in each country's GDP. The result is a general underestimation of the relative GDP of low income countries. (The application of different measures of value is justifiable in so far as the quality of goods and services differ.) Measurements in Purchasing Power Standards (PPS) make allowance for national differences in the prices of goods and services and in the purchasing power of national currencies applying a common set of prices representative of the international price structure to quantities of commodities and services entering each country's final expenditure on GDP. These measures which are an index of the volume of goods and services that different local economies produce and indicators of differences in living standards are used throughout this article. Measurements in PPS raise the estimated GDP of low income countries relative to high income areas.

2 It is important to note that there is a difference between regional and county GDP series. In the regional GDP series income and output are attributed to place of residence, whereas in the county series commuters' incomes are included in their county of work rather than in their county of residence. In the case of cities where commuting is substantial the consequences are dramatic: in 1991, for example, according to the county data, GDP per head in Greater London was 145 per cent of the national average while according to the regional series it stood at 124.4 per cent of the national average.

Part II

National experiences

7 German regions in the European Union

From joint policy-making to multi-level governance

Arthur Benz

Since the mid-1980s, the Federal Republic of Germany has been in the vanguard of the development of a Europe of the regions. The Single European Act and later the foundation of a European Union induced the German *Länder* governments to assume a leading role in the battle of European regions to defend their interests. Europeanisation of regional policies and regionalisation of the EU are now topics which rank high on the agenda of German regions. Since Maastricht, the federal government can no longer monopolise the representation of national interests in the EU, as the *Länder* governments became important actors in European policy-making. In addition, the implementation of the Common Market Programme and the growing involvement of the EU in regional structural policy, infrastructure, environmental regulation, culture, etc. have had considerable repercussions for regional governments and administrations. On the one hand, regions are exposed to intensive economic competition, which can no longer be smoothed by national government's interventions, on the other hand, they have to implement an increasing number of European programmes and regulations.

It is not very astonishing that demands for an explicit formulation of the subsidiary principle in the Maastricht Treaty and for institutional arrangements enabling the regions to participate in European policy-making were primarily advanced by representatives of the *Länder*. In the institutional framework of the German federal system, *Länder* governments were not only in a powerful position with regard to the federal government and had sufficient administrative capacities to elaborate proposals and lobby for them both at the national and the European level. Compared to regions in other Member States, they would also have been the main losers if European integration had implied an increasing centralisation of policy-making. What is more astonishing is that the German *Länder* reacted in a more defensive way than regions in other Member States to the institutional development of the EU. While the latter saw the EU as a chance to gain power *vis-à-vis* their national government, German *Länder* saw Europe as a centralised organisation which threatened their autonomy.

This reaction is even more surprising as, at a glance, a federal state with a strong regional level like the German *Länder* seems in a good shape to meet these challenges. However, regionalisation of European policy-making has revealed structural problems caused by a peculiarity of the regional level in Germany. It is composed of different regional units operating in different territorial boundaries and institutional settings. Therefore, the definition of regions is far from being clear. It is true that the German *Länder* governments are represented in the EU Committee of the Regions and understand themselves as European regions. Nevertheless, planning and important infrastructure policies as well as the implementation of regional economic policies are fulfilled either in regions which encompass parts of a *Land*'s territory or in trans-border regions. The regional level of the German federal system is rather differentiated, and there are ongoing debates about which regions are adequate Euro-regions. Germany is currently still looking for them.

The following chapter avoids the unsolvable task of determining what a region in Germany is. Instead, it intends to clarify the complexities of the German regional level and its relations with the EU. It presents an overview of the territorial and institutional framework and a short analysis of the integration of regions in the EU. It aims at revealing the divided regional structure in Germany, which may explain the specific situation of the German *Länder* in Europe. As so far our empirical knowledge is limited, my remarks concerning consequences for political practice and conclusions for future research should be taken as preliminary.[1]

THE TERRITORIAL AND INSTITUTIONAL FRAMEWORK

The territory of the regions

The idea of a Europe of the Regions is founded on two basic arguments. The first refers to economic aspects while the second emphasises culture, i.e. language, values, orientations and identities of people. These arguments adopt the reasoning in theories of regionalism, according to which the development of regions can be explained either by territorial differentiation of economic structures or by specific historical traditions and cultures. Common definitions of regions, which can be found in resolutions of European organisations, mostly combine both arguments.[2] EU policies affect both cultural and economic dimensions of regions.

From such a point of view, Germany's regional level consists of a set of overlapping territories and is not clearly organised. The cultural or historical basis of the *Länder* is rather weak. This assumption may sound surprising given the long history of German federalism and its development from a fragmented territory. However, in the course of the varied German history, the territorial patchwork was in a constant flux. During the twentieth century, the outcome of two disastrous wars overturned the territorial boundaries of the state and its parts. After the Second World War, the regional structures of the German state were re-established in a territorial setting which was primarily defined by the artificially created occupation zones. The *Länder* which formed the Federal Republic after 1949, as well as those which existed in the GDR until 1952 and which were re-established in 1990, were for the most part pragmatic creations of the Allies and lacked traditions. A recommendation of the Western Allies and the provision of the Basic Law (article 29), to reorganise the territories of the *Länder*, were never fulfilled apart from the creation of the *Land* of Baden-Württemberg, which came into being in 1952 by the merger of the original three south-western *Länder*. The formation of a united Berlin–Brandenburg failed in 1996. Moreover, the flood of refugees from the East and migrations after the war altered the existing population structures in the German regions and led to a mixture of ethnic communities. They undermined chances that specific *Land* cultures would emerge and that previously existing regional traditions would be revived. As a consequence, the identification of people with 'their' *Land* is not well developed. Although the federal system and the *Länder* as part of a decentralised government are widely accepted, the Germans feel themselves to be more members of a nation or of a local community than members of a *Land* [Mayntz, 1995, p. 135].

Nevertheless, opinion polls revealed that, despite the relatively low estimation of the *Länder*, social identification with regional units exists and is rather strong. But apart from the city–states, these regions are not identical to the territory of the *Länder*. While several *Länder* governments again and again tried to foster *Land* identities (as slogans like 'We in North Rhine-Westphalia' show), real patterns of orientation and valuation refer to regions characterised by specific dialects, meals, customs and culture (e.g. the Rhineland, the Palatinate, Badenia; Franconia). Despite the homogenisation caused by the wars and the modernisation of society, these regional identities play a considerable role in politics of the *Länder* governments, which is influenced by competition between political elites representing cultural regions inside the boundaries of the *Länder*. But this is only another indication that the territorial framework of the sub-national level of government does not match the cultural regions.

The same can be said if we look at economic regions. Although the federal and the *Länder* governments have implemented regional policies in order to achieve a balanced economy in the whole territory of the Federal Republic of Germany, disparities between regions have persisted. Meanwhile, policy-makers have learned that an equalisation of regional economic structures is neither feasible nor desirable. They have adopted new theories of regional economics, which regard coherent regional patterns of loosely coupled industries, adequate sets of infrastructure and public institutions and 'cultures' of communication and co-operation as decisive prerequisites to economic competitiveness [Grabherr, 1993; Rehfeld, 1995]. In addition, it is acknowledged that regions gain from specialisation and from their specific 'endogenous' potentials rather than from attracting external financial resources aimed at equalising economic structures. Hence, the territorial differentiation of economic structures has been followed by a regionalisation of public policies in areas which concern the promotion of economic competitiveness and improvement of locations [Hesse *et al.*, 1991; Heinze and Voelzkow, 1991].

Yet, if we compare economic regions defined by existing 'industrial districts', regional 'production clusters' or networks of public-private co-operation, we again find that they do not coincide with the *Länder*. They are either a part of a large *Land* or go beyond the *Land* territory. Most of the important economic regions in Germany, namely, those surrounding the cities of Berlin, Bremen, Hamburg, Frankfurt, Cologne, Leipzig/Halle, Mannheim, Ulm, are divided up by existing boundaries of the *Länder*. Thus it is common that policies aiming at competitiveness of regional economies have to be co-ordinated between two or three *Länder* governments.

While cultural regions are – from a political point of view – more fiction than reality, economic regions do exist as institutional units. The large *Länder* established planning regions that were made responsible for *Land* use planning and often for specific infrastructure policies too [Fürst *et al.*, 1990]. Moreover, federal and *Länder* governments defined regions to implement regional economic policies. Economic regions also provide the territorial framework for new forms of co-operative policy-making determined to mobilise information, knowledge and organisational, financial and personal resources of public and private actors for regional development [Heinze and Voelzkow, 1991, 1995; Hesse *et al.*, 1991; Jochimsen 1992; Krafft and Ulrich, 1993]. However, viewed as political or administrative institutions, these regional units are rather weak compared to the *Länder* or local governments.

In sum, regions in the sense of European policies, i.e. those defined by economic and cultural aspects, exist in Germany mainly outside the institutional framework of government. The sub-national level of the German state organisation is constituted by the *Länder* as parts of the federal system. The territorial demarcation of the *Länder*, which are politically defined regions, differs from the territory of economic and cultural regions. Together they form a regional level which makes up a differentiated structure of overlapping territories.

The framework of the federal system

Further peculiarities of the regional level in Germany come to the fore when we clarify the functions and positioning of the *Länder* in the federal system. As scholars working on comparative federalism agree, regionalisation of the German political system and the role of the *Länder* cannot be justified by claims of minorities. 'German Federalism today does not, therefore, reflect a society divided by significant ethnic, social, cultural, or religious tension' [Gunlicks, 1989, p. 4]. It is designed to reduce the power of central government and guarantee a stable democratic system.

Unlike the Constitution of the United States, which stipulates a separation of powers between the federation and the states, the German Basic Law places greater emphasis on the sharing of powers, responsibilities and resources [Abromeit, 1992; Hesse and Benz, 1990]. To a certain degree, this distinctive feature of intergovernmental relations is anchored in the tradition and constitution of German federalism. It further developed in political practice soon after the foundation of the Federal Republic in 1949. While the federal government extended its legislative powers, the *Länder* more and more became responsible for implementing the law. At the same time, governments of the *Länder* gained influence at the federal level via the *Bundesrat*, which has a veto right on federal legislation in more than 50 per cent of all cases. From this follows that federal and *Länder* governments are forced to co-operate in order to carry out intended policies. This system of joint policy-making or 'interlocking politics' [*Politikverflechtung*; Scharpf *et al.*, 1976] is supported by strong commitments to maintaining a 'uniformity' or 'equivalence of living conditions' (*Einheitlichkeit* or *Gleichwertigkeit der Lebensverhältnisse*). This commitment has in the practice of intergovernmental relations outweighed the subsidiary principle, which is laid down in the German constitution. A lot of conferences and committees involving members of government and administration of the federation and the *Länder* were established to co-ordinate policy-making. These structures resulted in a greater uniformity of regional policies than may be expected in a federal system. At the same time, they impeded any far-reaching centralisation as the federal government, too, has lost autonomy and has to co-operate with the *Länder* governments in most policy fields.

Of particular importance for regional policy-making in the federal context are the 'Joint Tasks', which were introduced by a constitutional amendment in 1969. Since then, the *Länder* government have had to co-operate with the federal government in matters of regional economic policy, agriculture and planning of universities. They lost their original responsibility, which is now partially delegated to a joint planning committee [Scharpf *et al.*, 1976]. Even more significant is the system of revenue sharing and fiscal redistribution along vertical and horizontal lines [Renzsch, 1991]. The autonomy of both the federal and the *Länder* governments is limited by the fact that the lion's share of their fiscal resources comes from joint taxes. These are regulated by federal laws, which cannot be passed without the consent of the *Bundesrat*. This gives the *Länder* governments a significant influence over federal fiscal policy. A complicated system of redistribution of financial resources between the federal and *Länder* governments and between rich and poor *Länder* further contributes to the linking of politics at the central and regional level.

Thus, the *Länder* as part of the regional level in the federal system are integrated in joint policy-making and revenue sharing both along vertical and horizontal lines. The same can be said if we look at regional institutions below the *Länder* level. The existence of these units is based on the remaining legislative powers of the *Länder*, which are responsible for the regulation of regional planning and the administrative organisation. Therefore, we find different forms of regional institutions fulfilling different functions. In general, however, they are responsible for planning and co-ordinating activities of various governmental and administrative organisations in order to achieve specific goals of regional development. This is the reason why these units also do not constitute an institutional framework for autonomous regional politics but represent an additional example of interlocking politics. This is even more true of the new forms of regionalised economic policy-making, which are carried out in loosely organised patterns of intergovernmental and public–private co-operation.

EUROPEANISATION OF REGIONAL POLITICS

The integration of the German federal system into the European context gave rise to different expectations as regards the future of intergovernmental relations and regional autonomy. Some scholars assumed that European integration would lead to a 'redoubling of interlocking politics' [Hrbek, 1986; Scharpf, 1985, 1992] which would further reduce the discretionary power of *Länder* governments. Others saw chances for a revival of regional autonomy in a 'Europe of the Regions', because the *Länder* governments could gain power by directly contacting European institutions and by-passing the federal government [Borkenhagen, 1992; Clement, 1993]. Actually, evidence from first empirical studies and practical experiences reveals that reality is more multifaceted than political theories have predicted. In a nutshell, European integration caused at the same time dissolution and intensification of interlocking politics at various levels. Given the insufficient state of empirical research, statements on the interplay between regional and European politics and policy-making have to be understood as hypotheses. The following explanations are also made under this proviso.

Institutionalised participation of regional interests in the EU

The assumption of a redoubling of interlocking politics is, as a rule, based on observations of institutional developments of the EC/EU. In fact, the regional or 'sub-national' governments are now incorporated as a third level in the institutional structure of Europe. They became actors in the system of intergovernmental negotiations which constitutes the EU. The process of the Europeanisation of regional policies parallels the process of opening possibilities for regional governments to participate in European policy-making [Benz, 1993; Fuhrmann-Mittlmaier, 1991; Hrbek and Weyand, 1994; Morass, 1994; Morawitz and Kaiser, 1994].

As regards the Federal Republic of Germany, a precise analysis of the institutional integration of the regions in the EU has to take into consideration two points: first, regional interests are represented by the *Länder* governments. This is easily understandable because only the *Länder* governments have the political legitimacy and administrative capacities necessary for an effective representation of interests, whereas regional units below this level lack both prerequisites. In order to improve the flow of information and co-ordination between the *Länder* and the EU, they set up special ministries or departments in ministries designed to deal with European policies, and they organised information bureaux in Brussels which serve as their embassies. Thus, the *Länder* governments monopolise formal relations with European institutions, while other regional units are excluded from them.

Second, representatives of the *Länder* have two ways of achieving interest intermediation in European policy-making [Benz, 1993; Morass, 1994]. They can gain direct access to the EU as members of the Committee of the Regions or as participants in the European Council. Alternatively, they can try to influence the federal government when the national position for negotiations at the European level is prepared.

Opportunities to participate in European institutions did not significantly strengthen the power of regional governments. The effective role of the German *Länder* in the Committee of the Regions does not meet their expectations, which they had before the Maastricht Treaty was implemented. Due to the heterogeneity of European sub-national governments and due to failures to co-ordinate their policies, the *Länder* governments cannot take advantage of the Committee as a forum for their genuine interests. In contrast, the rights to participate in decision-making on European affairs, which are granted to them by a new Article 23 of the constitution, seem to provide a more effective source of regional power. When decisions of the EU affect the jurisdiction of the *Länder*, the federal government must seek the approval of the *Bundesrat*. In this case, with a majority of two-thirds of their votes in the *Bundesrat*, the *Länder* governments can impose their will on the federal government, which is then committed in negotiations of the European Council to assent to the proposals of the *Bundesrat* [Ress, 1995].

By the right to veto decisions which concern their responsibilities, the *Länder* governments are in a position to obstruct European policy-making. Some scholars warned them to exploit this position and to impede further steps towards European integration which could go against their own interests [Scharpf, 1992]. In practice, however, co-operation between federal and *Länder* governments functions well. The *Länder* governments obviously recognise the leading role of the federal government in European policies. They know that a commitment of the federal government to fixed proposals of the *Bundesrat* can cause decisions or non-decisions at the European level which may be disadvantageous from their point of view. Therefore, *Länder* governments support national interests more than might be in accordance with a purely regionalist standpoint. At the same time, in order to pursue interests of individual *Länder*, they resort to informal channels of communication with national and European authorities [Börzel, 1995].

Although it is too early to evaluate the new institutions designed to improve the participation of regions in European policy-making, one should not overestimate their effectiveness. At any rate, formal procedures and institutions contribute to limit access of regional actors. Both in European and national institutions, regional interests are represented by *Länder* governments, while representatives of other regional units are excluded. Moreover, in the processes of intergovernmental bargaining at the national and European level, the *Länder* governments are in a weaker position compared to the federal government. Final decisions of the EU are dominated by the national governments negotiating in the European Council.

Yet as theories of two-level games show [Putnam, 1988b; Evans *et al.*, 1993], complex patterns of intergovernmental relations do not simply constrain regional actors, but also provide strategic opportunities. Even the institutionalised linkages between regions, federal government and the EU open different access points, which a creative *Land* government or other regional actors can exploit simultaneously. The set of strategies of interest intermediation and the number of actors participating in European policy-making is in fact even wider, if informal, network-like patterns of intergovernmental relations are taken into consideration.

Sectoral and inter-regional policy networks

After long debates, an increasing number of experts on European integration seem to acknowledge that the EU 'is best characterised as neither an international regime nor an emerging state but as a network involving the pooling of sovereignty' [Keohane and Hoffmann, 1991, p. 10). Studies on policy-making reveal that it is more accurate to comprehend the structure of the EU as constituted by sets of interlinked networks. These networks include European, national and sub-national actors both from the public and the private sector. Compared to national policy networks, they are less stable, more heterogeneous as regards to participants and based largely on informal relations and not on institutional structures [Grande, 1993, p. 187; Héritier *et al.*, 1994, pp. 8–11; Peters, 1992, pp. 106–7]. To an increasing extent, regional actors are integrated in these networks. There are indications that German regions have discovered European networking as a promising strategy to promote their individual interests. From an analytical point of view, we can distinguish at least three types of networks, in which regional actors participate: transnational networks of regions, public–private networks of interest intermediation and intergovernmental policy networks. They differ as regards to actors included and their functions.

Transnational networks of regions [Leonardi and Nanetti, 1990, p. 11] connect regional actors of different Member States. Although they are often regarded as an important contribution to European integration, often they serve merely symbolical purposes. At present, they constitute rather weak forms of co-operation and co-ordination of interests. Nevertheless, German regions are intensively engaged in transnational networks. A well-known example is the co-operation between Baden-Württemberg, Catalonia, Lombardy, Rhône-Alpes and Wales. Similar relationships exist between North Rhine-Westphalia, Nord Pas-de-Calais and the West Midlands and between Lower Saxony and European regions in which automobile industries are concentrated.

As these networks have no institutional framework, their composition and boundaries are fluid. This gives actors representing economic regions opportunities to become involved. Their participation contributes to making inter-regional co-operation more problem-oriented. The drawback of this flexibility of structures is that transnational networks of regions do not provide a basis to influence European politics. Although these co-operations link regions with similar economic structures and problems and with common interests, they are used primarily to exchange information and experience.

The second type of networks results from lobbying activities of interest groups. In the fragmented structure of decision-making of the EU, these interests find access to a variety of committees of the Council and the Commission, in which policy proposals are elaborated. During the 1980s the EC experienced 'a growth of complex multi-level patterns of informal influence' [Andersen and Eliassen, 1991, p. 178] in different policy fields [Eissing and Kohler-Koch, 1994; Mazey and Richardson, 1993].

These sectoral networks, which are dominated by private interest organisations, can be used by regions to transmit their interests to the European level. Although empirical evidence is rather weak, there are not only theoretical reasons to assume this is the case. In order to influence the policies which affect their regional economy, some German *Länder* governments actively engage in sectoral networks and lobby EU institutions in a coalition with private interests groups. While this strategy is at present primarily pursued by representatives of *Länder* governments, such informal patterns of interest intermediation are in principle open to other regional actors, too. We can expect that in particular members of quasi-governmental organisations of economic regions like chambers of industry and commerce or economic development corporations will increasingly participate in the sectoral networks of the EU.[3] In their dual function as representatives of economic interests and as the important public administration of an economic region, they may strengthen the vertical links between European and regional policy-making.

Finally, European and regional administrations are immediately linked in intergovernmental policy networks, which serve the implementation of structural policy of the EU. They developed as a result of the 1988 reform of the Structural Funds, which overhauled implementation procedures. With this reform, the EU advanced the regionalisation of policy-making as now operationalised development programmes and projects, which are co-financed by money from the Structural Funds, are elaborated at the regional level. The partnership principle guiding the new regional policy implies that hierarchical control structures are removed and that regional actors participate in decision-making on the allocation of regional policy grants. In contrast to the federal–*Länder* Joint Task, the partnership between the Commission and regional actors is manifested not in institutionalised co-operation but in informal policy networks. In addition, EU rules for the structural funds require that regional administration responsible for deciding on development programmes should include all relevant public and private actors into the decision-making processes in order to gain comprehensive information and to achieve broad consent on policy goals. The idea was to open policy-making to new interests at the regional level beyond those taking part in existing institutions.

With the reform of the EU regional policy, the traditional form of interlocking politics in the German federal system has turned into a more complicated pattern, whose exact shape is at present not entirely clear. Apparently, there are narrow links between the Commission and representatives of the *Länder* governments or – if they exist – of the subdivisions of the *Länder* that are designed to organise regional co-operation. Regional policy schemes of the EU are mostly implemented in networks in which delegates from the Commission interact with leading actors of the regions, while the federal government is bypassed [Hooghe, 1995b, p. 182]. This structure provides opportunities for the regions to develop their strategies and programmes aimed at an improved competitiveness of their economy. Thus it effectively contributes to a strengthening of the regional level.

However, beyond these new patterns of policy networks, the new regional policy of the EU stands at the same time as an example of a separation of functions between different levels of policy-making. The adaptation of the working structure resulted in an increasing centralisation of the traditional instruments of regional policy, namely the allocation of funds to low-developed regions, while functions such as the formulation of regional development concepts, the co-ordination of public and private activities, the organisation of information exchange and co-operation between government and industry are fulfilled at the regional level [Hooghe and Keating, 1994, pp. 66–9]. Policy networks linking European and regional organisations focus on implementation of joint development programmes and projects, while distributive policies of allocating money to different regions are at the same time centralised and negotiated between national governments, without notable participation of regional interests. As a consequence, the joint policy-making between federal and *Länder* administrations in regional economic policy is weakened and possibly will dissolve during the process of progressing institutional development.

Interregional competition, intra-regional co-operation and dissociation of interlocking politics

Transnational, public–private and intergovernmental policy networks are parts of a complex structure of interlocking politics in the EU. They increase channels of information, communication and negotiation which counterbalance the predominance of *Länder* governments as representatives of regional interests in European policy-making. Nevertheless, the openness of policy networks should not be overestimated. At best, they are accessible to economic interests of regions, while social and environmental concerns are left out. Not only institutionalised linkages but also policy networks favour an elite of regional actors, who are able to play a role in the complicated multi-level game of European politics. Furthermore, the multitude of networks and linkages in the European Union should not lead us to ignore that the European intergovernmental system not only enables new patterns of joint policy-making but also establishes boundaries between policy arenas, which are hardly permeable to interests from outside. Networking simultaneously integrates and dissociates actors from different levels of government.

Structural divides in the European multi-level system are not only caused by institutional settings or by limited power or skill of the actors. They can be traced back to a fundamental dilemma of linked policy arenas characterised, as is the case in the EU, by networks and bargaining [Benz 1992a]. If policy-making processes cross the boundaries of different arenas of bargaining, the problem arises that each of them limits the discretion of participants in the other arena with negative consequences for the effectiveness of negotiations. This problem is well known in negotiation theory and in theories of international relations. In their pioneering study on negotiations, Richard Walton and Robert McKersie pointed out the dilemma of linking two levels of inter- and intra-organisational bargaining, when they wrote:

> Very often integrative bargaining is impeded by intra-organisational pressures which require negotiators to act in a specific way. The constituents may not tolerate off-the record discussions, subcommittees, and other tactics necessary for integrative bargaining. Nor may the constituents be satisfied with an agreement that had been reached via problem solving.
>
> [Walton and McKersie, 1965, p. 350]

As Walton and McKersie stated, the problem can be managed by 'isolating the membership' of the organisation in order to remove constraining influence from the bargaining room in the inter-organisational arena [ibid., p. 351]. Recent theory on international relations which is influenced by Robert Putnam´s [1988b] analysis of the 'paradoxical interactions of domestic and international politics' [Moravcsik, 1993b, p. 4], supports the proposition that the dissociation of policy arenas can solve the constraints of interlocking politics. Yet it is more optimistic that strategies of a 'double-edged diplomacy' of actors participating in boundary-spanning positions in both contexts may be successful. Similar arguments can be found in management theory, which states that the 'negotiator in the middle' between inter-organisational and intra-organisational bargaining can choose to keep the two processes separate, join them, or approach them separately [Lax and Sebenius, 1986, p. 360]. In any case, mutual adjustments of agendas, interests, strategies and structures in the linked arenas are assumed to be necessary [Evans, 1993].

The strategy of 'double-edged diplomacy', which aims at a simultaneous or sequential development of policies in two arenas, reaches its limits in complex multi-level structures. This seems to be the case in the European Union, in which the problem of linking international bargaining and domestic politics is complicated by the integration of the regional level. The complexity of decision-structures is intensified when the regional level is composed of different arenas, as is the case in Germany. In such a multi-level system, networking and joint decision-making are restricted by the actors' cognitive capacities. As Fritz W. Scharpf has shown, real actors react to information problems in connected arenas by drawing boundaries [Scharpf, 1991]. Boundaries become even more relevant if information problems are accompanied by decision problems, which are caused by institutional contexts of policy arenas. Apart from the fact that conflicts of interests between actors, who operate in different arenas, are intensified by specific action orientations, selective perception, and strategies defined by an institution, linkages of arenas reduce the likelihood of an agreement in bargaining [Benz, 1992a]. This argument gives reason to assume that an unlimited extension of interlocking politics in further levels of government is not possible. Rather, we have to expect that intergovernmental bargaining and co-operation at one level will be accompanied by separation of policy arenas or dissociation of interlocking politics at other levels.

Given the predominance of national governments in institutional structures and formal procedures, from this reasoning it seems to follow that the integration of regions in the intergovernmental system of the EU is hardly successful if integration means effective participation in joint policy-making. However, empirical evidence should prevent us from jumping to such a conclusion. There are ample indications to assume that the institutional development of the EU will lead to a variety of patterns of intergovernmental policy-making in different policy fields, and that the role of the regions varies accordingly.

First impressions from our research project[4] support the hypotheses that decision-problems in multi-level policy-making are solved by simultaneous rearrangements of intergovernmental relations and intra-regional networks, which differ from region to region. In Germany, we find the paradoxical result that regions, that are strong from an economic and political point of view, i.e. the densely populated agglomerations with a highly developed economy, have only weak ties to the European level, while the economically and politically weak regions are better integrated in European policy networks.

This outcome is brought about by the particular institutional setting of the policy fields. Policies relevant to the central regions, e.g. industrial policy and planning of transnational infrastructure networks, are highly centralised. European and national actors prevail in intergovernmental negotiations concerning these matters, while the *Länder* governments, as well as other regional actors, are mostly excluded. Decisions of transnational infrastructure projects, aimed at supporting European networks of cities and regions, are obviously based on package deals between national governments. Any participation by affected regions would threaten to disturb such bargaining tactics. Actually, the *Länder* governments are still influential in national infrastructure planning, but their power may decline with the advancing Europeanisation of large-scale infrastructure networks, despite the fact that they are undoubtedly affected by them. Moreover, in the EU, economic development of the great agglomerations is expected to be stimulated by inter-regional competition. Consequently, regions by themselves are regarded as responsible for improving their competitiveness, while the EU promotes competition by deregulation.

Further research will reveal whether regions can gain influence in centralised industrial and infrastructure policies via sector-specific networks of interest intermediation. However, apart from institutional settings of European policies, internal structures of the relevant regions work towards a separation of both levels, too. What we know so far is that economic regions try to adapt to the changing European context by intensifying intra-regional co-operation [Heinze and Schmid, 1994]. This contributes to the separation of regional and European policy-making for two reasons. On the one hand, economic regions arise as a powerful arena at the sub-*Länder* level. In the large *Länder*, the government is now confronted by divergent regional policies which imply different demands *vis-à-vis* federal and European programmes. Thus, in as much as policy networks or political organisation of economic regions become effective, the *Länder* governments are weakened *vis-à-vis* the national and European institutions. On the other hand, in highly diversified agglomerations, co-operation must include a broad range of interests and actors both from the public and the private sector. Intra-regional decision-making is further impaired by redistributive conflicts, which here are more intense than in peripheral regions. Generally, such conditions are unfavourable to the emergence of leading actors who achieve a powerful boundary-spanning position in European policy arenas and are able to play the game of 'double-edged diplomacy'.

In contrast to policies focused on agglomerations, European policies aimed at regional development in peripheral and less developed regions are implemented in co-operation between the EU Commission and regions. Given the provisions of the Structural Funds and the selection of target regions, the elaboration of regional development programmes and the choice of projects take place in collaboration with regional and European authorities. This new pattern of interlocking politics is based on bilateral intergovernmental relations as the federal government is mostly by-passed. Although the discretion in the implementation of regional policy is constrained by European regulations and programmes, individual regions profit from the fact that the range of measures which can be supported by EU money is wider than those financed by the Joint Task committee of federal and *Länder* governments. This is the reason why the Europeanisation of policies supporting less developed regions has worked towards a powerful mobilisation of regional actors [Hooghe and Keating, 1994, p. 71].

Internal structures of policy-making in less developed regions correspond to these vertical links with the Commission. They are characterised by an elitist pattern of co-operation, in which boundary roles between the regional and the European arena exist. As a rule, the *Land* ministry responsible for implementing regional policy programmes is the central actor in co-ordinating regional decisions with the Commission's policies. Regional partnerships between public and private actors in fact focus on a limited core group, which normally includes representatives from local governments and chambers of industry and commerce, while e.g. unions or environmentalists are left in a marginal position. Thus regions pay the increase in influence and money from EU funds by a centralisation of regional network structures in which the *Land* government controls decision-making.

To this must be added that the interplay between (vertical) intergovernmental relations between regions, national government and the EU, on the one hand, and (horizontal) intra-regional and international bargaining and co-operation, on the other, produces a dynamic structure. Therefore, patterns of regionalisation in agglomerations and less-developed regions might change in the near future. It is quite probable that the position of regions in the multi-level system of the EU will fluctuate between separation from and interlocking into European politics. Besides, it is also likely that the intergovernmental dynamics varies from region to region.

BETWEEN INTEGRATION AND SEPARATION: A DIVIDED REGIONAL STRUCTURE

The reasons outlined above may explain why the German regions do not easily manage to find their role in the EU. The problem is that the regional structure of the German federal system is divided along two lines. On the one hand, we have to bear in mind the division between *Länder* and sub-*Länder* regions. Although the *Länder* governments claim to represent all regional interests, the rise of intra-*Länder* and transborder co-operation of regional actors and, to a limited degree, cultural cleavages in several *Länder* challenge their representation monopoly. As far as regional co-operatives and councils, dealing with regional planning and economic development, are transformed into powerful networks or even organisations, the *Länder* government must take their decisions into account. Given the complexity of multi-level governance in the EU, the representation of the region's interests (including those of the *Länder*) in intergovernmental policy-making at the European level will presumably remain limited since the multiplication of regional arenas requires increasing co-ordination at the *Länder* level.

On the other hand, relations between regions and the EU are characterised by a second dividing line between central and peripheral regions. They differ in their interests as the latter favour support from European funds and cohesion policies, whereas central regions refuse policies which reduce inter-regional competition to their disadvantage. But they differ also in their opportunities to co-operate with European institutions. It is therefore understandable that both types of regions use different strategies to advance their objectives in the EU. Taken seriously, these strategies are going to end in divergent conceptions of the role of regions in the EU. Central regions favour a *Europe of the regions* with strong concern for the autonomy of regional institutions, the subsidiary principle and co-determination of important decisions in a chamber of the regions [Jochimsen, 1992, pp. 99–100). In contrast, policies of peripheral regions amount to a *Europe with the regions* [Leonardy, 1992, p. 133] in which regions, national governments and European institutions co-operate in a system of joint policy-making.

This reasoning can clarify the paradoxical result that while Germany is the vanguard of a regionalised Europe and while the German federal system is often cited as a model for the future institutional development of the EU, the German federal state is currently poorly integrated in the multi-level governance of the EU. The analysis outlined above can also explain why endeavours of the German *Länder* governments to promote their interests in European institutions are doomed to fail. Not only does such a strategy ignore the divergent objectives of German *Länder*, but it also underestimates the intricacies of the EU's political system. It is simply not possible to transfer the German practice of joint policy-making between federal and *Länder* governments to a system of multi-level governance as is characteristic for the EU.

CONCLUSIONS FOR FURTHER RESEARCH

As a federal system with a heterogeneous regional level, Germany represents a special case for the study of regionalisation in Europe. Yet some general conclusions for research may be formulated.

First, the notion of a 'Europe of the regions' is hardly helpful either as an analytical or as a normative conception. It obscures the fact that even in a federal state the region as a solidly organised autonomous unit does not exist and it is rather doubtful whether it is desirable that it should exist. The variety of regional interests often prevents a definition of regions by clearly drawn territorial boundaries. Moreover, development of regions is influenced to an increasing degree by national and international factors, which prevent us from viewing the region as an isolated arena of policy-making. In modern societies, a region must be comprehended as an intermediary structure. It incorporates activities which are bound to a specific locality and have to be co-ordinated due to their interdependencies, but it is also embedded in wider economic, cultural or political contexts and forms a constitutive part of them. Therefore, regional policy-making should be characterised by network-like patterns which – whatever the institutional framework may be – is open to public–private and intergovernmental communication and co-ordination [Thierstein and Leuenberger, 1994].

Second, even if we take such an analytical view as point of departure, the integration of regions in the EU differs not only due to the divergent institutional structures of the Member States but varies from region to region too. Future research on regions in the EU should therefore not solely focus on international comparisons but also compare different types of regions. Regarding the relations between regions and Europe, not only the institutions of Member States make a difference, but their policies as well.

Third, the institutional development of a multi-level structure of the EU is marked by contradictory movements towards increasing interlocking politics and a dissolution of joint policy-making. The latter follows from decision problems of the former. As a result, new co-ordination problems arise. However, while structures of joint policy-making dissolve, informal communication channels crossing new structural divides may persist or emerge. It is possible that developments in the 'hardware' of intergovernmental structures may well be counteracted by changes in the 'software' of communication patterns. Further research on these 'weak' ties of intergovernmental relations has to show whether this still speculative thesis is convincing.

Finally, the German federal system with its divided regional structure may be taken as an example of regionalisation without regionalism. This means that regionalisation in Germany is promoted by pragmatic considerations rather than political ideologies, by administrative concerns rather than political conflicts, by economic development rather than ethnic cleavages. The ambivalence of such a regionalism is obvious. It lacks strong support of regionalist movements, but avoids separatist trends and destructive inter-regional or centre–periphery conflicts. Despite its problems, is seems to be a model which is worth considering in a comparative perspective.

NOTES

1 This article presents first and mostly hypothetical ideas of a comparative project on 'Institutional development and regionalisation of the EU' (Arthur Benz, Gerhard Lehmbruch, Burkhard Eberlein, Susanne Ast, and Albrecht Frenzel). It is part of the work of a research group at the University of Constance, which is dealing with problems of 'Europeanisation in sectoral and international comparison'. During the elaboration of this text, I profited from stimulating discussions with the members of the project team. Nevertheless, I bear the full responsibilitiy for the following discussion.

2 For example, the Convention of the Council of Europe from 1978 (Declaration of Bordeaux); Resolution of the conference 'Europe of the Regions' of 18 October 1989.

3 Our interviews conducted so far reveal that relationships between chambers and the Commission of the EU are still not well developed, but there are reasons to assume that this situation may change in the near future.

4 The following assumptions are based on a first series of interviews carried out by Albrecht Frenzel.

8 Provinces versus urban centres

Current developments, background and evaluation of regionalisation in the Netherlands

Theo A.J. Toonen

INTRODUCTION

Regional government reform policy in the Netherlands is a continued struggle for the meso [Toonen, 1993b]. A seemingly clear-cut and widely supported government policy to create new forms of urban regional government over the past five years came to a stop only two weeks before the first legislation that would translate this policy into tangible results was to be adopted by parliament at the beginning of the summer of 1995. All administrative preparations had been completed. Sufficient political support had been secured. The proposals carried broad political and bureaucratic support. Parliamentary decision-making was considered a formality; a political festivity, just before Parliament adjourned for the summer. The prospect of future regional government reform seemed clear for the years to come.

Only a few months later and the outcomes of the whole regional government reform process of the last five years were wide open again. Nine months later, and the whole regionalisation process as envisaged by the government had stopped. The government withdrew the proposal for law on the province of Rotterdam during the parliamentary debates that eventually took place in the first half of February 1996. In the space of less than one year, therefore, the outlook on Dutch regionalisation policy had completely changed. A deeply felt, broadly carried and self-assured political consensus on the 'Rotterdam model' as the guidelines for future urban government reform – the splitting up of the central municipality in exchange for a consolidated urban agglomeration government for the city–region was replaced by a deep political and administrative crisis in the Rotterdam urban area.

This chapter tries to present, explore and analyse the ongoing business of regional government reorganisation policies in the Netherlands and the renewed last minute 'failure' of the most recent efforts from a broader institutional perspective. To begin with, the update of a continued story on regional government reform in the Netherlands will be presented. Next, the backgrounds of regional reform efforts in the Netherlands will be described and analysed. The first step is to provide some general background information on the Dutch administrative system. The second step is to explain why regionalism politically has never been a real item in the Netherlands, and why, in a way, this is remarkable. The logic underlying the most recent regional reform policies will be briefly presented next. This logic will be briefly evaluated by way of conclusion.

THE UPDATE OF A STORY: CONTINUING REGIONALISATION 'DUTCH STYLE'

The beginning of the summer of 1995 presented a bleak picture for the proponents of the fourth generation regional reform policies that the Netherlands has experienced since the Second World War, more notably since the late 1960s. For the first time in decades reform efforts and governmental reform policies actually seemed to have achieved tangible results. A frustrating period, at least for some participants, of over twenty years of effortless regional reform policy and politics seemed to have been brought to a conclusion. A proposal for a law – a *lex specialis* – for a totally new form of regional, or better metropolitan government organisation – a 'city–province' – for the Rotterdam agglomeration had already been presented to parliament. Other areas, most notably Amsterdam and The Hague, were expected to follow soon.

Sufficient political support had been secured. The proposal for the law merely needed formal approval. In 1994 a Framework Law for regional reform had already been adopted by parliament and was reconfirmed during the negotiations about the new government coalition in the summer of 1994 after the general elections. The elections caused a major shift in Dutch politics. They brought a new government coalition into power: a historically unprecedented combination of social-democrats (PvdA), liberal conservatives (VVD) and neo-liberals (D'66), leaving the Christian Democrats (CDA) for the first time this century in the opposition.

The Framework Law on regional reform of the previous (CDA/PvdA) government provided for a process in which the municipalities in seven designated areas – around the cities of Amsterdam,

Rotterdam, The Hague, Utrecht, Arnhem-Nijmegen, Enschede-Hengelo and Eindhoven – would be enabled to explore the opportunities and feasibility of a new form of consolidated 'regional' government. This would take the form of a so-called 'city–province' (*stadsprovincie*). Upon agreement between the municipalities involved, and after evaluation according to standards set by parliament, these designated areas could be granted the status of a province with extra duties and competencies in policy areas related to urban policy and city development.

If all of these areas reached this status, the number of provinces would be expanded to nineteen. Since it would not be unlikely that the splitting-off of the 'city–provinces' would result in the necessity of some additional territorial readjustments within the remaining territories of the existing provinces, a total of about twenty-five provinces 'new style' to fill a perceived 'regional gap' could easily be anticipated as a likely outcome. In any case, the reform process could be anticipated to amount to a drastic reform of the meso-level of government, changing both the scale and the nature of 'regional government' in the Netherlands.

The existing provinces as a whole were not very much in favour of this development. They presented alternative reform proposals to reduce the number of provinces and therefore to enlarge the scale of meso-government in the Netherlands. These proposals gained much less political support and have, altogether, not been taken very seriously. They were generally perceived as merely tactical moves in an effort to avert the proposed reorganisation of provincial government.

The Rotterdam model

The established national reform policy had drastically been pushed forward and had gained real momentum by the introduction of the so-called 'Rotterdam model' in the early 1990s. This model entailed the building of a metropolitan council – city–province – for the Greater Rotterdam region, the so-called Rijnmond Area. This city–province was to be entrusted with strong powers to deal with the harbour interests, big city problems (social questions; unemployment; urban decay; drugs; crime) and intermunicipal co-ordination. In exchange for this strong urban regional government, the central municipality of Rotterdam would be split into a number of municipalities.

The division of the existing municipality of Rotterdam was demanded by the neighbouring municipalities which feared the domination of a large central city in the new regional configuration. There was also fear that the new provincial structure would be paralysed by a permanent bureaucratic struggle of the administrative organisations of the central city and the city–province. This fear is called the 'Rynmondsyndrome' which refers to all kinds of real and perceived problems which led to the earlier failure to build a regional authority for the greater Rotterdam region (for a description and analysis see Hendriks *et al.*, 1994). In the eventual proposal for law, the municipalities in the region and the Ministry of Home Affairs had reached a compromise to divide the existing municipality of Rotterdam into ten new municipalities. Together with the other seventeen municipalities in the area, these would form the new municipal tier of government in a newly integrated urban agglomeration of about 1.1 million inhabitants.

The concept of a strong provincial government with extended legal authority in areas such as urban finance, economic policy, physical planning, public housing, social policy, police, public transport, environmental policy – tasks which in the Dutch context are traditionally carried out by municipalities – became the model for the administrative reforms in other urban agglomerations as well. The only question in other regions was whether there, too, the central municipalities needed to be partitioned in exchange for the consolidated urban regional government.

The Rotterdam area was way ahead of the other designated areas in translating the general concept into draft legislation under the direction of the Ministry of Home affairs. Five years of costly, intensive, complicated and time-consuming preparations were almost brought to completion when the high expectations were virtually shattered by the outcome of two local referendums – interestingly enough a phenomenon which at the time was not yet formally recognised in the Dutch legal system nor the tradition of Dutch public law. The ongoing debate on the desirability of referendums was not concluded on a national level until February 1996, two weeks after the *Lex Specialis* Rotterdam had been withdrawn from parliament. Parliament has in the meantime adopted a proposal for a law to introduce the institute of a referendum into the Dutch administrative system (February 1996). Citizen action groups and local political parties in Amsterdam and Rotterdam had managed to use experimental local bylaws within their municipalities, to push through a referendum on the desirability of a city–province that would be characterised by the division of the central municipalities.

The administrative elites in both the cities of Amsterdam and Rotterdam – both officially very much in favour of the proposals for reform – had seen this development coming since the municipal government elections of 1995. They were either confused, they underestimated the resistance, or they, at least some of them, were in silent agreement with the growing protest to 'split up the city'. In any case, for a long time they ignored the building up of this protest among the general public within their municipalities. With a completely unexpected but, for Dutch standards, impressive turnout of almost 50 per cent, more than 90 per cent of the voters in Amsterdam (17 May 1995) and Rotterdam (7 June 1995) voted overwhelmingly against the proposals.

These results had no legally binding status. Yet they created an important political fact. The mayor and the municipality of Amsterdam immediately concluded in public, on the night of the referendum, that future models of city regional government could no longer be founded on the splitting-up of the municipality of Amsterdam. In Rotterdam the reactions were less clear, initially only blaming those responsible for organising the referendum for the embarrassment. The Rotterdam suburban municipality blamed Rotterdam politics to hide behind the predictable outcome of a referendum. They were insisting upon the implementation of the original proposal, including the division of Rotterdam.

Many observers concluded that 'ordinary citizens' should not be allowed to have a decisive say in these complex matters. Citizens, after all, were basically 'uninformed', 'emotional' in their considerations and by definition 'conservative' in matters of administrative reform. These comments unintentionally displayed the major weakness of the whole reform process: a possibly technically brilliant masterpiece of consensus politics among administrative elites, but virtually unconnected to the forces of social support and external legitimacy.

Current policy

The Minister of Home Affairs postponed the parliamentary treatment of the *Lex Specialis* Rotterdam until after the summer, and called for 'time out' to explore the situation. At the beginning of the autumn he disclosed the strategy to be adopted. The Rotterdam and Amsterdam agglomerations would still have to become 'city–provinces'. The central cities would still have to be split up in order to take away the fears of the suburban governments that the large central city would dominate decision-making in the new province. For Amsterdam, somewhat more time was considered to be necessary to develop appropriate proposals. In the Rotterdam area, an earlier proposal to restore the historical pre-WWII borders of the central city of Rotterdam resurfaced in an effort to reach a compromise. The proposal became to contain the municipality of Rotterdam within the 'Ring' of highways around the central city and to grant municipal status to the residential quarters built after the war to absorb the population growth. This entails a splitting up of the current municipality of Rotterdam in five instead of ten municipalities and reducing the central city from 600,000 to 400,000 inhabitants.

For the other five designated areas, an earlier evaluation was announced to establish the need and the possibility of becoming a city–province along the lines of the Rotterdam model by the beginning of 1997. The ministry expressed a preference to restrict the whole operation to the creation of only two new provinces – Rotterdam and Amsterdam – but this met with a massive administrative and political lobby by most of the other regions who would like to keep the central government to its 'promise' to also grant them the special status of city–province. This was the case, despite the fact that municipalities within these regions were clearly divided among themselves about the actual necessity and desirability of such an operation. By announcing the evaluation, the government bought itself some time.

Thus a situation arose in which future developments of Dutch regional government reform were wide open again, even though official policy-makers would like to create a different picture. The original procedural scenario of exploring the necessity and desirability of the creation of seven additional provinces remained official policy. This policy could still easily develop in two completely different directions.

The original administrative interests and political forces supporting the ongoing process and actually favouring a division of the Netherlands into about twenty-five provinces 'new style' were still very much alive. Once all seven designated areas were granted the status of a province, it would be administrative logic to expand the number of areas becoming a province and to grant provincial status to the about twenty-five nodal central city areas distinguished within the structure of the Dutch spatial economy since the early 1970s. This alternative was represented by the dominant Christian Democratic party, which has been in opposition since the 1994 general elections.

Proponents of this reform model within the other parties seemed to have been compelled to opt for a step by step 'salami-technique' to reach their goals, if at all. Fierce and effective resistance of the united provinces against an overall 'blueprint' – reorganisation into twenty-five regions earlier on in the reform process led the proponents of this model to keep silent, if only for tactical reasons. They still do form an important current within the reform ideology, but they lack sufficient political power, and seemed to rely on the 'systemic logic' that follows when a few of these nodal city regions have been granted provincial status. The domino strategy: 'with one sheep over the bridge, the rest will easily follow'. That one sheep was Rotterdam.

On the other hand, it was also clear that major forces in government would like to restrict the proposed reforms to only the urbanised areas of Amsterdam and Rotterdam. Amsterdam, however, announced that it would resist any reform model based on a division of the central city. The suburbs have already announced that they will resist proposals for an integrated regional government for the metropolitan area which would be dominated by a large central city. In Rotterdam the forces to resist the ultimate compromise of a less radical division of the central city were quickly mounting up, both within the central city and in the suburbs.

Vested interests were divided, which made it possible up to the very last minute that the coin could flip either way. Given the previous history, and forces – reputations, vested interests, and firm beliefs of having developed the best possible system for managing urban affairs in the region – to continue the reform, despite resistance of the population were strong. At the same time one could see a development in which a seemingly clear-cut and decided case of regional reform once again would not result in any formal regional government reorganisation. Nobody wanted to be politically blamed, however, for another policy fiasco in regional reform in the Netherlands. This amounted to a tense two-week parliamentary poker game in the first half of February 1996. It became clear that the Social Democrats wanted to support their colleagues within the municipality of Rotterdam who had committed themselves to the outcome of the Referendum. D'66 – up until that time a firm proponent of the Rotterdam model and more than once an outspoken proponent of the '25 regions model' suddenly supported the Social Democrats and opposed the division of the Municipality of Rotterdam, knowing that this would be unacceptable to government, as well as the suburbs in the Rotterdam region. The changing opinion of the D(emocrats)'66 may be explained by the fact that ever since the 1960s, this political party in particular had been advocating the introduction of the referendum into Dutch public law. In addition, their recent electoral successes in local elections had put some D'66 politicians into municipal executive boards of some of the larger municipalities, which might have changed the outlook at the nature of urban problems.

The conclusion of the parliamentary debate was that a majority of parliament accepted a proposal for an undivided municipality of Rotterdam within the proposed city–province, which was unacceptable to the government. It withdrew its proposal for law, leaving the question of future development in the Netherlands (again) wide open.

REGIONS IN THE NETHERLANDS: SOME BASIC BACKGROUND INFORMATION

Compared to the majority of UN members, the Netherlands is among the bigger countries: compared to the great powers in the world and, more specifically in Europe, it is rather a small country. It has a population of 15 million people living in an area of 42,000 sq. km., including 1,600 sq. km. of sea water. The population is 442 people per sq.km, making it one of the most densely populated countries in the world.

As to its social–economic performance, it is possible to distinguish some territorial differences and disparities. It is striking that more than 40 per cent of the Dutch Gross National Product is produced in the two western provinces, Noord-Holland and Zuid-Holland. For this reason they claim to be the economic heart of the country. Together with the centrally located province of Utrecht, these three are well known as the Randstad-region. Nine of the sixteen cities of more than 100,000 inhabitants are part of the Randstad-region including the four biggest cities (Amsterdam, Rotterdam, the Hague, Utrecht). In 1987, these three highly urbanised provinces institutionalised their co-operation, claiming more attention for the specific economic and infrastructural problems of this region.

Until the middle of the 1980s, the northern and southern provinces clearly were the economically weaker regions, showing a gross regional production and rates of employment significantly below the average levels. In the second half of the decade, the southern province of Limburg greatly improved its regional economic circumstances, leaving the rural northern part in a somewhat peripheral situation. In the past, both regions have been targets of specific regional socio-economic programmes in charge of the Ministry of Economic Affairs. They have also gained support from the European Union. The south and south-eastern provinces of Noord-Brabant and Gelderland in particular have gained importance from an economic point of view. Together with the province of Limburg, they seem to have benefited most from the development towards a common European market so far.

A country of minorities

When dealing with the political structures of the Netherlands, Dutch political scientists often refer to their country as a country of minorities [Andeweg and Irwin, 1993, p. 23]. In this century no national party has ever gained a nation-wide electoral or political majority. All Dutch cabinets have been coalition governments. The political system formed a unique two-cleavage system in which the socio-economic and the religious dimension bisected each other. The leading parties have their specific socio-economic, ideological or religious background. Until the end of the 1960s, the character of Dutch politics had been determined by a system of tightly organised social groups or subcultures. 'The strong institutional build-up of Calvinist and Catholic organisations led to a strong segmentation of the Dutch nation in separate subcultural communities of Calvinists, Catholics and more secular groups' [Daalder, 1971].

The political system of the Netherlands and the development thereof have mostly been described in terms of a 'pillarised system'. Dutch society for a long time consisted of Catholic, Calvinist–Protestant and 'humanist' subcultures at the mass level. The latter group is subdivided into a socialist and *liberale* (free) pillar. Each of these were more or less societies in themselves, with their own political parties, newspapers, radio and television stations within a centrally co-ordinated broadcasting system, trade unions, employer associations, agricultural associations, cultural, recreational and social organisations. Based on these patterns of pillarisation, the main features of Dutch 'consociational' politics have been analysed in terms of the 'politics of accommodation' [Lijphart, 1975].

The simultaneous process of pluralisation, unitarisation and centralisation was one of the most significant results of pillarisation. Although some major changes have taken place in Dutch politics in the past twenty-five years – which can be characterised by catchwords such as secularisation, depillarisation, democratisation and professionalisation – the Dutch political system is still strongly influenced by a continuous search for consensus, by a strong developed pluralistic political culture, a multi-party system and a policy style where multi-actor negotiations play a prominent role [Daalder and Irwin, 1989].

A country without regions?

As indicated earlier, regions in the sense of a formal governmental organisation with a constitutional status do not exist. As a result, the term 'region' is not fixed, but is used as a sort of container definition:

different people, different sciences and different 'branches' inside the Dutch public administration have different kinds of region in mind, while using the same term. The Dutch province comes closest to what a foreign observer would label a 'region' [Kleinfeld and Hesse, 1990; Kleinfeld, 1990), but to a Dutch administrative mind, the province, until now, is by far the least important level of government. There are twelve provinces, varying in size and population. The boundaries of most provinces are historically determined. Therefore, provincial boundaries no longer conform to the territorial shape of actual socio-economic or infrastructural activities. Apart from the splitting of the province of 'Holland' into a South and a North province during the nineteenth century and the formation of a new province, Flevoland, out of the land reclaimed from the sea in the Zuiderzee Lake, no major changes have occurred until today. However, plans for a reorganisation of Dutch provinces have become a permanent item on the public administration agenda for the past thirty years.

Provincial politics usually do not feature prominently in the analytical framework of regional sciences. When Dutch observers speak about 'regions' they generally refer to an administrative level between provinces and municipalities (*gewesten*). Outside observers would identify the 'regional problems' which are of concern to the Dutch administrative minds probably as inter-local, inter-municipal or metropolitan government problems. The Dutch concept of 'a region' is therefore in terms of scale much smaller than what is commonly understood, internationally, as a 'region'.

The fact that 'regions' do not formally exist is probably one of the reasons why 'regionalisation' has been one of the most prolonged and intense debates in the history of Dutch home affairs and the subject of many recurrent efforts to 're-organise' the Dutch intergovernmental system.

EXPLAINING THE (NOTABLE) LACK OF POLITICAL REGIONALISM IN THE NETHERLANDS

The Dutch government likes to present itself in the international European arena as a country without regions. Many observers, particularly those (silently) in favour of the twenty-five 'regions' model, claim that the concept of regionalisation does not apply to the Netherlands. They would place the Netherlands in the same category as, for example, Denmark and England. They, in fact, prefer a two-tier government system consisting of national and local governments only. In this perspective, provinces may easily be eliminated or be transformed into a second, upper-tier local government form next to the municipalities.

The problem with this position is that it confuses 'regionalisation' with 'regionalism' [Loughlin, 1994b]. Indeed, the Netherlands has not seen any forms of regionalism for a long time. It is often overlooked that this is the case precisely because the Dutch political and administrative system for almost a century has been characterised by a specific and rather unique form of 'regionalisation', which prevented regional issues from developing into expressions of 'regionalism'. It is actually rather striking that despite the traditional reputation of being a comparatively pluralistic, religiously divided and culturally diversified nation,[1] the regional issue in the Netherlands of today is hardly ever associated with the socio-cultural and ethnic cleavages that dominate the debate on regionalisation and regional government reform in so many other countries. The only 'regional' group which sometimes claims an identity in terms of culture and separate language is the Northern province of Friesland. But the 'Frisian Republic' is more symbolically and culturally than politically or administratively a social movement. In cultural scope and political ambition, there is no equivalent in the Netherlands of the socio-cultural movements that have captured the debates on regionalisation in other European countries. This is true, despite the fact that for a long time, and still, there has been a fundamental regional disparity in terms of the strong major religious groups of pillars (*zuilen*) in which the Dutch population and political structure have been mutually divided.

The hidden dimension

The fact that regionalism is in fact considered an unimportant dimension in Dutch politics is actually quite strange in light of the historical picture [Toonen, 1996]. It is often overlooked by Dutch as well as by many foreign observers, that in terms of political majorities, the different 'pillars' largely had their pedestals in different geographical regions of the country: the Catholics in the south and south eastern region, the Protestants in the band which runs from the south-western to the north and north-eastern region, and the smaller and anyway less well organised social-democratic and conservative ('free' or *liberale*) 'pillars' in the urbanised and therefore automatically more heterogeneous western part of Holland. If one simply looks at the picture, it becomes immediately clear that the Dutch political system over the past 100 years has been characterised by strong regional disparities, particularly on religious grounds.

In his comparison of the Netherlands and Switzerland, Kriesi [1990] shows that Swiss federalism and Dutch pillarisation have fulfilled much of the same functions in coping with the plurality of both societies and corresponding political systems: 'federalism and pillarization constitute two alternative mechanisms for the integration of subcultures into a larger national community'. Among other things, he concludes that the 'enormous difference between the two countries concerns the intermediary level of government, which is most important in Switzerland, while it turns out to be almost non-existent in the Netherlands' [ibid., p.437].

In representing their functional interests, the different pillars implicitly, almost on a continuous basis, were also dealing with many 'regional' interests of the subcultures involved, even though, or perhaps because, these issues were seldom represented as interregional political problems. The rules of the politics of accommodation 'to agree to disagree', to conduct 'politics like business' and to stress 'points of agreement instead of conflict', implied that the fundamental regional differences and different regional backgrounds of the pillars were defined as non-issues in Dutch politics. Distributional problems were resolved by the rule of 'proportionality'. Dutch politics of accommodation have never been characterised by a 'winner takes all' position. The strategy has been to distribute the costs and benefits of all kinds of policies – from budgets for schools and welfare organisations to appointments of mayors and top civil servants – in proportion to the relative size of the various pillars. This is also the way in which the 'regional' distributional issues have been resolved.

Seen in this way, the pillarised system constituted, not formally or legally, but *de facto* the system of regional governance of the Netherlands. Because of the exclusive attention on the sociological and political aspects of pillarisation and consociational democracy, it has been systematically overlooked that one is also dealing with an institutionalised system of public organisation and administration. The fact that they were not formalised in the legal sense, does not make them any less 'real' as a part of the constitution of the Dutch system of governance up until the 1960s.

Provinces on the back burner

This perspective also explains why the provinces have never been really able to play the regional government role which they were meant to play in the constitutional set up of the Dutch intergovernmental system. The system of pillarisation started to emerge from the middle of the last century onward. The Netherlands at that time was still a rural society with few 'regional' problems. Regional and interregional issues and conflicts of a somewhat larger scale and more complex nature did not arise until the turn of the century. They followed from the social and economic transformations caused by the industrial revolution which washed over Dutch society from the 1880s onward. The situation, thus, was ripe for dovetailing the constitutional steering capacity of the provinces with the emerging regional economic problems of an industrialising and urbanising society. However, by that time the institutionalisation process of pillarisation had already taken shape at the local level. The institutional system of pillarisation overtook the legal constitutional set up. It provided the institutionalisation for regional governance, already before the constitutionally defined 'regional government' – the province – had properly been able to assume its designated job.

REGIONAL ADMINISTRATIVE REFORM: THE UNDERLYING LOGIC

For more than thirty years now, there has been an ongoing debate concerning a fundamental reform of the vertical structure of the Dutch state and the Dutch administrative system. Provinces have been simultaneously criticised for being too large and too small. Compared to the size of the majority of bodies of interlocal co-operation, most provinces appear to be relatively too large. For planning purposes provinces sometimes appear too small.

The same argument was revived in the European context. The European meso – the interrelated cultural and socio-economic spatial entities – has not yet been clearly identified. So the Netherlands decided to form the NUTS I-level regions not according to provincial borders, but instead chose four inter-provincial units (*landsdelen*) which do not correspond to any administrative level. The same option of creating regions for statistical purposes that do not fit any administrative units was taken for the NUTS III-level. Here, too, only statistically used socio-economic districts (sixty-two so-called COROP districts) were chosen. Thus, only the provinces, which form the Dutch NUTS II regions, correspond to existing administrative units.

Multiple meso

Provinces are a prominent part of the Dutch meso-level but not the only one. Instead of deploring a 'regional policy gap' as some Dutch politicians and scientists have done over the years, it would actually be more appropriate to speak of the Dutch meso as a crowded if not overpopulated level of government. There are at least seven different kinds of administrative 'regions' in the Netherlands operating at the meso-level somewhere between local and national government.

The twelve provinces constitute a fully fledged layer of general purpose government with its own constitutional, legal and democratic legitimation and a directly elected representative body. Compared to national and municipal government, they only carry a limited administrative weight. Provincial budgets cover less than 10 per cent of direct public expenditures, leaving the remaining expenditures to national and municipal governments on an almost equal basis. Provinces mainly fulfil co-ordinating tasks and planning functions. In terms of policy, they are traditionally active in the 'hard sector' (waterways, regional highways, infrastructure) and in recent years also environmental policy.

The local meso is formed by the more than sixty intermunicipal co-operative districts in which a far greater number of almost a thousand bodies of functional co-operation between groups of municipalities are integrated. Newer proposals try to concentrate all activities in less than thirty districts.

There are about 100 government field organisations of the national government in the regions which are called 'deconcentrated government agencies' (*gedeconcentreerde rijksdiensten*). They are considered a form of functional deconcentration (mostly they act as regional boards of supervision of sectoral policies such as education and welfare).

There are some new functional regions, in which sectoral policies are co-ordinated, planned and implemented at the regional level. The initiative for the design and establishment of these regions lies with the ministry in charge, which also spends a special budget for running the regions. There are functional regions, for example, in the field of transport and traffic or in the field of labour market administration. The role of provinces varies here from a non-participating to a leading status. A peculiar case is the forming of regional police corps as basic units instead of a provincial police which originally should have taken the place of the traditional division between national and local police forces. This reform took more than twenty years and is still a hot political item. Talk about a provincial police force has re-emerged in the context of the debate on 'city–provinces' where the Queen's Commissioner is supposed to take over the role which is currently played by the Mayor within the municipal structure.

The Dutch water boards can be considered the oldest systems of functional administration. Today, there are only about 100 water control boards left (*waterschappen, veenschappen, zuiveringsschappen*); their number was much greater (about 2,000) some forty years ago.

At the Dutch border there are five Euregios in which local and provincial authorities participate; they vary in status and intensity of co-operation. During the last few years a new spirit in most of these regions could be observed due to the influence of the process of European integration.

Since the end of the 1980s, central government and also the big cities have been busy making plans to shape new regional authorities or city-provinces as a new kind of regional government in the biggest metropolitan areas.

Urban regional reform

This complex picture has been a reason in itself for the Dutch government to strive for regional administrative reform, in order to streamline the system ever since the 1950s, but particularly since the late 1960s. These efforts have not led to actual reforms. They merely added to the complexity of meso or regional government in the Netherlands. By the middle of the 1980s 'regional reform policy' was associated with 'failure' and no sensible politician dared to touch the subject.

In 1989, however, a Committee (named after its chairman: the Cie Montijn) which was set up by the government to explore the problems of urban development in the Netherlands particularly from the perspective of private business, issued its report. The message was very clear: Europe 1992 is about to arrive, the world is internationalising, the economy is becoming more global and internationally competitive and the urban city and regional government will become more important in the Europe of the future.

According to the vision of the Committee, internationalisation primarily required attention being given to the strengthening of the position of central city government within the urban agglomeration, in order to be able to meet the demands of international competition. The message fitted remarkably well with the thrust and philosophy of national government physical planning policy formulated at about the same time and heavily concentrated on the importance of urban centres in the international economic developments.

In due course, twelve cities were selected as 'municipal junctions' (*stedelijke knooppunten*) for the spatial targeting of national investment policies, infrastructural developments, social housing, public transport and cultural affairs. These cities were supposed to play a regional role *vis à vis* other municipalities. The status of a 'municipal junction' was greatly desired because of the preferential treatment by the national government. These 'junctions' also required some specific administrative arrangements, particularly in order to be able to cope with the 'regional' function ascribed to them.

The Ministry of Home Affairs seized the opportunity to try and restore something of its long-lost prestige due to the inconclusive previous struggle to reform the administrative system and the failure to achieve any real substantive results in terms of its decentralisation policy. They developed the policy which eventually led to the selection of the six designated areas where the feasibility would be explored to constitute a city–province as the administrative infrastructure for carrying out the special tasks assigned to the central cities in those areas.

Thus, the shaping of city–provinces became one of the 'hottest' items in the regional public administration debate in the first half of the 1990s. The aim has been to arrive at a reinforcement of the development of the big cities as motors of economic development. The basic strategy has been to combine the centre of an agglomeration with the surrounding suburban communities in a new regional body, which gives both a greater development potential, a greater policy freedom to solve problems and to improve the quality of the public administration system.

The renewed interest in regional reform has partly been prompted by the discovery of the European dimension of urban and regional management, although this concern has only been indirect and Dutch municipalities still seldom situate themselves in the broader European regional context. The discussion on optimal size, type of decision-making structure, legal powers and financial arrangements is heavily dominated by rather local concerns, particularly the selected tasks in urban regional development which the new regional administrations are considered to carry out. The city–provinces are understood to have mainly a mission in urban planning, housing, infrastructural and economic development. Relieving big city problems is added particularly for the larger city–provinces. All this of course constitutes an important mission, but it is somewhat restricted as the 'core business' of a general purpose government which a 'province' in the Dutch legal context is supposed to be.

EVALUATION AND CONCLUSION

The indecisiveness and circularity of Dutch regional administrative reform policy have often contributed to a lack of political courage in a consensus democracy. Indeed, the whole process is an illustration of the point that the Netherlands are ill-understood as a centralised country in which top-down policies prevail and local and regional governments are at the mercy of national government departments. Actually, just the opposite seems to be true. Administrative reforms are the outcome of a complex, multi-level negotiation game in which joint decision traps do frequently occur, but in which at the same time administrative reform and modernisation should not be mistaken for (formal) administrative reorganisation, and vice versa. Administrative modernisation might quite well flourish in the absence of a formal governmental reorganisation policy.

There are at least three viewpoints from which one may evaluate the processes described in this chapter: the functional, the historical and the European perspective. From a functional point of view it is important to note that current reform efforts have been explicitly geared towards solving metropolitan and big city problems. Dente [1990] has aptly illustrated that we are at least dealing with three different definitions of these problems, each requiring a different problem-solving strategy and administrative 'solution'. The Dutch reform process has been presented as a 'bottom-up' reform strategy allowing for differentiation and promoting a variety of solutions. In fact, the process has been prematurely closed and unified by declaring the 'Rotterdam model' *de facto* the standard for judging regional reform proposals from the other city regions.

The nature of the urban problem in the Rotterdam area is rather straightforward. It is the typical case of a 'capital city' whereby an international regional function requires regional reform. The overriding economic importance of Rotterdam harbour as the still – but threatened – largest harbour in the world, gives the area a rather unique 'hierarchical' structure in which all other concerns might be subordinated to this overriding economic interest. As a capital city function, a harbour has a very physical, spatial impact in terms of spatial development, physical planning, traffic, highways, railroads, environment and economic outlays which cause all kinds of intermunicipal 'agglomeration problems' on top of those which are characteristic for nodal central city relationships anyway. In addition, the 'big village problems' which Dente distinguishes, in which diseconomies of scale (bureaucratism; lacking responsiveness; inefficiency) and the accumulation of urban problems (drugs; unemployment; decay; crime; inequality) are at the core of the urban definition, of course also applied to the Rotterdam case. They could all be tackled by the same integrated model.

The amalgamation or annexation of all municipalities in the region into one 'decentralised unitary agglomeration municipality' has been proposed by some, including the Council of State as the highest legal adviser to the government, but has systematically been rejected. Some feared that the resistance of neighbouring municipalities could not be overcome. Others argued that a municipality of over one million inhabitants would not fit into the overall Dutch municipal structures.

The choice of the structure of a 'city–province' in the Rotterdam area could be justified as a special case, since the underlying 'hierarchical' problem structure would potentially enable the province to act as if it were a unified agglomeration municipality. The problems with the reform process began once the Rotterdam solution started to become a model for the reforms in the other urban regions and also the provinces started to ask what precisely was the difference between a 'province' and a 'city–province' except for granting the latter formal powers and financial resources which were withheld from the former.

The international 'capital city' functions of Amsterdam do not have to be denied to recognise that the problem structure in this respect is far more 'polycentric'. Amsterdam harbour, Amsterdam Airport as a major European airport, the central city as the cultural capital city, international tourist functions, and major functions in the international financial world, each pose their own demands upon the administrative system which can hardly be resolved within one, unified structure. For the other areas the functional logic of the Rotterdam model is even more remote, since the nature of the problems are dominated by typical urban agglomeration problems and (redistributive) 'big village problems' which require a different solution in terms of Dente's typology. The confrontation of a diversity of problems with a single model is only one of the causes of stagnation caused by an administrator's administration in which, for bureaucratic and political reasons, everybody likes to be treated 'equally'. This easily creates 'errors of the third kind': the right solution for the wrong problem [Dente, 1990].

The problems with the nature of the regional reform strategy are compounded when looking at the historical background of the regional issue and the way it has been resolved in the Netherlands. The system of pillarisation started to crumble from the end of the 1960s onward. This has, by now, contributed to an even more complex situation at the intermediate or regional level of government. Many of the para-governmental organisations (PGOs) with which the Dutch administrative structure has been richly endowed, and that used to carry out state functions in the region as an integrated part of the larger pillarised structure have started to take on an organisational life of their own. They have become independent of the formerly integrative institutional structures and forces of the pillarised system. Policy sectors like culture, welfare and social policy were among the first to experience these institutional changes in the 1970s. Now, twenty years later, there seems to be a developing social consensus, that the 'regionalisation' of social security and labour policy is a necessary prerequisite to modernise, if not 'rescue' the Dutch welfare state. The precise nature of this 'regionalisation' is the subject of ongoing political debate.

The overall trend towards 'regionalisation' has now also extended itself to local housing corporations that 'free' themselves from their former national ('pillarised') associations and is even manifesting itself in such diverse strongholds of the pillarised system as physical and mental healthcare, hospitals, homes for the elderly and other welfare institutions, the broadcasting and even the educational system. The 'drying up' of the political power of the national 'domes' of the pillars had as a consequence that the organisations which carried out the national policies have become institutionally insulated, looking for new ways to link up with the system of government.

Some of these formerly pillarised organisations have merged and others have evaporated. The net result of all this is an increased institutional complexity which manifests itself at the regional level of governance. Their organisational domain was, after all, located at the regional level of government. There is, again, no agreement as to the specific 'location' of this region, but in many cases – particularly outside the larger Rotterdam and Amsterdam regions – this will exceed the 'logical' borders of the city–provinces which are drawn on the basis of a relatively restricted mission in urban economic development, housing and physical infrastructures. More generally, one wonders whether the technocratically and bureaucratically inspired regional reform process is actually linked to the social forces of the broader regionalisation movement which is implied by the depillarisation process.

The pillarised structures played a particularly important role in policy areas which are presently of particular interest to the European integration process: economics, cultural affairs and education. From a European perspective it will be easy to identify the Dutch 'regional' reform policies as various efforts to resolve 'upper-tier' local government problems. The creation of a city–province – other than in the Rotterdam and Amsterdam regions – would have to be perceived as the introduction of an upper level local government structure.

The recent debate in the Netherlands has been triggered by 'European' considerations, but in fact the broader regional European perspective is largely lacking from the Dutch reform process. Some would maintain that this perspective is irrelevant to the Dutch case. From a European perspective, it comes as no surprise that not only the provinces but also the Dutch municipalities generally perceive the 'city–province' as a rival competing for scarce local resources and legal powers. There is no European model for regionalisation but within the Dutch context, the meaning of the concept seems to have been stretched too far. Furthermore, the whole case illustrates that regionalisation may be presented for quite a while as a technical and a functional issue, but in the end it inevitably reveals its political character. Regionalisation is a social, cultural and symbolic process. The Dutch case may illustrate the frustrating experiences with functionally brilliant government policies which are not rooted very well in the underlying institutional state structures and the deeper socio-cultural developments within society.

NOTE

1 H. Daalder, 'Consociationalism, centre and periphery in the Netherlands', in P. Torsvik (ed.), *Mobilization, Centre–Periphery Structures and Nation-Building: A Volume in Commemoration of Stein Rokkan*, Oslo/Bergen, 1981; A. Lijphart, *The Politics of Accommodation: Pluralism and Democracy in the Netherlands*, Berkeley, University of California Press, 1968; J. Lane and S.O. Ersson, *Politics and Society in Western Europe*, Sage, London, 1991.

9 Italy*

'Le trompe-l'œil' of regions

Arnaldo Bagnasco and Marco Oberti

Italy has acquired the image of a very regionalised society. It seems to be economically, socially as well as institutionally regionalised, to the extent that the Region[1] has come out as an important actor in the economic development of the country. In reality, the large territorial differences in the peninsula's economic development, linked to very differentiated and specific types of local societies, have led to an illusion about the real role of the Regions. This illusion was all the more effective as in certain cases, particular forms of economic development became territorialised at the regional level, the most famous being the third Italy, with Emilia-Romagna as the model Region due to its economic and institutional performance.

It is useful to recall the factors which have helped to strengthen this image of Italian society and sometimes, to exaggerate the importance of the Regions. In 1970, Italy was in the vanguard of creating the regional institution and at that time, it was often cited as an example of a regionalised society. However, the real activity of the Region in the framework of its powers, which none the less remained rather modest, as did its available resources, remained largely unexamined [Cammelli, 1990; Trigilia, 1989].

More recently, some studies, which have become famous in Italy and elsewhere [Putnam *et al.*, 1985; Putnam, 1993], have tried to evaluate the 'institutional performance' of Italian Regions. Putnam concluded that the 'efficiency' of the Region was linked to the strength and the historical tradition of 'civicness' which has an uneven dispersal in the peninsula. This particularly stimulating and attractive thesis gave rise to numerous critiques, but was also instrumental in presenting a very distorted picture of the regional institution. By showing quite unremarkably and with questionable criteria [Bagnasco,

* Translation Uttam Bharthare and Claire O'Neal.

1994; Oberti, 1994], that the Region worked best in territories where the economy was already very regionalised and efficient (again employing the example of Emilia-Romagna), these studies reinforced the confusion between 'regional societies' (territorialised forms of economic and social organisation) and the level of their political representation. This approach risks exaggerating the importance of the Region in the planning and regulation of these local societies which have often favoured other politico-institutional levels such as the *comune* or the *provincia* [Bagnasco, 1988; Trigilia, 1986, 1989].

Finally, this debate on Regions took place in a very troubled political context characterised by the crisis of the old political system, and the emergence of the *Lega* which made regional autonomy its main objective. Its secessionist stand forced other political parties to address the theme of regionalism. Yet only the *Lega* adopted it as the essence of its movement, and the regionalist push expressed itself forcefully in only a few parts of the country – in the north and especially the north-east [Diamanti, 1993].

To address the question of the regionalist push in Italy and to clarify the role and perhaps future of the region, we move away from the classical studies of Regions, which belong either to the institutional or socio-political current (as Putnam understands it), preferring an approach which endeavours to link regionalist themes to the more profound changes in the social structure. To be more precise, the trends of socio-economic transformation must be simultaneously related to current political changes and the regional question. The territorial cleavage, of which regionalism is an ideological and political aspect, is not necessarily the main axis around which politics is organised or reorganised in Italy.

We begin by recalling the economic and political foundation on which post-war Italy was rebuilt, with the already existing marked territorial differences that cannot be reduced to the north–south divide, although this is a fundamental economic and social cleavage. In the next section, we identify the different paths that capitalism has taken in Italy, by highlighting logics and interests that find different political interpretations, posing the regional question in specific terms. This will enable us to identify the place of Regions, to assess the importance of the regionalist push in Italy, and thus to better understand these elements once shorn of all the sensationalist aspects tied to the perspective of the break-up of Italy.

THE THREE ITALIES WITHOUT REGIONS

The industrial triangle

Even though the regions only came into existence at the beginning of the 1970s, post-war Italy was transformed by a real economic miracle that did not affect the whole country in the same way. Industry based on large production units was concentrated in the north-west which was already more economically advanced. In the 1960s and the 1970s an urbanised industrial society emerged. This model of economic development was based on mass production and consumption, with social groups integrated as much by paid work as by the consumption which accompanies and feeds it. This model can be seen in authentic Fordist cities such as Turin [Bagnasco, 1986] which absorbed large numbers of workers coming from the south. The result was a very polarised social structure with, on the one hand, a very politicised and aggressive working class, and on the other, a large industrial and financial bourgeoisie. Political and union organisation reflected this social polarisation. A strong Communist Party backed by a powerful union such as the CGIL co-existed with the right-wing Christian Democrats. This is also the period when the struggle for social protection and workers' rights was at its most intense.

Integration and forms of social identification were dependent on salaried and guaranteed work, social security cover and political membership along social class lines. In this case, more traditional forms of social identification such as those which mobilise territory and local communities disappeared, giving way to modes of integration and identification which accompany industrialisation and mass consumption. The strong presence of a popular party such as the PCI ensured this integration at the political level by encouraging a class rather than a local or regional sense of belonging.

The modernisation expected to arise from industrialisation was supposed to benefit the whole society, including that of the south which in turn was to take off. At that time, even though this form of capitalism was clearly limited to the north-west of the peninsula, economic and social development did not have a regional dimension. On the contrary, the logic was rather a national aid logic which aimed to spread the Fordist model throughout society, and more particularly to the Mezzogiorno. The working class and the main industrialists did not consider the region or locality a pertinent level for the organisation of political or economic activity. Social regulation rested on agreements between the employers, the state and the representatives of the working class.

The Mezzogiorno

Most of the south remained untouched by the Fordist economic miracle. The Mezzogiorno already appeared to be an assisted economy characterised by large agricultural and public service sectors. The industrial sector on the whole remained less developed, less productive and was dependent on the north.

The economy was largely regulated by politics through the mechanism of the state. The latter intervened in the management of economic development with public spending in the Mezzogiorno, and generated a demand in consumer goods which mainly benefited the industrialists in the north. At that time, it was the region most characterised by political regulatory mechanisms and had the most developed informal economy.

There were few skilled industrial workers and an entrepreneurial class did not really develop. Alongside them, there was a massive layer of underpaid, precarious and part-time workers. Everywhere was witnessed the decrease of agricultural wages, the stabilisation of a stratum of small farmers, the reorganisation of small-scale producers and traders around the Mafia and political clientelism, and finally, most importantly, there was a sharp increase in the stratum of public sector employees highly dependent on the political sphere.

The whole local system was riddled with family ties, local connections, and political links which intermingled in complex relationships marked by clientelism and reciprocity [Graziano, 1980; Gribaudi, 1980]. From the 1950s the Christian Democrats began setting up a clientelistic system based entirely on political exchange, to distribute state resources, which helped it to stay in power for more than forty years. Political clientelism rested on the mobilisation of networks of 'friends' organised around local and family ties. Various social groups thus exchanged their vote for pensions and other benefits in the field of taxation or health, or to obtain secure public employment. Invalidity allowances were generously distributed in entire regions of the Mezzogiorno, retirement pensions were given in conditions which were unique in Europe, public employment was controlled by the local political elite, and tax evasion had became largely institutionalised. Many different kinds of advantages and privileges linked to the welfare state, but also to the public sector in general, were put in place. All sectors of society benefited. The most disadvantaged strata availed themselves of generous social aid, and public sector employees received sound social protection and good working conditions. Large numbers of the self-employed (liberal professions, small businessmen, traders and craftsmen) enjoyed flexible taxation and benefited from the distribution of public contracts.

Political, union, and professional organisation was weak and traditional relations were resilient even in urban environments (personal dependence, loyalty to a protector or a restricted group, etc.), where they formed the basis of all forms of clientelism. This context was particularly conducive to a lack of confidence in institutions, which allowed the economy to develop on an illegal terrain, where the Mafia was often present which, however, remained very localised in some regions of the Mezzogiorno (Campania, Calabria, and Sicily). These are regions that according to Putnam lack *civicness*, which militates against the 'smooth functioning' of the regional institution.

Southern society seemed so dependent on the political and economic centre situated in the north that the regional question was raised in terms of economic backwardness but not in relation to autonomy or independence.

The third Italy

The strong presence and dynamism of small-scale industry from the 1960s onwards are a well-known fact of Italian economic development [Becattini, 1987; Fuà and Zacchia, 1993]. A more differentiated and fragmented demand, adapted technologies for small-scale production, better communication instruments, among other factors, explain the return and success of flexible small-scale industry. In the regions of the centre and north-west, local societies left untouched by Fordism were characterised, on the one hand, by strong traditions in business, artisanship and small-scale industries and, on the other, by a rich tissue of medium-sized cities which facilitated the spread of urban functions (banks, schools, services, business, cultural resources). Finally, the sons of farmers and tenant farmers left the country in these regions to become very mobile workers on the market, ready to go out on their own if family savings permitted [Bagnasco and Trigilia, 1984, 1985].

Industrial districts specialising in one or several kinds of production grew up around these cities which were characterised by a capacity to economically, culturally and politically integrate the entire local society. In the industrial districts of the urbanised country and main cities, a powerful economic mobilisation, consolidated largely by shared values and perspectives, took shape. High social mobility, intense local relations which overcame social categories and economic relations within companies, facilitated a social and cultural continuity which did not polarise the class structure (employers against employees) and favoured instead negotiations in interest relations.

A 'regionalised' social structure which was very different from that of the typical Fordist society was apparent in some Italian regions. Red and white subcultures helped to maintain marked local identities despite a clear perception of different class interests. In the catholic and red regions, these interests were redefined for the benefit of the locality and differentiated from those of heavy enterprise in the industrial triangle or from underdevelopment in the south. Close relations between the working class and small entrepreneurs pushed local governments to strike a balance between economic growth and transformation of the entire local society. This partially explains the original reformist transformation of Italian Communism: forced to represent the interests of different classes, the Communist Party could not limit itself to the defence of the working class alone, which, moreover clearly differed from the working class of northern big industry.

Thus before the appearance of the Region as an institution, a model of local societies based on small and medium-sized firms became regionalised. Later, specific economic and political conditions which favoured a regionalist discourse were effective in mobilising a whole series of local factors – not only economic ones – that facilitated the emergence of a regionalist push.

The political system and the white and red subcultures

At this point, it is important to emphasise the original nature of the Italian political system during this period. On the one hand, it rested on imperfect bipartism and consociationalism [Pizzorno, 1993, 1995], and on the other, on the presence of territorialised political subcultures. In the wake of fascism, the state remained very centralised and retained some fascist elements in its organisation despite constitutional changes. It was tied to a political system fluently captured by imperfect bipartism. Two parties polarised the electorate but did not alternate in government: the Christian Democrats (DC) and the most powerful Communist party in Europe (PCI). Alone, neither party was strong enough to obtain a majority. The DC remained in power with minor allies, whereas the PCI was not legitimised by any other party to participate in coalitions. Thus the working classes and their interests were under-represented and on the margin of official politics. Ideological issues (the Catholicism/Communism divide), the radicalisation of the socio-economic cleavage (the PCI did not choose a social-democratic path after the war), but also political links prevented the PCI from associating itself with the government. Opposition parties were, however, *de facto* and systematically associated with informally negotiated political decisions. This informal consensus-seeking mode of Italian politics ('consociationalism') developed further over the years.

Territorialised political subcultures are also a characteristic of the Italian political system. The 'white' regions of the north-east, under the hegemony of the DC and Catholic associations, and red 'central' Italy (especially Emilia-Romagna and Tuscany), under the control of the Communist Party and all its offshoots, represented the third Italy of small entrepreneurs and of the urbanised country. One of the two big parties dominated, constituted the centre of social life, and did not share local power. Politics was at the service of the community. Although the two regions had different political colours, they constituted fairly similar types of local societies, where the family, local identity, as well as artisan and entrepreneurial traditions were all mobilised for the economic development of very integrated localities.

These differences in political culture have their origins far back in history, but the regionalist culture, despite ideological differences, is very much rooted therein. These aspects were reinforced in the last century during unification when Catholics could not consider national political action due to the controversy surrounding the choice of Rome as the capital. For their part the Socialists, who were weak and marginalised, could not hope to come to power at the centre. Thus for Catholics in Catholic regions and for Socialists in Socialist regions, regional investment became the preferred means of doing politics and they specialised in that [Trigilia, 1986]. The regionalism of the Veneto and other 'white' regions was tempered when the DC came to power at the centre. Conversely, Communist hegemony in the central regions constituted a fundamental element of the strength and strategy of this party which was excluded from power. In the absence of real Regions and despite the statist tendencies of orthodox Communist tradition, the PCI had the most active role in setting up these institutions. Later its capacity to lead the more dynamic and the richest regions of the country facilitated its legitimation.

RECENT CHANGES AND THE REGIONAL QUESTION

Each of the three Italies presented above had to deal with the demands of the economic game in its own way. They were completely transformed during the 1980s and 1990s, and although profoundly modified, they sometimes retained some traits which even now allow us to distinguish the socio-economic worlds particularly related to the regional question.

Large industry on the path of modernisation

Large industry in the north-east underwent a massive modernisation programme and diversification of production. Technological innovations were especially important and they profoundly modified the landscape of large industry. Although large industry did not lose its basic importance in the economic system, it no longer structured society. Social categories which gave rise to specific classes in large industry were changing and diversifying. The crisis of standardised work brought to an end the large homogeneous working class although the resulting differentiations do not seem to have provoked any real fragmentation. For mass production, fixed establishments needed organisational stability and forward-looking strategies, thus reducing flexibility and forcing large-scale production to maintain an organisation culture. This socio-economic world could not function on short-term profitability and financial speculation. It needed a larger and more stable labour force, as well as dialogue with organised partners representing different interest groups.

Forms of social and political integration linked to Fordism were largely damaged by these technological innovations and global changes in life styles. The salaried factory work and forms of political identification linked to it are today undoubtedly less integrative than before. The political level showed more visible signs of the crisis of this model with the radical transformation of the Communist Party and of political and trade union action. However, organisationally and professionally, aspects remained and continued to characterise this socio-economic world of large-scale industry on the path of modernisation, distinguishing it from the other more recent one which produces intangible goods. This has consequences for politics and the regional question. Maintaining more stable forms of mobilisation and organisation, as well as a negotiation policy based on economic and professional interests, continues to limit spaces available for the more traditional forms of identification which could mobilise territorial 'belongingness' and consequently, vitalise the regionalist discourse.

The headquarters of large industry undergoing restructuring are still situated in the north-west but many parts of it have spread to other areas. Currently Fiat is producing 800,000 automobiles per year in the north and 600,000 in the south in several regions and plants. The regions of the north-west which have emerged from Fordism and with large cities with expanding service sectors, certainly have specific interests to exploit and may favour regional decentralisation. But these interests do not seem to express themselves as clearly and forcefully for all actors as in the regions of the third Italy. The territory of large modernised industry does not coincide with the Region at a time when this sector is becoming globalised.

The emergence of the service sector

Parallel to large industry undergoing modernisation the second main trend of socio-economic change is the appearance of a huge tertiary sector powered by an autonomous economic dynamism. Even though Italy is characterised by a strong presence of assets in the traditional service sectors, the more innovative and profitable activities of the tertiary sector are now being aggressively invaded by markets. This concerns, in varying degrees, expanding market sectors such as information technology, communications, entertainment, advertising and leisure businesses, along with health, finance and job training, etc. This sector clearly differs from large industry because of its economic logic, social organisation, and how it relates to territory.

Actors in this sector operate in a market whose rules, controls and constraints are weak. This social world is very fragmented and within it the value of resources increases in so far as the market can free itself from collective constraints and favours differentiation and specialisation. Firms operating in this sector show great flexibility and are capable of adapting to short-term fluctuating markets. They are neither limited by the immobilisation of large capital in fixed establishments, nor daunted by the necessity of confronting organised partners.

The social relations of production can take two forms. For the more simple tasks or those requiring a greater but subject-to-demand know-how, part-time work and temporary contracts are the rule. For activities which require specialised and very competent human capital, semi-professional and individualised relations tend to prevail, and are free from more formal contracts and interest representation.

The possibility given to Berlusconi to 'land' and succeed in politics reveals the importance of social forces linked to the growth of the sector producing intangible goods. *Forza Italia* built its programme on watchwords and values which are directly tied to this social world: individualism, economic liberalism, market expansion, anti-statism, etc. Of course, the pressure of this kind of capitalism based on liberalism, financial speculation, short-term profit and individual success, on its own does not explain the success of *Forza Italia*. The political event, however, demonstrates clearly the increasing presence of this sector in Italian society. *Forza Italia* did not limit itself to this socio-economic domain and certainly channelled a part of the discontentment of the aforementioned small producers. However, wage earners have a small electoral representation through this movement, compared to other political parties.

The new producers of intangible goods and their worlds, which are changing, heterogeneous and mobile, seem to be less tied to space and less bound by territory. It is perhaps excessive to talk about indifference to place, when referring to this post-modern world of imagery and communication. The organisational and cultural modes of this advanced tertiary sector are not attached to the cultural and structural roots that favour a strong regionalist movement. The values currently mobilised by advocates of greater regional autonomy do not always coincide with those prevailing in this sector which is less tied to tradition.

Small enterprise and the return of the regional question: the limited territory of a regionalist movement

Even though the societies of the third Italy have considerably changed in these past decades, this type of social formation has, however, managed to develop in an almost pure form in some regions. Politically, it is mostly the economic vitality of the regions of small enterprise, and not the persistence of underdevelopment in the south, which has reintroduced the regional question in Italy, sometimes in a provocative and extremist way.

In small enterprise regions, social cleavages can be presented and interpreted as centre–periphery or local–global-type territorial cleavages. The cities and districts of the Veneto in a way constitute the ideal–typical case of a society with a diffused economy and a Catholic subculture. This subculture, much more than the reformism of the left, facilitated exchange between classes, and culturally guaranteed the spread and acceptance of the free enterprise model peculiar to these societies. Subsequent to the decimation of the DC, the *Lega* recovered and reinterpreted this culture of diffused entrepreneurship, by radicalising it and by presenting it as the cultural inheritance of a regional people in a difficult economic context. Tax increases to fill the treasury of an inefficient and corrupt state and to continue redistribution in the south, provoke strong reactions in these regions. This sense of a general disorder becomes unbearable when it is seen as something capable of calling into question the 'order' of these regions.

The leagues phenomenon clearly illustrates the structuring power of this social formation based on small enterprise. This economic form which facilitated the anticipation of the demise of Fordism, also foreshadows political change. Political actors in this context can join together and express in a united and relatively homogeneous fashion, the interests and values of these regional societies by differentiating them from those of national society and thus achieve a diffused consensus facilitated by a feeble social polarisation. The factory worker, tradesman, entrepreneur and employee in Treviso are not the same as those in Turin or Palermo. In specific local contexts such as those in north-eastern Italy, these interests can produce alliances between different classes at a local level. In a way, this is what the *Lega nord* has achieved. Presenting itself as the guarantor of the interests of independent small enterprise, it unites different social categories, on a local and community basis, and even has a higher proportion of factory workers than all the other political parties. Thus the *Lega* finds its original and most stable bases in medium-sized cities and urbanised country in the heart of Veneto (Belluno, Vicenza, Verona). Subsequently, it won over the sociologically similar regions of Lombardy (Brescia, Bergamo, Sondrio, Como, Varese), and then the peripheral zones of the Po plains not belonging to the red Italy.

The strong link between the social base of the diffused economy of the north-east and the *Lega* is clearly illustrated by two other phenomena. First, the *Lega* encounters some difficulties in conquering big cities. The exception of Milan is explained, among other things, by a particularly indistinct initial phase, marked by the anti-establishment stands of the *Lega* when Berlusconi had not yet entered the political scene. Later, he in person regretted having called 'his' people to vote for Bossi's party. The values which Berlusconi's party, *Forza Italia* (FI), is capable of mobilising find an echo in the big cities which do not provide a favourable ground for the *Lega*. Therefore, it is a regionalist movement which, given its social bases, is not in a position to conquer and hold the main regional capitals. These large cities contain very different local societies which are far more complex and diversified, and have experienced other paths of modernisation.

Second, recently, in an electorally difficult moment, the *Lega* retreated to its true original base in traditional Veneto. When political supply becomes diversified and the political market becomes more competitive, the *Lega* loses its ground in urban environments to *Forza Italia*. It thus withdraws to its real stronghold, the world of small enterprise in the north-east. The *Lega* is decreasingly the party of the north, as it claimed in the latter half of the 1980s but is becoming rather the party of the northern industrial periphery.

The social world of small enterprise is also caught between two extremes. When small entrepreneurs along with not only the artisans and tradesmen dependent on their success, but also the workers who work for them, can no longer put up with tax and public expenditure increases, they turn to *Forza Italia* and its liberal ideology. When they think about the growth of districts and the spread of social co-operation and public property in traditional society, they look rather to the Left. When they think that they have to simply protect their own particularity, they tag along with the *Lega* as in the Veneto. The *Lega*'s separation from Berlusconi's party on this account is significant.

The small enterprise society will certainly support the more autonomous Regions of the northern white zones, even though the *Lega* there is actually losing ground; as in the red zones such as Emilia-Romagna or Tuscany, where we should find a confirmation of the Left's regionalist tradition in central Italy. The 'new' regional institution, however, remains to be built. Putnam has shown that Regions with diffuse economies in the centre and north-east are much more efficient and in a position to act more potently in the economy. However, all things considered, even the regional institutions of these territories had but a minor influence on economic development. Thus even in the most favourable situations for the functioning of these Regions, we are faced with what Carlo Trigilia has called the 'paradox of the region'. Since their creation they have had only minor institutional powers in matters concerning economic policy, and they do not have autonomous institutionalised representation within the European Union unlike some other countries. Economic and political forces still seem to be reticent about the idea of making the regional level a first-rate political domain.

In Italy, the regional organisation of union and employers' interests has always been weak from an organisational and financial point of view. Politics also continues to be organised on a local rather than a regional basis, and leads local interests towards the centre rather than formulating and redefining regional interests. In sum, with some exceptions, social and political actors never really believed in the possibility of Regions playing an important role.

In fact, there is a kind of Italian paradox which makes the regionalisation of this society a recurring characteristic though the Region still remains to be institutionally built. As we demonstrated, this is due to the illusion of Regions in Italy. They refer more to a multitude of local societies which have their networks, strategies and cohesion at the municipal and the provincial levels, than to real societies and regional governments. Because the regions are only aggregations of localisms, they are unable to provide dynamism or to establish a coherence among different actors.

The Region as a place and level of planning and organisation of Italian society, remains to be built. It is really localism rather than regionalism that has characterised this Italian reality of a diffuse economy, and this is also true for other parts of the country, including the Mezzogiorno. The crisis of regulation on the macro level did not benefit the Region but nor did it affect the vitality of the micro-levels.

The ever-dependent south diversifies

Although the 'engines' of the economy were not very active in the south, it is not possible to disregard the Mezzogiorno (one-third of the country's area and a little more than a third of the population) which, despite its internal diversity with some examples of economic vitality, represents a vast, disadvantaged territory.

Even though the state has intervened massively in the Mezzogiorno, this has rarely induced real economic dynamism. Overall – even though it is difficult to give a homogeneous picture of the south – this part of the peninsula remains marked by 'development without autonomy' [Trigilia, 1992].

These general trends mask substantial disparities from the point of view of industrial development which has not spread to more than a few zones on the Adriatic coast. Among the zones with limited industrialisation it is necessary to distinguish the peripheral provinces and the cities of Naples and Palermo where industry has lost ground. More precisely, Trigilia identifies four development logics according to public intervention, socio-economic traditions, and the level of social tension. None of these zones, which have different levels of economic and institutional development (the way Putnam understands it) refer to the regional question in the same terms.

Politically managed public transfers have always been decisive for the southern economy and the alternatives do not seem clear. From a political point of view, the break-up of the DC has made room for the Right, especially for the *Alleanza Nazionale* which arose from the ashes of *Movimento Sociale Italiano* (MSI), the former fascist party, from which it has inherited its statist tradition. Even if it is true that the crisis of public expenditure has imposed serious constraints on transfers, it is difficult not to envisage a national policy for the future of Mezzogiorno, albeit somewhat different and supporting economy and society. In other words, *laissez-faire* policies cannot be seriously considered and would be strongly resented by southerners. However, it remains difficult to make a link with political changes. *Alleanza Nazionale* is clearly rooted in the South. Favouring state intervention, it gains a sizeable portion of the DC electorate dependent on various social allowances and the generosity of the welfare state. At the same time, the Left is gaining regions and important cities and *Forza Italia* has scored decently (especially in Sicily). It is difficult to give an overall interpretation of these phenomena when Naples has just been conquered by the PDS (the former Communist Party) and Palermo, which shortly after having assured the success of the Left, voted massively to the Right in the last elections. Thus the situation remains quite unpredictable. We may witness, on the one hand, a reconstruction of a system of clientelistic redistribution with new political intermediaries or, on the other, a non-clientelistic use of national resources oriented to an upgrading of local resources. The Region would then undoubtedly have a role to play. The reconstruction of politics in the Mezzogiorno, however, in many cases has to face a dramatic situation of close ties between political corruption and the criminal economy.

Entire zones of the Mezzogiorno are still characterised by underdevelopment, while others have economic dynamism. There is no regionalist push and the possibility of a national withdrawal on the southern question remains delicate. Only a part of the progressive pole cautiously think that greater regional autonomy, commencing with fiscal autonomy, could facilitate a political renaissance based on greater direct responsibility of political elites.

The economic and political dependence of the south is not a very favourable factor for the strengthening of the Region. The redistribution of public resources according to a clientelistic logic leads to dependence on state intervention, which is not conducive to dynamising the Regions.

THE UNCERTAIN FUTURE OF THE REGIONS

Some elements, however, seem to indicate the increasing necessity of taking into account the regional level in the economic and political organisation of large, developed countries. In the new context characterised by the uncertainties of the market, the differentiation of economic organisation and the loss of efficiency of centralised Keynesian mechanisms, economic policy interventions could be differentiated and managed at a level where needs are more apparent and easier to organise. This could equally apply to the management of welfare states which authorities are trying to make more efficient. The Region could thus become the pertinent level of government, and as a 'middle' level of organisation could enable obtaining sufficient economies of scale.

Similarly, development based on small firms requires significant investment in infrastructure and collective equipment which cities and local collectivities are unable to produce alone. In addition, the inefficiency of the state and the public sector constitutes a real problem for small firms which previously managed to adapt using local resources. A collective guidance for this kind of economic activity becomes necessary more than ever within a national policy marked by budgetary constraints.

Our socio-economic arguments enable us to explain how the regionalist push appeared in some parts of Italy, without making recourse to hypotheses based on ethnic elements. However, it must be said that all this cannot be reduced to economic logic alone. Social and cultural differences must also be taken into account. Although these differences have far-off origins, the fact that they now constitute 'new' differences which are tied to modes of adapting to changes in the contemporary world, must be emphasised. This avoids over-evaluating the importance of original cultural differences and also possibly their reformulation as ethnic differences in the context of the 1990s. The recent electoral decline of the *Lega* and its move away from ethnic references clearly demonstrate these aspects. Moreover, some linguistic minorities who have long since obtained significant institutional recognition such as the French minority of Val d'Aosta, or the German minority of Alto Adige, and who have a sufficient cultural base for independence movements, are not active at the moment. The financial transfers and tax advantages from which they benefit are too important to jeopardise with independence claims formulated on cultural grounds.

In sum, apart from the world of small enterprise in the third Italy, none of these areas under consideration seem to constitute a favourable ground for cogent regionalist options. The break-up of politics and the gravity of economic risks in a country with one of the highest public deficits in Europe have contributed to the return of the regional question, in a particularly agitated climate.

What conclusions can be drawn in relation to the development of the Regions? The present situation is undoubtedly too confused to see clearly or to determine precise orientations. Really interested actors with solid experience to take up the matter are rare. Yet, the problem of the institutional renewal of levels of government exists and is a serious issue. It is one variable in the complex game of representation of interests and identities. If we put aside once and for all the improbable dissolution of the national state, it seems impossible to remove the question of regional autonomy from the political agenda. Moreover, the process of strengthening regional autonomy will progress, but still seems ill-mooted and uncertain. Italy is still looking for its regions.

NOTE

1 Region with a capital R refers to the regional institution while the lower case indicates the regional society, that is, the regional formation attached to the territory.

10 Autonomous Communities and the state in Spain*

The role of intermediary elites

William Genieys

In Spain, the democratic transition has brought about a profound change of relations between the centre and the periphery, much faster than in any other country. It has passed from a strongly centralised state to an extremely decentralised state. The trajectory of the Spanish state is a very pertinent example of the unfinished construction of a nation–state [Linz, 1993]. For Juan Linz, the comprehension of this phenomenon requires an understanding of the distinction between *state-building* and *nation-building*. This analytical distinction allows to approach the relationship, generally thought to be convergent between the state and the nation, from a new angle. In Spain, in the nineteenth century, the birth of some nationalist movements within some peripheries, developing a 'fundamental identity' based on language and cultural revivalism altered the building process of a nation–state. Hence on the Catalan periphery, certain ideologists, with whom the bourgeois elite associated itself to form the *Renaixença*, invented a project of autonomous national construction: political catalanism. Confronted with such a phenomenon, the Spanish state had two options. The first, the one followed by the authoritarian regimes of Primo de Rivera and Franco, consisted in trying to destroy the existing fundamental identities in order to impose the nation. The success of such an undertaking depends as much on the international context in which it takes place, as on the resources (education system and the army among others) available to the state to invent a strong integrating national ideology. Keeping in line with the same reasoning, the authoritarian regimes, in order to succeed in their endeavour of statification of the nation, had to integrate the peripheral elite into the power structure. The sociology of the Francoist elite underlines the limits of pluralism of this regime, with the failure of political institutionalisation of the Basque and

* Translation Uttam Bharthare and Claire O'Neal.

Catalan peripheral elites [de Miguel, 1975; Jerez Mir, 1982]. The second alternative consisted in the recognition of the duality of national identities, within the Spanish nation, leading to the development of a new form of state. According to Linz, the states which have not succeeded by their own efforts to form a nation–state, can be called 'multinational States' when the nation–state offers a *roof* to cultures and identities, without pursuing a policy of exclusive identification to the nation.

The state of Spanish Autonomous Communities, built at the time of the democratic transition, can be analysed as a particular form of multinational state: in fact, political and institutional autonomy was devolved by favouring the peripheries where the elite was strongly mobilised around a nationalist movement. The new formulation of the statist link results from the political exchange between the host of networks which are made up of competing systems of action within which the elite acts and struggles to impose its own logic. Thus, the birth of the state of 'autonomies' can be interpreted as the institutionalisation of a compromise between the peripheral elite in the quest of representativeness and the centralist elite looking for a kind of legitimate state [Genieys, 1996]. To understand the transformation of the Spanish state we want to centre the analysis on its political dimension alone. The sociology of the elite underlines the specific role of the leaders of the transition in shaping the democratic institutions [Gunther, 1992]. In the same way, the comparative analysis of the different strategies of institutionalisation of the Catalan and Andalusian elites shows how the peripheries behave, when faced with the change in the statist link. The comparison, of the forms of mobilisation of the Spanish peripheries, highlights the influence of the Catalan model on other peripheries, as is attested by the policy of institutional emulation [Mény, 1993] followed by the Andalusian elites. The creation of autonomies then participates directly in the emergence of a double level of institutionalisation and representation of the Spanish political elite within the *Cortes* (Congress of elected representatives and the Senate) and the parliaments of the autonomous regions. It is this connection between the institutional change and the change of political personnel that we want to analyse here.

THE ACTION OF THE PERIPHERAL ELITES IN THE PROCESS OF REGIME CHANGE

Right from the democratic elections of 1977, the claims for self-determination of the 'Spanish nationalities' appeared in the programmes of PSOE and PCE, bringing in a higher bid from the regionalist parties [Gunther *et al.*, 1986]. However, this revenge of the peripheries operated through highly differentiated logics of action. The process of devolution of the state's legal powers fitted in to this political dimension by the legal recognition of *el hecho diferencial*. This gave rise to a differentiated devolution of the state's legal powers, in which the peripheries, which had been historically mobilised, played the double role of matrix and referent. So the regions with a strong political identity such as Catalonia, by referring to the historical precedent, imposed a return of the institutional autonomy on the political centre, whereas the other peripheries such as Andalusia took advantage of the situation and following the others demanded the same status. The diversity of relations between the peripheries and the Spanish State leads to focus on the comparison of sub-national entities within the same nation. Thus the political mobilisation which founded the autonomous state of the Catalan elite countered the importation strategy deployed by the Andalusian elite. In addition, the comparative analysis of the process of institutionalisation of these elites strengthens the contrast between the logic of the founding action developed by the Catalan elite and the importation logic of the Andalusian elite. Therefore, the analysis of the political action of the peripheral elites at the time of the change of the regime shows how the differentiated mobilisation of the peripheries imposed itself on the state.

A process of imported mobilisation

In Catalonia the transition paved the way for a demand of the restoration of the *Generalitat*. Thus the return of the democratic regime constituted a political opportunity for the peripheral elites attached to this form of autonomous government. Right from the death of Franco, the claim for democracy and access to political economy could not be separated for the elite of the Catalan periphery. In February 1976, on the call of its elite on the theme *Volem l'Estatut*, the Catalan masses were mobilised. On 11 September 1976, at Sant Boi de Llobregat, the Catalan political elite created an 'Assembly of Catalonia' centralising the Catalan political forces which were still illegal. A massive demonstration was organised in Barcelona where a million people filed past in the streets to support the project. In the face of such a strong mobilisation and to get out of the political crisis the Suarez government decided to call a highly symbolic mediator, Joseph Tarrandellas, the exiled president of the *Generalitat* [Benet, 1992]. Following this mediation a decree temporarily restored the institutions of Catalonia. President Tarrandellas then formed a coalition government within the *Generalitat* of Catalonia which neutralised the Catalan claims regarding participation in the planning of the autonomous statute project. Later began a period of negotiations on the final form of the autonomous status/statute between the Catalan elite and the government elites in a parliamentary commission set up for this purpose. The debate on the 'nationalities' provoked strong conflicts between the different protagonists. The disagreement about the scope of the legal powers of the *Generalitat* was settled through negotiation between its president and Prime Minister Suarez. In the end, the final project based on a consensus between the UCD, the PSOE-PSC and the CIU was adopted by a referendum on 25 October 1979 in Catalonia. The *Cortes Generales* approved the statute on 13 November 1979 before the recognition of the king which came on the 25 of November 1979. Thus, following their mobilisation, the Catalan elites secured the possibility of having access to political representation at the intermediary level of the Spanish state. In this Catalonia created an institutional precedent which tended to spread to other peripheries.

This form of mobilisation was imported by the Andalusian local elite who took advantage of the political situation to claim the status of autonomous communities. Referring to the actions of the Catalan elite, the Andalusian elite mobilised itself to obtain a status on the model of 'historical nationalities'. This strategy of imitation translated itself first by an identity revivalism built on the Andalusian folklore. For these elites which denounce the traditional dominance of the North on the South, the constitution of a 'regional conscience' strongly inspired by Basque and Catalan models imposes itself as an alternative to the centralism of the Spanish state [Lopez-Arangen, 1983]. This strategic imitation serves as a dynamism for a call to the 'Andalusian people' (*el pueblo andaluz*). This 'neo-populism' developed in particular in the political rhetoric of the Spanish Socialist Party which tried to channel democratic legitimacy in Andalusia. The mobilisation of local Andalusian elite is relayed by Andalusian leaders such as Félipe Gonzales and Alphonso Guerra. Thus in autumn 1977, after the first legislative elections, the Andalusian deputies asked the Suarez government to grant autonomous status which Catalonia and the Basque Country had just acquired. On 26 November 1977, the Andalusian minister, Manuel Clavero Arevalo (UCD) in charge of the regionalisation, granted the pre-autumn community status to Andalusia. From there on a dispute broke out between the centrists (UCD) and the Socialists over the constitutional procedure to be followed to attain autonomy. The Andalusian Socialist parliamentarians had the recourse to the special procedure of the article 151 ratified in the assembly of local elites of Andalusia, so that their region might attain/gain the status of autonomous community in the same way as the 'historical nationalities'. This strategy of institutional imitation turned out to be perilous, Andalusia having refused democratically this form of political autonomy during the Second Republic. Despite the lack of support of the central government, the socialist parliamentarians and the local elites obtained an absolute majority in 97 per cent of the municipalities in all the Andalusian provinces except Alméria. In the face of a strong electoral mobilisation of the Andalusians in favour of this project, the Suarez government retroactively modified the referendum law and gave the status of Autonomous Community to Andalusia by an organic law, on 30 December 1981. This institutional reform should be examined in relation to the political personnel on the intermediary level of the state: the intermediary elites.[1]

The first studies carried out on the peripheral political personnel insisted on the difference in nature between the political resources of the local elites and those of the deputies of the Autonomous Communities. Our sociological study on the deputies of the Andalusian and Catalan Autonomous Communities put forward the peculiarities of resources of these political actors. In fact the majority of these, with some exceptions, were born in the regions which they represent, and a large majority of them are relatively young (56 per cent – 30/44 years). Their higher level of studies and their professional positions show that these actors are a product of the social change which Spain underwent in the 1970s. On the other hand, these elites show the features of professional politicians as is attested by their autonomy in relation to economic and financial elites and their strong partisan militancy. The analysis of the institutionalisation process shows the integration of the peripheral elites at the meso-state level. The study of the careers of deputies of the Andalusian and Catalan autonomies shows the contrast between two different types of career paths. The first type of career path concerns the Catalan elites which entered politics under the authoritarian regime of Franco and by their action participated, in different degrees, in the founding of the democratic political institutions. These are *career paths with a founding characteristic*. The second type of career path, to be found largely among the Andalusian elites, corresponds to that of the elites who entered politics at the time of the change of the regime. These are *career paths with a predominantly militant characteristic*.

The careers with a founding characteristic are mainly to be seen in the peripheries which have historically been opposed to the centralising action of the Spanish state, such as Catalonia. In fact in Andalusia, with some exceptions, we do not find any parliamentarian who had openly taken a stand against the Franco regime. Hence, it is in the parliamentarian elite of the Catalan periphery that we find the strongest presence of the founding characteristic. In the Convergence and Union party, which was born of a strategic syncretism of different clandestine components of political Catalanism, we find a majority of founding careers. As a general rule these actors took an active part in the mobilisation organised by the Catalan Church against the Franco regime. This form of political commitment constitutes a political resource which turns out be highly legitimising when the democratic institutions return. In this perspective the trajectory of the present president of Catalonia's *Generalitat*, Jordi Pujol, appears to be particularly significant. Right from 1954, his actions and his political stand in favour of Catalanism within the Christianity and Catalonia group allowed him to weave relational networks on which 'Pujolism' was slowly built [Marcet, 1987]. Following a slightly different logic, the president of the Parliament of Catalonia, admits having been an active militant of the Christian Democratic Left (EDC) from 1956 to 1974, before joining, in 1975, the Christian Democrat faction of the CIU, the Catalan Democratic Union. Emerging stronger by this legitimacy he began his national career by getting himself elected in 1977 as the deputy of the *Cortes* for the Madrid constituency. He participated in the efforts to get autonomy status for Catalonia introduced on the institutional agenda and later won the presidency of the Catalonian parliament after the 1984 elections.

Similarly, the invention of Catalan democratic socialism was the result of the founding action of some young Catalan Socialists in the 1960s. Two symbolic figures of the students' movement of 'February 1962', Pascual Maragall and Raimon Obiols, laid the foundation of the Catalan democratic socialism. The political careers of these two leaders have been strongly linked. After taking over the leadership of the anti-Franco students' mobilisation in the 1960s, from 1974 they took up the task of creating Catalonia's Socialist Convergence (CDC). Later Maragall joined the municipality of Barcelona and went over to financial management (1981) whereas Obiols devoted himself to the task of institutionalising the Catalan Socialist Party (PSC-PSOE), and became its leader in 1983. In 1982 the former took over the municipality of Barcelona and it is only in 1988 that he reached the Catalan Parliament to join his comrade-in-arms. We find similarities between the founding dimension of the political careers of these two actors and those of other Catalan Socialist deputies. This kind of political commitment characterises the Catalan Socialist elites and by this can be distinguished from their counterparts in the Andalusian Parliament. In sum, the founding careers are characteristic of the peripheral elites who opposed the authoritarian regime, either from within religious associations of the opposition, among university students or from underground political party organisations. These elites, legitimised by their past political commitment monopolised the political party resources during the transition, thus gaining easy access to recently institutionalised representative functions.

The Andalusian intermediary elites had different political careers. In fact, the absence of political mobilisation against the Franco regime was replaced by a strong associative and partisan commitment. The associative militancy tolerated by the Franco regime allowed the constitution of a democratic culture [Pérez-Diaz, 1990a] which later became the socialising mould for elites of the transition. Very much attached to social change, the propensity for associative commitment was stronger in the economically more developed regions. However, this phenomenon grew more vigorously in Andalusia where the associations of farmers and Catholic Action were a favourable ground for weaving powerful relational networks [Bonachela Mesas, 1983]. As a result, a new kind of clientelistic relationship was established between the peripheries. Partisan militancy occupied an important place in the political career of these parliamentarians. For these elites, the political parties indeed served as real training schools. The federal organisation of the parties and the mode of selection of the candidates for autonomous parliaments' elections favoured partisan militancy within the intermediary elites. Hence, the Andalusian elites affiliated to centralist parties present the greatest proportion of careers with a militant characteristic. Generally these parliamentarians entered politics during the democratic transition [Genieys, 1994, pp. 447–70]. For these actors, new to the political game, owning militant resources turned out be decisive as is illustrated by the model career of this secondary-school teacher who joined the PSOE in 1975 in order to help the party set up locally. Then quickly he assumed responsibility at the provincial and regional levels and later in 1982 got himself elected to the Andalusian Parliament and became its leader in 1990. Similarly, careers with a militant characteristic occupy a central place for the deputies affiliated to the Andalusian People's Party. A perfect example of this is the career of this 51-year-old public engineer who in 1979 joined the Popular Alliance and right from 1980 occupied local-level responsible positions such as the post of secretary of the province of Grenada. In 1981, he joined the PP and became representative of

Andalusia within the 'national Junta' of the party before taking up the post of deputy of the Andalusian Parliament in 1986. In this way, commanding partisan resources often allowed these militants to obtain a party ticket for Autonomous Communities elections and was a basic requirement for gaining access to elective resources.

The analysis of careers with a militant characteristic reveals two dimensions which are specific to the institutionalisation process of the intermediary elites of the Spanish peripheries. The first one is the strong associative commitment prior to any partisan activity. This for historical reasons is very evident in a region with a weak identity such as Andalusia. The second rests on the conquest of partisan resources which one can change in political resources at the level of autonomous institutions. Finally, what becomes evident from all this is that there is a certain specificity of political careers of the Spanish peripheral elites. The mobilisation of the peripheral elites against the Franco State, in Catalonia, is oriented towards the restoration of institutions guaranteeing political autonomy as is illustrated by the careers with a founding characteristic whereas in Andalusia, it is the political parties who play a major role in the process of reconstruction of the democratic institutions.

The changing dimensions of the logics of institutionalisation

The emergence of a political elite at the intermediary level of the state can be understood only by the reformulation of the links with the state. In this way the Autonomous Communities modify the rules of the political game by opening up the possibility, for the peripheral elites, of an institutionalisation on the intermediary level of the state. We would insist on the integrative role of these institutions by stressing the functional variations attributable to the partisan affiliation of the elites [March and Olsen, 1988]. Indeed, if the political autonomies offer new political resources, such as the electoral mandate of the parliament member, the career of the peripheral elites varies according to the representation these actors have of the state institutions. Thus the deputies associated with the centralist political parties (PSOE, PP) often see their action as a stage which adds to their worth and helps their political career acquire a national dimension, whereas the regionalist deputies generally aspire only to win power at the Autonomous Community level.

The dynamics of Spanish institutional change considerably modified the traditional overrepresentation of the Castilian elites at the top level of the state [Beltran, 1977]. During the process of democratic consolidation the renewal of the political class happened thanks to the institutionalisation of the young leaders who had emerged from the peripheries [Botella, 1995]. This phenomenon developed with the support of the political parties who selected their office bearers amongst the Spanish intermediary elites. The federal organisation of the PSOE facilitated the integration of the 'young reformers' and the formation of a winning party of government. On the other hand, the Catalan elites also secured ministerial offices. Thus, Narcis Serra who began his career in 1982 in the Ministry of Defence, in 1991 became vice-president. He was the first Catalan, after General Prim in 1870, to hold such a high office in the governmental hierarchy. This was also the case of Jordi Solé Tura, a Catalan academician and ex-member of the Catalan Communist Party, who joined the Catalan Socialist Party and was elected deputy of the autonomous parliament and in 1991 became the head of the symbolic Ministry of Culture. In the same way the renewal of the executives of the different federations of the Socialist Party takes place through the integration of leaders who come up in the autonomous parliaments as is shown by the change which came about during the congress of 1994. This phenomenon is also to be found in the right-wing conservative parties. The first attempt at renewal by the leaders of the Popular Alliance concerned the leaders who came from the autonomies. The attempt to challenge the leadership of Manuel Fraga Iribarne as the head of the PA was made by a senior civil servant, Antonio Hernandez Mancha, the regional president of the party in Andalusia and elected senator representing the Autonomous Community. These particular strategies adopted by the intermediary elites for the conquest of the summits of the state were confirmed at the time when José Maria Aznar, the young president of the government of the Castilla Y Léon, was elected president of the People's Party (PP).

The analysis of the careers of the deputies of the Andalusian and Catalan autonomies allows us to show this new mode of institutionalisation of the peripheral elites. The translation of this process is often the nationalisation of the political career of the elites, members of the centralist parties (PSOE/PP). Indeed, the deputies who are members of the Socialist Party generally consider their passage in the Autonomous Community as a prior requirement favouring their integration in the political centre. These strategies increasing the value of the political resources are to be found specially amongst Andalusian Socialist deputies. The young elites point out that their political experience on the level of the Andalusian parliament is often considered a stage where one learns the profession of politics. These elected members, while showing their strong territorial identity, insist on the professionalisation by 'daily practice' which favours 'political experience'. As a general rule these deputies perceive their stint in the autonomous institutions as an experience which will help their career acquire a national dimension. In Catalonia if the strategies of adding value to the political resources of the Socialist elites follow the same logic, they differ by putting forward the role of the party. The Socialist deputies of Catalonia insist on the dominant role of the political parties and on the electoral system's own logic. On the other hand, these Socialist deputies wish to be able to use their institutional resources to take up political responsibilities at the national level. Similarly, the intermediary elites, members of the People's Party develop strategies to join the government at the centre. In sum, the outcome is that the intermediary elites, members of the centralist parties tend to add value to their institutional resources by developing strategies to allow them to join the central government. Seen in this way, the political party organisations benefit from the logic of the electoral system and help push the peripheral elites in an upward integration into the higher levels of the Spanish state.

If attaining the political centre appears to be an aim in itself for the elites belonging to the centralist parties, it is quite different for the deputies of the regionalist parties. Analysis of the internal conflict of Convergence and Union, which took place on the eve of the legislative election of 1993, between Jordi Pujol and Miquel Roca on the possible participation in the coalition government is here very enlightening. Miquel Roca, who was heading the list of the party proposed a direct participation of the Catalans in the government, whereas the president of the *Generalitat* of Catalonia refused and reminded him that only the meso-governmental institutions were legitimate for the regionalist parties. Jordi Pujol then imposed the principle of not joining the national party system nor the government, coupled with the strategy of negotiated support for the central government, and thereby modified the logic of relations between the centre and the Catalan periphery. This option of the regionalist parties is confirmed by the analysis of the institutional strategies of the Andalusian and Catalan regionalist elites. For them the conquest of Autonomous Community institutions and more particularly of the governmental institutions constitutes the main objective of their political action. These deputies see this representative mandate as a fundamental and essential political resource. For these actors autonomy is the legitimate framework for political action [Genieys, 1994, p. 449]. In this way we understand, on the one hand, the strategic difference which exists between the centralist elites whose final aim is to arrive at the top level of the state and the regionalist elites whose aim is to conquer the meso-government. This phenomenon provides fresh encouragement to the study of different forms of institutionalisation of the elites on the issue of centre–periphery relations. The multinational Spanish state allows a vertical integration of the elites who are members of the centralist parties, while it offers the opportunity of a horizontal integration to the regionalist elites [Robins, 1976]. This phenomenon is translated by very strongly differentiated representations of the institutional logic of the autonomous state.

THE DYNAMICS OF THE AUTONOMOUS STATE

The dynamics of the autonomous state wield enormous influence on the institutional position of the intermediary elites on the representation of the autonomous state, notably because the left–right divide is transcended by the institutional representations of the state. State institutions are perceived as repertoires of thought or of coherent behaviour which in the long run produce political results. So the institutions are meaningful: on the one hand, as concrete structures (autonomous parliaments and governments) and, on the other, as abstract structures (nationalist ideology) [Stone, 1992, p.164]. So the interaction taking place between the concrete and cognitive structures at the level of representations of actors in their institutional configurations deserves attention. Analysis of the institutional representations of the intermediary elites allows us to interpret the new form of legitimation of the state–society relationship [Nordlinger, 1987]. This demands an awareness of the change in behaviour of these elites when faced by the new logic of institutionalisation of the state. The different discursive strategies of the intermediary elites within the national state are analysed here as *repertoires of legitimation* [Genieys, 1996]. The repertoires of legitimation of the intermediary elites point to the birth of the real power of the Autonomous Communities which is strengthened by the dynamism of European public policies.

The integrative dimension of the autonomous community: the different *repertoires of legitimation* of the intermediary elites

The first repertoire of legitimation, based on the discursive strategies announcing a 'loyalty option' with respect to the institutions of the autonomous Spanish state, is shared by the elites belonging to the Andalusian Socialist Party and that of the Catalan Regionalist Party of Convergence and Union. Most of the Andalusian Socialist deputies insist on the legitimacy of the state institutions. The legal framework outlined in the 1978 constitution is sufficient for the Andalusian Socialist elites. They want the institutional representation of the Andalusian territory defined by autonomous community status to be respected in its present form. The regionalist elites of CIU use the same kind of legitimation repertoire to show their loyalty to the state institutions, while denouncing the central government's restrictive interpretation of the statute. However, for these actors the evolution of the Spanish state needs a more open reading of the Constitution ensuring the full expression of the *hecho diferencial* and not a questioning of the statute. Similarly, for the Catalan deputies, the policy of European construction is a very important factor in the further evolution of the statute of autonomy. The loyalty option shows the elective affinities which exist, concerning the legal legitimacy of the state, between the regionalist Catalan party, CIU, and the Andalusian Socialist elites. From there one can understand the basis of the governmental arrangement worked out between the centre and the periphery.

The second repertoire rests on the 'voice option' of the intermediary elites wanting reform of the Autonomous Community statute. This regroups institutional representations as diverse as the Catalan Socialist deputies, partisans of a federalism-oriented evolution and the deputies of the People's Party claiming the necessity of centralism in order to avoid the fragmentation of the Spanish state. The discourse of the Catalan Socialist deputies on the autonomous community is singular in that, in its objective, it somewhat differs from that of the governing elite of the PSOE. In fact, while the Catalan Socialist members perceive the status as *globally good*, they none the less propose the adoption of a *federal status*. For these deputies, the federal evolution of the state would stabilise the relations between the central government and the Autonomous Communities while helping Catalonia and Spain join the European construction. For this purpose, institutional reforms such as transforming the Senate into a genuine chamber of territorial representation have to be envisaged. The will of the Catalan socialist elites to reform the state institutions has to be interpreted with reference to a specific political context. In fact these deputies have to distinguish themselves, on the one hand, from the repertoire developed by the Catalan government party (CiU) and, on the other, by the defection strategies put forward by the Catalan Left (ERC). In fact, in Catalonia the Socialist deputies' discourse favours evolution towards a federal status and in this is opposed to the institutional loyalty of the Convergence members. On the other hand, the repertoire of legitimation proposing a reform of the state does not question its legitimacy. In fact the representations which are put forward here by the intermediary elites show the will to perpetuate the policy of institutional arrangement characterising the passage to democracy. For its minority peripheral elites it is a matter of struggling to impose their idealised representations of another model of the state. Thus the debate on the evolution of the autonomous community permits some understanding of certain forms of thinking specific to Spanish politics such as the differentiated perception of the development of the autonomous community between the Andalusian and Catalan Socialists, or again the problematic relationship of the elites of the People's Party with the new state institutions.

The third repertoire of legitimation of the intermediary elites which occupies a marginal position within the autonomous parliaments is characterised by a 'defection' in face of the present status. In fact, these members of parliament (MP) consider that gaining political autonomy is a necessary first step to independence, notably in Catalonia. The elites of the Catalanist left launched a discussion which appeared as a radical criticism of the present form of the state. These discursive strategies of going beyond the present form of the Spanish state are less radical among the Andalusian regionalist elites. In fact these MPs concentrate their criticism on the elites governing Andalusia. For these MPs the logic of political autonomy cannot express itself within autonomous institutions of their regions because they are dominated by a centralist party. Finally, these regionalist MPs see the examples of the Catalan and Basque autonomies as models of government to be followed. What results from the analysis of the repertoire of legitimation of the regionalist elites, occupying a marginal position within the autonomous institutions, is that the reform of the state during the change of the regime has to be surpassed at the theoretical level and even in practice.

The evolution of the state: the institutionalisation of autonomous power

The institutional changes in the state bring about a modification in the logic integrating the elites into the power structure. The autonomous governments and parliaments become territorialised political institutions endowed with a strong potential for political representation. The increasing development of policies at the level of meso-government tends to turn the Spanish democracy into a peculiar political regime [Pérez Diaz, 1994]. We are witnessing the beginnings of an intersecting regulation game between the central government and the peripheral authorities, where politics and politicians are in constant interaction. This has the effect of perpetuating the method of doing politics which was very much used during the democratic transition, i.e. negotiation. This phenomenon has almost been institutionalised since the 1993 and 1996 general elections. In fact, the arrangement between the government party of Félipe Gonzales and the Catalanist party of Jordi Pujol was made in the form of a political pact which placed the growth of autonomous authority at its centre. Thus the political elites are taking advantage of the current political situation to change autonomous policy in their favour.[2] Then the transfers of legal powers and administrative decentralisation become a major stake. An increasing number of sectoral policies are transferred to the level of intermediary governments [Subirats, 1992]. The action of the central government in certain sectors has to take into account the Autonomous Communities which in turn regularly calls for the ruling of the constitutional Tribunal, as was the case for the harmonisation law of the autonomous process (LOAPA), the law on the littoral and the law on the ports. More recently, the reform bill on the organisation of the administration (LOFAGE), put forward by the minister of Public Administration, Joan Lerma, perfectly illustrates this phenomenon.[3] In fact Lerma proposed a reform of the status of the civil governor, the emblematic figure of Spanish centralism, and a transfer of legal powers and staff with respect to Catalonia and the Basque Country in the sectors of justice, agricultural production and the Navy's social institute. Lerma also advocates the setting up of a round table of the presidents of all the Autonomous Communities, which will deal with inter-Autonomous Communities disparity and will put on the agenda the Autonomous Communities' participation in the cohesion funds' policy in the framework of European integration. However, the logic of public action is often called into question by the logic of political exchange proper to the democratic life of Spain. So, the new constitutional configuration of the Spanish state is inducing a complex interaction between the intermediary elites and those of Madrid, and this constitutes the uniqueness of democratic life in Spain.

On the other hand, the singular dimension of the autonomous community is strengthened by the dynamic relations between the intermediary governmental level and the European Community institutions (Llamares, 1995, pp. 69–77]. In this way, this form of state becomes a privileged place of interaction where networks are institutionalised according to differentiated sectoral logics [Keating, 1995]. Some authors have described Southern Europe as a territory where the interest groups openly lobby within the European political institutions

[Sidjanski and Ayberg, 1990]. This dimension is deemed so central in its political dimension towards the European Union that Catalonia is often cited as an example. The role of the Catalan Employers' union (pro Europa) is presented as decisive despite the recent clarification made by the president of the *Generalitat*.[4]. We can none the less criticise these neo-corporatist approaches for neglecting the main political aspect of the question of nationalities [Lopez-Arangen, 1994]. The problematic question of terrorism carried out by ETA in the Basque Country is the reflection of the marginal elites' violent refusal of the current autonomous institutions. On the other hand, the conquest of European representative institutions by Catalan intermediary elites, with Pasqual Maragall as the President of Europe's Committee of the Regions and Jordi Pujol as the President of the European Association of Regions are a matter for autonomous and competitive political strategies. This entry into representative political institutions occurs thanks to the alliances between the peripheral elites which go beyond the nation–states and the interest groups, which at the time Jacques Blanc (Languedoc-Roussillon) led, at the head of the Committee of the Regions. Finally, the different European policies implemented in Spain are based rather on the territorialised and singular political logics than on the concerted action by interest groups [Ritaine, 1994b; Smith, 1995]. Hence, to understand these processes which are progressively giving shape to the political reality of Europe, it is necessary to go back to the relational approach of the political processes as was suggested earlier by Stein Rokkan [Tilly, 1995].

NOTES

1 Intermediary elites are the political elites who are active at the Autonomous Community level.

2 This dimension has been explicitly expressed in the official communiqué of Convergencia I Union dated 17 May 1995 [cf. El País, 18 May 1995].

3 We will mention here that Joan Lerma is a typical example of an intermediary elite which has succeeded in its integration into the central government. In fact, he was the president of the Autonomous Community of Valencia until the elections of 28 May 1995 when he lost his seat. This did not, however, prevent him from becoming a minister after Félipe Gonzalez's cabinet reshuffle [see El País, 16 October 1995].

4 During an interview given to El País, Jurdi Pujol answering the journalist who was insisting on the weighing of the employers' union on the action, said: 'It has more weight than power' [see El País, 16 October 1995].

11 The French region as a space for public policy*

Richard Balme

INTRODUCTION

In a comparative perspective, the French region and the successive reforms which gave birth to it seem to be the perfect example of the administrative and technocratic character of a particular form of regionalism. The region has institutional or constitutional foundations as in the case of the German *Länder*, and is the result of the political handling of the unity of the nation as, for example, in the case of Belgium or Spain. French regions should not be seen in that sort of light. They have little to do with a federal conception of a state which is known for its centralising tendency. Also, regions respond minimally to autonomy-seeking or secessionist movements that wish to affirm a regional socio-political identity. In fact, the regionalist logic of constituting a region remains limited and confined to insular situations such as Corsica or the overseas *département*. French regionalisation is rigidly linked to the development of planning [Viot, 1971; Sharpe, 1994]. It responds to state modernisation as defined by the Fifth Republic, which is based on significant powers for initiative associating the executive with high public function and the *Grands Corps* [Grémion, 1976]. It is one of the characteristics of the French-style modernising state, that is to say, a sovereign state that is enterprising, mobilising, but also tutelary, and permeated by elitist and corporatist tendencies. The region, in the top-down perspective, appears to be a mere springboard for state action. This is functional regionalism [Quermonne, 1963] which becomes meaningful only in relation to state intervention in the form of public policies. This raises a number of questions. Thirty years after their inauguration as well as a decade of decentralisation, what is the purpose of the French regions? What is

* Translation Uttam Bharthare and Claire O'Neal.

the precise function of this regionalism? Does it make public policies more efficient? Has it adapted or changed its characteristics, thus creating a new model of public policy? Is it appropriate to talk of regional public policies, or does the term cover a reality more complex and more difficult to define?

This chapter wishes to illustrate the comparative interest of the study of French regionalisation from a public policy approach. The reform of decentralisation leads much less to the constitution of a regional government endowed with autonomous public policies, than *a regionalisation of public policy, that is to say, the establishment of a regional space of interdependence and collective action among participants taking part in public policy processes*. Since then the difficulties of public policies have been linked to co-ordination, co-operation and representation challenges rather than to autonomy problems of the different government levels involved. It follows, therefore, that first in order to restore their meaning and scope, public policies have to be perceived as processes which are essentially inter-organisational. This has become a truism in public policy analysis, but it is somewhat forgotten in the study of decentralisation, due to the development of local and regional policies. More fundamentally, an analysis of intergovernmental relations woven by public policies is necessary for an understanding of the origin and dynamics of regional institutions. Thus, because of its specific features associated with state modernisation, French regionalisation can provide a revealing indication of the changes in public policy fairly common in Western democracies.

THE INSTITUTIONAL CONFIGURATION OF THE FRENCH REGION

The prefiguring of the region, first, with the creation of the *Circonscriptions d'Action Régionale et des Commissions de Développement Economique Régional* (CODER) in 1964, and second, the *Etablissements Public Régionaux* in 1972, following the failure of the 1969 referendum on reform, marked the end of the republican administration of the notables, and through planning, established complex relations between the state administration and modernist local elites. The decentralisation reform, especially the laws approved in 1982, 1983 and 1986, strengthened the region by developing its powers and resources, and direct elections endowed it with political legitimacy [Ollivaux, 1985; Rondin, 1985; Turpin, 1987; Chevallier, 1993; Douence, 1995].[1] This reform handed over new powers to the regions in the fields of regional and economic development, education, culture and vocational training. These powers have remained quasi-specialised attribution competencies, which means that regional initiatives are in principle limited to fields of intervention defined by law. Their role is to conduct and co-ordinate regional development while respecting the powers of communes and *département*, over which it does not exercise judicial supervision.

A number of ambiguities characterise the process. These ambiguities relate to the *objectives* of a reform which seems to succeed when it becomes less necessary; to the uncertain *status* of the region in the enacting terms of decentralisation; and finally to the problematic *legitimacy* conferred on the institution by the chosen voting system.

First, the current reality of the region is characterised by a paradox. While it is the result of planning and regional development policy begun in the 1960s, the regional institution asserted itself in the 1980s, at a time when neo-liberalist macro-economic policies were rendering these forms of state intervention almost obsolete. Planning and development were forms of public policy in decline during this period, along with the institutions which animated them, such as the *Commissariat Général au Plan* and DATAR. This was before their luck changed in a European perspective or public policy evaluation. In fact, the region came to maturity in a context very different from the one into which it was born. Planning loses its fundamental meaning in an internationalised economy and if regionalisation makes territorial development an intergovernmental process, it also diminishes its imperative character in the eyes of the state. This factor, as we shall see later, is borne out by the evolution of the procedure of contractual plans.

In fact, the paradox is only a relative one. The crisis induces the region to seek new functions in the search for economies of scale such as territorial adaptation in the programming of infrastructure and above all, in the management of public finances. Its creation introduces an interesting room for manoeuvre effect in that it enables budgeting investments by externalising their costs for the central authorities. In retrospect at least, the region responds to the known principle of no taxation without representation. By voting for an increase in tax rates, regional representatives served both their own interests and those of the state and the extension of their prerogatives coincides with the relative decline of public expenditure at the central level.

Moreover, national regional development actually faded away during the 1980s, until the genesis of delocalisation policies and urban policy, and its new formulation and reintroduction to the political agenda by the Balladur government with Pasqua's law. However, this retreat was in line with the progress of European integration and the development of EU regional policy, and particularly with the reform of the Structural Funds in 1988. Thus the region has served as an administrative and political support for the elaboration of European Community programmes. During this period, regional policy appears to be the result of the connection between state–region contractual plans, on the one hand, and the Community Support Framework, on the other. Even though leadership of the regional institution in these policies remains problematic, at least it furnishes its partners with a legitimate negotiator. Above all, it determines a reference space within which public policies are negotiated through collective action procedures, that is to say, justification and modes of distribution of opportunities which they create.

The second ambivalence relates to the legal framework of the regional institution in the decentralisation plan. The creation of a new level of territorial authority which is comparable in law to *communes* and *départements*, is certainly a striking development in the French state and its territorial management methods. The Jacobin conception of the state is much too unitarian and rationalistic to prevent the introduction of regions from bringing about a change that would affect the entire politico-administrative system. The region, along with the transfer of prefects' executive powers to elected representatives, is one of the most innovative decentralisation measures. For a while, that is, before the definition of its election rules and the implementation of the state–region contractual plans, it appeared to be the potential keystone of the reform and the radiating centre of the modernisation of territorial institutions and their relations.

However, the reality is more moderate. The French region has a comparatively limited budget. It faces strong competition from *département*, city, and even state initiatives in its areas of competence. Its technical and social resources, that is to say, its capacities for contact and mediation with interest groups or central administration, remain less than those provided by state services in the region. Its attributions, although considerable, are specialised rather than general and it has no supervisory powers over other local collectivities. This specialisation choice which in practice is not exclusive, and the absence of supervisory powers is a double constraint on the region as it is constrained by its means and in its field of action. The innovation introduced with regionalisation, although not erased, is contained and used to amend the existing institutional set-up rather than to replace it.

The final ambivalence is tied to the democratic legitimacy conferred on the institution by the introduction of direct elections. This legitimacy is limited by proportional voting in a departmental framework which leads to a number of consequences. In practice, the electorate does not have a say in designating the executive, and regional politics remain subject to the partisan coalition game which often favours small parties. Incidentally, this departmentalisation of regional political stakes inhibits the emergence of a regional level of political party organisation, which might favour debate during election campaigns. Compared to *communes* and *département*, thus, the region suffers from a lack of visibility in the public arena and this is not sufficiently compensated by the regional organisation of the press. While opinion polls show that the public give credit to the region, they also indicate a relative lack of information regarding its functions and leaders. The most civic clause of the decentralisation laws, which opens up a new field of electoral participation, seems to prefer the risks of indifference to those of identification and political mobilisation. The caution and contradictions characteristic of the motivations of those who brought forth the regions are evident.

Thus, the regional space clearly appears to be a social space, that is, a set of relations among actors whose resources, representations, and strategies are conditioned by the position they occupy in this space. Conditioning more than determinism brings a social space closer to a stabilised configuration, rather than a closed system or a self-reproducing field. None the less, these relations are kept in line with the hierarchy of positions and within time constraints. Regional territory, in the geo-political sense of the term, furnishes a probable dominant representation of this social space by indicating the field of legitimate interaction, the actors in the configuration, their more or less central or peripheral positions, and the motives behind strategies adopted (clearing roads, rural development, urban renewal, the defence of agricultural interests or the promotion of political or bureaucratic careers). Although spatial and geographical factors are only part of the resources and constraints that define positions, they are essential to the organisation of this relational configuration as they formalise a collective representation. This space, however, is structured more by the interactions derived from public policy procedures than by those provoked by political markets, that is to say, by elections and other forms of exchanges that regulate access to and preservation of representative positions.

The constraints organising relations which structure regional reality are far from exclusively exogenous, for example, those defined by law, or local representatives' national political influence. These elements enter naturally into the composition of actor resources. Their relations are essential. They are also determined endogenously as the product of tactical interactions or co-ordination problems, on the one hand, with the effects of temporal deadlines, and co-operation, on the other, with confidence and reputation factors. Here, interaction is not considered in relation to its social determination, in the Durkheimien sense of the term, but *vis-à-vis* its sequential constitution where cognitive factors linked to time, memorisation and anticipation, are of crucial importance. The interest in studying the French region lies precisely in its institutional adolescence, its obvious ambivalences and thus 'the game on the game' introduced to interpret juridical texts in relation to local situations and to build regional institutional reality with public policies. Obviously elected representatives and regional bureaucrats do not play 'this game' alone and they may not necessarily have the knack of it either.

Regionalisation reveals both rupture and continuity traits in the territorial system, but its analysis shows above all that its mutation and progressive evolution through decentralisation has prevailed over harsh and radical transformation. The ambiguities that characterise the regional institution can be seen as points of equilibrium between conflicting interests. The line separating these interests can rally on one side functional agencies tied to the modernisation of the state and regional planning, elected members with federal or regionalist sympathies, representatives of certain local socio-economic interests, elected members of Corsica and overseas *départements*, and the pre-1981 Socialist Party in its strategies of electoral mobilisation. Strictly speaking, they did not form a coalition, still less a lobby pressing for regionalisation. This is because these interests remained varied, unstable, and lacked co-ordination. However, they provided case by case support and justification for putting regionalisation on the political agenda which remained a governmental initiative, and thus clearly faded away once the process of decentralisation had begun. In fact, it met with resistance from a part of the executive including President Mitterrand, and from a large number of elected representatives who had national and local mandates, all of whom were attached to the departmental model from which they drew their resources. In this case the 'republican spirit' coincided with an expected reduction in uncertainty introduced by change. Central government and state decentralised services were obviously reticent about the emergence of a strong regional authority. They were joined by local socio-economic agents who, despite the fact that they had been mobilised at the beginning of regionalisation in the 1960s, notably in Brittany, remained generally indifferent to a reform which hampered their access to the political system, and disturbed the agreed upon and often suitable methods for interest mediation.

The process of regionalisation is, however, less rigid than it seems. Far from being the forced result of confrontation between divergent interests, the modest but relatively loose configuration of the regional institution seems to present the margin of uncertainty necessary for the progressive adaptation of the French territorial system. Its final form constitutes the incremental product of a series of circumstances and multiple rationalities, rather than a grand design conceived *ex ante*.

THE PARTICIPATION OF REGIONS IN PUBLIC POLICIES

As already mentioned, the limited budget of regions gives the measure of the reform which set them up. In 1992, local authorities spent 606 billion francs, of which 27.3 million was for the regions. The volume of their contribution represents only 8.2 per cent of the whole, compared to 28.8 per cent for the *département*, and 63 per cent for the communes [Ministère de l'Intérieur et de l'Aménagement du Territoire, 1994b]. Regional expenditure is practically lower than that of individual communes which, in France, are not well developed and are largely ignored by democratic debate. This situation puts the region in a delicate position to decisively influence public policies implemented on its territory.

That said, the evolution of regional finances gives proof of the region's progressive affirmation as a producer of public policies. Between 1979 and 1992, this expenditure increased with an annual average of more than 16 per cent [Gilbert, 1995]. A large part of this growth is naturally due to the transfer of powers. However, between 1986 and 1992, when the institutional structure was constant, the average annual growth rate remained at 13.7 per cent, far higher than that of other territorial governments. (Ministère de l'Intérieur et de l'Aménagement du Territoire, 1994a).[2]

An examination of the structure of this expenditure is also revealing. By comparing their distribution between the years 1986 and 1992, some main trends become apparent:

- *Current expenditures decreased* from 44 to 34 per cent. Among these, personnel expenses are comparatively small and stabilise at around 2 per cent. The grants allocated by regions bear the principal brunt of this decline.
- *Investment expenditures had a corresponding increase*, from 55.8 per

cent in 1986 to 65.8 per cent in 1992. It was mainly large infrastructure that caused this increase.

- The explanation of this movement is provided by an *increase in education expenses*, from 14 per cent to 33.7 per cent of the total, mainly due to the pressure of investments made in building schools.
- The evolution of the revenue structure was characterised by the *growth of loans* necessary to contain pressure from tax increases, while transfers remained relatively stable. Despite this increase, regional debt remained moderate compared to other territorial authorities.

Observers thus underline two major trends in regional finances. The first one is their dynamism, since their increase in terms of volume and structure is relatively rapid, and the proportion of investment expenditure, somewhat naturally, turns the region into a collectivity innovating in the field of public policies. The second trend appears to be the counterpart of the first one, as it is due to the volatility of this expenditure, the distribution of which varies on an annual basis as well as across regions. The proportion of investment expenditure largely explains this element. The fact that its relative growth is closely associated with the cost of construction and extension of schools in 1986, and that the proportion of this expenditure probably decreased from 1993 onwards, must be noted.

These temporal fluctuations were accompanied by an inter-regional dispersion brought about by the sectoral distribution of this expenditure. In keeping with methodological exactness, the analysis of regional public policies requires comparative and longitudinal methods. A single case study, or comparisons drawn from a particular budgetary year can be accepted here only by default. Taking only the metropolitan regions in 1992, and excluding the exceptional cases of Corsica and Ile-de-France, investment in education and training varied from 150 francs per person in Lorraine to 491 francs per person in Haute Normandie; investment earmarked for culture varied from 3 to 60 francs per person between Picardie and Languedoc-Rousillon; finally, economic policy expenditure varied from 16 to 133 francs per person between the Centre region and Alsace. Regions do not make similar investments or more precisely, they do not carry them out at the same time. Thus their budgets reveal differential planning rather than different policies.

We note the global importance of education and training expenditure which was already underlined, as well as the relatively high level of investment per person in peripheral regions but also in Ile-de-France.

From a global point of view, regional investment is in regional development, where school and road infrastructure account for 65 per cent of expenditure. But regions also demonstrate a 'variable geometry' capacity for public policy. For example, Ile-de-France abandoned economic development to concentrate its efforts on transport and on problems on the margins of the regional responsibilities (health, social action, town planning), whereas peripheral regions are more active in economic policy, and in Corsica, rural development.

In 1990, state investment expenditure amounted to 189 billion francs, communes 123 billion, *départements* 64 billion francs, intercommunal grouping 41 billion francs and finally, regions 30 billion francs. [Ministère de l'Intérieur et de l'Aménagement du Territoire, 1993]. However relative it may be, the participation of regions in public investment significantly alters the political economy of French territory. How this comes about is assessed by examining their sectoral impacts and underlying political processes.

THE REGION AS PRODUCER OF SECTORAL POLICIES

Due to a lack of space and available data, we cannot present a systematic analysis of regional policies here. However, a sectoral analysis, beginning with economic policies which are the main vocation of the region, is necessary to refute the notion that regionalisation only amounts to the emergence of regional government.

The most specific power of the regions, at least from the legal point of view, is undoubtedly that of economic development. In a neo-Fordist perspective, regional intervention is often analysed as functional in an economy where the localisation of enterprises is more and more disputed for reasons relating to fiscal and employment resources, where information and communication are increasingly associated with production, where consequently the environment of firms increasingly determines their performance and where the activity of small and medium-sized enterprises is in a way the crucible of growth. In such a context, regions constitute an intermediary level between local and state ones, where micro-economic policy becomes functional and where competitive advantages can be offered to localised productive sectors. International competition does not take place between isolated enterprises but between socio-political territories and groups articulating (sometimes problematically) production systems, social systems and politico-administrative systems. Finally, these territories are regulated, and the endogenous or local parameters of economic competition such as salaries, labour conflicts, services to enterprises, access to bank financing, technology transfers and communications are modulated at a regional level [Trigilia, 1991]. These factors have become particularly decisive for the competitiveness of enterprises, especially small and medium-sized firms. Thus economic globalisation would functionally induce a form of regional neo-corporatism, articulating economic interests and political leadership through public policies. The issue of regional institutional design thus becomes crucial both empirically and theoretically.

This argument considers the implication of French regionalisation for public intervention modes particularly in the economic field. While this logic provides an undoubtedly rich discussion for political scientists, it does not necessarily lead the interpretation of regional public policy development in the right direction. Analysis of regional economic intervention identifies some general trends which cannot support such a thesis [Kukawka, 1989; Némery, 1993a; Morvan and Marchand, 1994]. As is evident from the budgets examined above, economic policy is not the main regional budgetary item, but expenditure on investment ranks third – far behind education and training as well as transport and telecommunications. In addition, more than half of the economic expenditure undertaken by territorial collectivities is incurred by communes, which are ahead of regions (about 30 per cent) and *départements*.[3] The regional share of these economic interventions is shrinking. Some analysts even describe regional economic policies as insignificant [Le Galès, 1995]. If they devote a diminishing part of their budgets to economic policy and are being outdistanced by communes in this field, how can regions spearhead the decentralised economic policies imposed by functional necessity?

However, it can be argued that regional economic interventionism is dynamic as it concerns more the environment for firms than firms themselves. It is centred more on the development of strong points than on helping sectors in difficulty, which for example is quite different from the policy of *départements*. While these policies are essentially indirect and primarily model the environment of firms, regional action in favour of job training and education as well as programming of transport and telecommunication infrastructure requires the same approach. Therefore, a change in the system of reference and legitimacy which subordinates all local public policy to economic development, is considered a sign of the emergence of regional policies [Gerbaux and Muller, 1992]. This emergence, as a result, would be measured by the capacity of regions to weave these different interventions into a coherent whole, and co-ordinate the public policy of other authorities active in their territory.

This capacity, however, remains very relative for three reasons. First, a sectoral logic most often prevails over a territorial logic in programming policies. The region mobilises repertories of actions which are provided by the state or the EU. Second, its status in practice enables it to act as the co-ordinating agent of other authorities only with great difficulty and depending on the whims of local political situations. Finally, the very impact of the measures (aid to enterprises, vocational training, regional transport) is difficult to evaluate, and thus to classify and plan. Consequently, its mobilising potential for regional economic development remains uncertain and indeed improbable. In the present state of research, it cannot, however, be ruled out and its variable nature certainly calls for further and more advanced comparative studies.

Regional initiatives may seem to be endowed with a greater latitude in other sectors, particularly vocational training, the environment and culture. Systematic and significant studies that could address these questions are missing.[4] None the less, in each of these sectors, regions face strong competition from other producers of public policy, chiefly the state, other local authorities and the EU. Culture and the environment are two fields in which decentralisation to regional level accompanied rather than followed devolution, and local-level state initiatives lead to the territorialisation of sectoral policies to which the regions react rather than anticipate. The case of the environment in particular, reveals a situation where regions are bereft of financial, regulatory and implementation powers.[5] Here, the regions play a role, the composition or access of which they do not control.

Secondary education is even more representative of public policies almost imposed by state co-financing, as the regions initially did not have any say except in choosing architectural projects. However, they seem to find ways of asserting themselves *vis-à-vis* the imperious power of the Ministry of National Education, by modulating and progressively orienting their projects, and mobilising the communes and the *départements* [Fontaine,1990 and 1992]. Lastly, vocational training is also a regional power disputed by the state with its policies of fighting unemployment. It is also disputed by enterprises through chambers of commerce as well as EU policies with the deployment of European Social Fund grants. While it is probable that regions can innovate in this complex world, tormented by the badly organised dynamics of need, the public, and training offers, it is at least premature to consider them the pivot of improbable coherence and unattainable co-ordination [Le Galès, 1995].

It is probably in the field of higher education and research that regions have found the opportunity to demonstrate their capacity for taking original initiatives. In fact, while in matters of secondary education, their role is reduced to that of financing, the preparation of the outline for *Université 2000* between 1990 and 1992 to meet the expected explosion of the number of university students, witnessed keen negotiations between regions and the state. They thus gained the power to influence the localisation of universities and the orientations of certain programmes. They obtained control of the more visible and prestigious infrastructure for which they claimed construction. Certain regions like Ile-de-France and Nord Pas-de-Calais, planned the creation of new universities. In all cases, they have contributed to regional development by developing higher and often technical training programmes in medium-sized towns. They influenced the planning of new courses, in particular by developing technological training that was related to the local economic environment. Finally, academics are well placed to know that regions make a considerable contribution to research by providing support to laboratories, granting scholarships and project-financing contracts. Naturally regions are not the only authorities to finance higher education.[6] However, there they have found an area of influence, planning and co-ordination where they make a specific contribution to public policies. Now it is up to research to identify conditions that determine possible variations in these policies and to make progress in the evaluation of their effects.

Regional sectoral policies seem to emerge where they are perhaps less expected than in economic development or regional development. This is far from neo-corporatism as it refers to a negotiated form of public policy where the political actor facilitates the elaboration of a compromise between divergent socio-economic interests which are then involved in the implementation of programmes. Regional policies are based more on loose interdependencies than on close interactions, and sectoral and politico-administrative logics are more prevalent than territorial or socio-political logics. Notwithstanding the potential difficulty of measuring their impact, the hypothesis of progressive affirmation of their effects on the regional political economy and, consequently a capacity for institutional guidance of social change, cannot be ignored. The structures of these public policies could thus contribute to the regionalisation of socio-political regulation.

THE REGIONAL PUBLIC POLICY PROCESS

Going beyond these sectoral analyses, we would like to shed some light on some common characteristics of these policies and thus illustrate their most significant transversal processes. The first element can be revealed by evoking the sequential approach of public policies. The definition of *problems* is severely constrained by the statutory powers of the regions, whereas the regional *agenda* is hardly differentiated in the jumble of local policies, and is sectorally fragmented. *Implementation* is also constrained due to limited capacity, for example, with respect to personnel and regulatory means and due to the often multi-annual character of programming, to the extent that it is generally imposed by consequent investments. Lastly, *evaluation*, the effectiveness of which remains to be seen, is often proclaimed to be a necessity and is laid down in the chosen procedures, which shows that these policies have a social experiment dimension. They also constitute an attempt to set up a reflexive practice and from a certain point of view a kind of a social control. In sum, evoking this sequential grid demonstrates that they are deployed in a restricted social area. Regional policies are a *collection of elements borrowed from a doubly limited repertoire*, on the one hand, because institutions do not control the register and, on the other, because in their use they are heavily dependent on competition from other political and administrative actors. Hence problems of co-operation and co-ordination become decisive for public policies in general, and for their territorial dimension in particular [Scharpf *et al.*, 1978; Scharpf, 1993b].

The second overall characteristic of these policies is precisely a *formalisation of inter-governmental relations*, as shown by the implementation of contractual plans or of the reform of the European Structural Funds in particular. These procedures have been analysed elsewhere [Balme and Bonnet, 1995; Balme and Jouve, 1995; Smith and Smyrl, 1995], and so we shall not take them up again here. We must, however, note some strong trends. First, the development of *conventional procedures* is quite generalised in public policy modes and is particularly noticeable in local policies. The contractual plans involve about 20 per cent of the regional budget and more than 30 per cent in the case of Ile-de-France. The Structural Funds, for their part, bring a contribution comparable to that of regional spending in contractual plans. Between 1989 and 1993, state spending in contractual plans increased to 60,198 million francs, that of regions to 51,783 million, whereas Structural Funding amounted to 45,723 million francs. We can hence see the importance of the interlocking character of regional policies, especially infrastructure policies in which the regional 'outlay' conditions by way of a 'cascade' the participation of the state in contractual plans, which in turn determines the contribution of the European Commission to the Community Support

Framework. This is a game of close interdependencies in which it must be emphasised that the tightening of the objectives of contractual plans and the Community Support Framework limits the scope of the regional policy repertoire.

The *banalisation* of these policies can also be stressed, as although they were designed as tools of regional development to reduce spatial disparities, their functions were extended to become a mode of managing inter-governmental relations at three levels, local, national and European. Finally, empirical observation of relations established in the preparation and implementation of these programmes reveals two important factors. While animation and co-ordination are formally left to regional authorities, they are in fact most often exercised by state services decentralised to regional level as well as SGAR and prefects, who in the formulation of public policies at the regional level recover a part of the influence they ceded with devolution to departmental and local administrative control. Furthermore, they must not hide the fact that the capacity for inter-sectoral variation and inter-regional variation of networks of public policies are important and are to be explored in their configuration as well as in their determinants.

An examination of regional policies also shows that they develop by the creation of an *inter-governmental bureaucratic technostructure*, consisting of all the agents who interact during their formulation and implementation. With the exception of the case of the environment, to which we will return later, we are struck by the technical character of the policies under consideration, and by the distance which most often separates them from the ideological debates that trouble politics. They demand resources such as social, legal and technical expertise which turns them into a matter for professionals, whether they are elected representatives, government officials or private bodies. This elaborate division of the politico-administrative work makes regional policies a product of an aggregation of poorly articulated networks which are not confined to the regional territory, and are not necessarily centred on the regional institution.

Finally, the last common characteristic of these policies is their contribution, which in practice is differential, to the organisation of the regional institution by turning it into a *political arena*. First, the peculiarity of the election model confers on regions a unique position in national political life, as proportional representation gives free reign to the expression of political currents and the game of partisan coalitions. Thus, during the 1992 elections, it was evident that the election of the president of regional councils was equivalent to a test in the elaboration of national coalitions. It must be recalled that it was in the stormy climate characterising these elections that the plan to introduce proportional representation for the 1993 general elections was abandoned by the government. The moderate right had rejected the possibility of an agreement with the National Front early on, but an exception occurred in Haute-Normandie, depriving the socialists and their leader Laurent Fabius of victory. In Nord Pas-de-Calais, the Socialist Party lost its dominant position and had to support the Green candidate, Marie-Christine Blandin, who won the presidency. Intense controversies erupted in Burgundy and Lorraine where elected presidents were suspected of having benefited from the votes of the National Front. The political climate worsened due to the election as each party accused its opponents of deceit and its allies of treason. After the Socialists were routed, Prime Minister Edith Cresson was replaced by Pierre Bérégovoy and the plan to introduce proportional representation for general elections in order to facilitate a reorganisation of political parties around new issues, was withdrawn from the government's agenda. The regional political arena when considered globally thus becomes a component of the national political arena [Habert *et al.*, 1992].

Each region also formed a relatively specific political arena, whose particular structure, in the circumstances of proportional representation and the presence of Green and National Front elected members, had repercussions for public policies. The absence of an absolute majority does not facilitate the adoption of budgets. In 1993, in Burgundy, only the support of the members of the National Front for a project cleared of all tax increases, enabled the vote of the budget. These incidents which were already quite numerous during the election of the president Jean-Pierre Soisson, multiplied further and forced him to resign. Also at that time, the budget of the Nord Pas-de-Calais region headed by an ecologist representative was adopted only with the abstention of liberal councillors who sought electoral support in the general election. In 1994, the contractual plan between the state and the Aquitaine region was adopted with the support of the only elected ecologist, following long debates about the Somport Tunnel. In December 1995, the executive of the Rhône-Alpes region put forward a plan for employment based on the reduction of working hours, which enabled him to increase his relative majority by mobilising the support of the ecologists, who occupied a pivotal position in the regional assembly.

Politics influence regional public policies, even if irregularly, during elections or voting on budgets. This politicisation also leads regional presidents to become public policy entrepreneurs and to expound a coherent programme of future plans, thus giving them greater publicity while regional powers remain limited. Thus public policies help the careers of regional representatives. The case of Charles Millon, President of the Rhône-Alpes region and later Defence Minister, is an example of this. However, by opening up to Europe the area of interdependencies and interactions which configures regional policies, this also transforms the political profession and the arenas in which it is practised. Through Atlantic inter-regional co-operation, the political enterprise of Jean-Pierre Raffarin, president of Poitou-Charentes and European deputy, subsequently Minister of Commerce and Artisan Business is a good example of this [Balme *et al.*, 1995]. It is also true in the case of Jacques Blanc, president of Languedoc-Roussillon then later of the Committee of Regions. By modifying the conditions of political leadership, regional policies also transform territories and forms of political representation.

CONCLUSION: MESO-GOVERNMENT AND REGIONAL GOVERNANCE

In conclusion, we wish to bring together some more theoretical observations at the end of the processes shown here. Four points can be distinguished. The first one relates to the interpretation of the phenomenon which is observed in French regionalisation. The argument advanced in this chapter is that the idea of the constitution of an institution understood as a regional mode of government is misleading, in that it overestimates the autonomy of regions, and conceals that which is essential, that is to say the development of inter-governmental relations. It is preferable to talk of meso-government [Sharpe, 1993b] or regional governance, if two elements are stressed. First, it is a matter of governance rather than government with envisaged public policies being somewhat limited to follow social change, and subject to the problems of co-ordination mentioned above. Regional public policy is infinitely more complex than the sovereign implementation of a clearly defined political intention suggested by the idea of government [Mayntz, 1993]. Second, thus we may talk of regional governance on condition that we recall that the political networks of this governance adopt variable empirical configurations and are not necessarily centred on the regional institution in the legal sense of the term. In any case, these factors demand important methodological considerations in the analysis of institutions and regional policies, and place the paradigm of collective action at the centre of these preoccupations.

The second conclusion to which these reflections lead is related to regional neo-corporatism. It would be absurd to claim that socio-economic interests have little to do with the political reality of French regions. Regional Economic and Social Councils do not have municipal or departmental equivalents and constitute a political scene in which these interests are represented, as well as a forum in which regional policies are debated. However, the concept of *neo*-corporatism supposes the elaboration of a compromise between conflicting interests through public policies. If such regulation exists, it is not at the regional level which operates an aggregate of sectoral interests. Furthermore, while these interests do not ignore new political opportunities offered by regions, they deploy their influence mainly around state administrations, in particular through the mediation of their professional bodies. Strictly speaking, such a pattern of corporatism is not innovative.

The third point is brief and takes a political representation perspective. It relates to the division which is established between the moving territories of public policies which are dominated by the flexibility of networks and variable geometry intergovernmental relations, on the one hand, and, on the other, more stable territories of political representation which are anchored in the permanence of electoral and administrative boundaries. There are two systems of interdependence, that of public policy and that of political representation. Their democratic principles implicitly suggest that they coincide and empirical analysis shows that they undergo a process of differentiation. Associated with what we may call a deficit of a local public space (the inadequate presentation of local problems in the media), this trend questions the notion of local democracy, and indicates in any case an important change in representation and the political profession.

To conclude, we would suggest an amplification of these conclusions by indicating that the same type of argument on inter-organisational governance could probably be developed in the institutional management of urban areas, on the one hand, and at the European level, on the other, where the political management of the Single Market is designing a model which is apparently much more integrated than an international organisation, and much less complete than a national government. We can formulate the hypothesis according to which these ('between two') intermediary arrangements define the mode of public policy characteristic of an era, or prefigure future institutional configurations. In any case, we can presume that the major socio-political stakes have shifted to these three levels: urban, regional and European, and the question of institutional design is the most determining one for the regulation capacities of public policies.

NOTES

1 The legislative texts dealing with the regions are: the law of 5 July 1972 supporting the creation and organisation of regions; the law of 2 March 1982 relating to the rights and liberties of communes, *départements* and regions; the law of 15 July 1982 on orientation and programming for research and technological development; the law of 29 July 1982 on planning reform; the laws of 7 July 1983 and of 22 July 1987, relating to the distribution of powers between communes, *départements*, regions and the state; the law of 25 January 1985 modifying and completing the law of 22 July 1983; the law of 10 July 1985 relating to the election of regional councils; the law of 6 January 1986 relating to the organisation of regions. Special statutes were adopted for the region Ile-de-France by the law of 6 May 1986; for Corsica by the law of 2 March 1982, of 30 July 1982 and of 13 May 1991; for Guadeloupe, Guyana, Martinique and Réunion Island by the laws of 31 December 1982 and of 2 August 1984.

2 See also Blanc *et al.*, 1994, and Saidj, 1992 for more developed analyses on these points.

3 In 1989, communes spent 5.1 billion francs on economic intervention; *départements* 2.7 billion francs and regions 3 billion francs [Gerbaux and Muller, 1992, p.104].

4 A study on Picardie is presented by François Rangeon, 1993.

5 Cf. Bodiguel and Buller, 1995, Pelletier, 1993.

6 The leading role of the state remains predominant. Let us also recall that the *département* of Hauts-de-Seine has undertaken the creation of a university.

12 Civic culture and institutional performance of the Belgian regions

Stefaan De Rynck[1]

INTRODUCTION

Inglehart [1990, 15] calls for a redressing of the balance in social analysis towards the role of culture. Seminal work on 'civic culture' and how it differs between nation–states had been published in the beginning of the 1960s [Almond and Verba, 1963; Pye and Verba, 1965]. But shortly afterwards, rational choice models took over as the dominant mode of political and social analysis. Based on strong assumptions about the behaviour of actors, these models predict how outcomes of political games occur irrespective of the cultural setting in which the game is played. Other 'comparative politics' approaches than rational choice similarly made abstraction of the historical and cultural context in which political phenomena happen. The balance is indeed being redressed lately by the rise in 'cultural theory' research. Inglehart's 'Culture Shift', for instance, provides an illuminating assessment of value change in advanced industrial societies. Some authors attempt to go beyond this theorising on cultural characteristics and developments of nation–states in a comparative context. Castles [1993], for instance, establishes a link between the historical and cultural tradition of given states and the observed patterns of policy outcomes. Putnam [1993] embarked with a similar research question on differences in institutional performance, but he took the Italian regions as units of analysis. His challenging book *Making Democracy Work* contends that the 'civic culture' of regional societies is a determinant for understanding the success or failure of their political institutions. This thesis adds an extra dimension to comparative public policy analysis, which concentrates mostly on political, economic and social conditions to explain policy outcomes.

In this chapter, the thesis of the overriding importance of civic culture for understanding institutional performance will be analysed with evidence from two Belgian regions, Wallonia and Flanders. In policy terms, Belgian regions are highly relevant levels of government, who taken together spend more than a third of all Belgian public expenditure (figures for 1992; [Hooghe, 1995b]). With this money, the regions subsidise enterprises, construct social housing, run schools and universities, organise health care, allocate welfare payments, decide and implement EU Structural Funds programmes in co-operation with the European Commission, distribute global and specific grants to local authorities, support libraries and public broadcasting companies, maintain roads and buy buses, invest in harbour infrastructure and provide employment schemes, amongst other things. Belgian regions have also full regulatory powers in areas such as the environment and land-use. They have a directly elected parliament that can organise the regional institutions autonomously. Moreover, they do all these things with a degree of autonomy that goes well beyond that of their average European counterparts. The Belgian constitution provides for no hierarchy between national and regional legislation.

Thus, Keating's question (see Chapter 1 in this book) whether regions constitute a relevant level of government receives an obvious 'yes' answer in the Belgian case, at least if one understands regions as political institutions with a coercive power over a given territory. The question that will be addressed in this chapter is how one could explain the performance of these regions. Are Flanders and Wallonia doing different things with their financial and jurisdictional resources and, if so, could 'civic culture' account for the observed differences? The limited number of cases will not allow us to draw any firm conclusions on that. However, the analysis presented here casts serious doubts on the determining impact of 'civicness'. While not denying the influence of the historical and cultural context on the policy-making process, the chapter will argue that a complementary micro-level analysis of specific policy sectors is needed to show how political and social actors and the structural constellation in which they operate come in as important variables between the civic culture and the production of concrete policy outputs and institutional performance.

THE HISTORICAL CONTEXT

A short overview of the transition from a unitary state to a federal one will contribute to a better understanding of the present Belgian institutions and their performance. The key event in the development of Belgian federalism happened in 1963, when a new 'state boundary' [Mabille, 1986] was drawn *inside* the Belgian state. With the introduction of the language border a firm commitment was given to the principle that the language of the region would be the only language for conducting public affairs. The constitution gives Brussels special treatment with its bilingual status: both Flemish[2] and French are recognised as official languages in the capital. Individuals living outside of Brussels are confined to the specific language of the area where they live.

On the independence of the country in 1830, the ruling bourgeoisie opted for French as the sole language for conducting public affairs due to its association with civilisation and modernisation. A first sign of protest against this monopoly of French came from some Flemish writers and poets. From the 1840s onwards they contended that the use of Flemish was an essential part of 'Belgian-ness'. In order to reinforce the feeling of a Belgian distinctiveness as opposed to France, they argued for a bilingual country. Gradually, this 'Flemish movement' gathered support and moved rapidly away from the original objective to strengthen Belgium as a distinct and multilingual entity towards the demand for political recognition of the Flemish group in its own right. At first, there was a minimal claim to give Flemish equal status to French. But the demand of the Flemish movement soon radicalised towards the exclusive use of Flemish in a unilingual Flanders, a demand that gathered broader support at the turn of the century and started to mobilise the masses in the interwar period [Wils, 1992, p. 186].

The process towards a full recognition of the Flemish language, legally as well as socially, took a bit more than 100 years, from the beginning of the Flemish movement until the end of the 1960s. This process of gathering support was a very slow one, despite the availability to the Flemish movement of some essential tools since the very beginning: a free press, freedom of association, urban centres such as Antwerp, Ghent and Bruges. The movement eventually broadened its base in a wider process of social change. Flanders developed from a rural society in the nineteenth century to an industrially based society. From the 1890s onwards the Catholic trade union that had strong roots amongst Flemish industrial workers became a powerful voice for expressing Flemish demands. Other factors that accompanied this economic transformation contributed to the power of the Flemish movement such as the increasing level of education which led to a greater desire for social mobility on the Flemish side, which was often frustrated due to the monopoly of top functions by Francophones.

Regionalism on the Francophone and Walloon side started as a reaction to the Flemish movement, and to the threat this posed to the vested interests of the Francophones inside the unitary Belgian state. The main speakers at the first Walloon congresses (1890s) were Francophones from Ghent and Antwerp, two Flemish cities. But gradually, a tension appeared in the Francophone and Walloon movement between the ones who stressed the importance of *la francophonie* as a binding factor between all French-speaking Belgians, and those who proposed an autonomous project for the Walloon regional economy. The former would argue that all Francophones of Brussels, Wallonia and of what is called the Flemish fringe around Brussels are united in a common interest against the majority of Flemish speakers in the country. The 'regionalists' would dispute this, and state that the regeneration of the Walloon economy has to rely on Wallonia itself in the first place, and not on 'Brussels'. There is a suspicion on the part of the Walloon movement towards the political and financial establishment of Brussels, which is seen as the external centre that ruled the Walloon economy at the time of industrialisation and deserted it as soon as decline started. The Walloon regional movement has its stronghold in the left of the political spectrum, which stresses that autonomy is the only alternative to a continuous exploitation of the Walloon minority and its economy by what is called *L'Etat Belgo-flamand*. This fear of being a minority inside the Belgian framework was fuelled by the economic development of the 1960s, when Flanders became richer than Wallonia in terms of Gross Regional Product for the first time in Belgian history.

Apart from economy and language, Flanders and Wallonia are also different from a religious viewpoint. This is linked to their different economic history. Flanders was for a long time a rural society where the Catholic Church was dominant in politics and in private life. On the other hand, Wallonia was one of the first European regions to industrialise and knew an earlier process of secularisation. As an expression of this, their autonomist movements have very different orientations. Flemish nationalists tend to be Catholic and more right-wing, while Walloon nationalists tend to be more anti-clerical and socialist. Accordingly, the centrist Christian Democratic Party has traditionally been the biggest party in Flanders, while the Socialist Party is the *parti incontournable* on the Walloon side.

The economy, the language and the religion are the three traditional cleavages in Belgian society. After 100 years of language legislation which failed to bring pacification between the two groups, the issue of language entered into a stage of heavy polarisation during the 1960s. This polarisation is explained by Huyse [1986] due to the fact that the mobilisation around the two other issues was seriously weakened by that time. Thus, free marketeers and socialists, as well as Catholics and free thinkers could align with each other much easier on each side of the linguistic border. The split of all political parties into purely regional parties expresses the diminishing saliency of the economic and religious issues compared to the linguistic cleavage, and it also reinforced the divisions between the North and the South of the country. At the same time, the social and economic transition of the Flemish society as a whole, which had a booming economy in the post-war years, remained the driving force behind the claim for autonomy. In particular, the ever increasing level of education seems crucial here. Maddens [1994, pp. 31, 55] shows that there is an impressive correlation between education and the consciousness of a Flemish identity, while such a correlation is absent as far as the Walloon identity is concerned.

Difficult political negotiations from the beginning of the 1960s until now have established a federal state with a far-reaching regional autonomy. The process of reform was an incremental one, during which the constitution has been changed on more than twenty occasions. In accordance with the consensual tradition of Belgian 'consociational politics', each of the parties involved had to find a sufficient amount of its demands in the political compromise. Thus, two models of subnational government were created, which exist parallel to each other and which operate on different territories. Cultural autonomy was institutionalised through the 'Communities' (French, Dutch and German). Community governments are responsible for education, cultural policy and language issues, amongst other things. The French- and Dutch-speaking Community Governments have also some jurisdiction in Brussels. Socio-economic autonomy was established in the constitution for the regions of Flanders, Wallonia and Brussels. They deal with issues such as economy, housing, energy, and the environment. The six subnational governments were then reduced to five due to the merger of Community and Region on the Flemish side. Each of these governments has its own executive, civil service and directly elected parliament. Unlike the German model of federalism, the Belgian reform aimed at giving each level exclusive fields of interest, which explains why no hierarchy between national and regional legislation has been foreseen.

INSTITUTIONAL PERFORMANCE

Governments have to be capable of delivering policies. This efficiency is one crucial aspect for evaluating their performance. The question of interest here is what are the policy outputs produced by the Belgian regional governments. Outcomes in the sense of a cleaner environment, better educated pupils or more passengers who opt for public transport are not considered as these depend on many more factors than the capacity of governments for delivering policies. What is taken into account are policy outputs such as environmental standards, changes in the educational system, amount of kilometres offered by public transport. These and the other indicators used are under direct control of public decisions. But institutional performance should look at more than mere efficiency. A second aspect concerns the process of governing and the way in which collective decision-making comes about. A third aspect has to be included as well. In the case of democratic governments we want their outputs to be in line with the citizens' demands. The issue of responsiveness will not be looked at in great detail here as the data that are available are rather scarce. Efficiency, the process of governing and responsiveness are the three key components of the performance of a democratic government. I will add a fourth dimension to the discussion which is situated at a different level. An indicator for assessing performance in terms of efficiency can be found in the satisfaction of the elite with the regional institutions, which is evidently not a constituent component of performance itself.

To consider efficiency, five randomly chosen policy sectors were analysed, namely education, environment, equal opportunities for women, public transport and vocational training for the unemployed. In their announcements the regional governments seem to attach equal importance to these issues for improving the quality of life in their societies. As reported earlier, however, the Flemish government is shown to have a higher capacity to deliver policies in all these domains. In the educational sector, the regionalisation released administrative and political energy to reform certain elements of the Flemish school system. Ideas for reforms had previously been frustrated in the unitary Belgian administration where the rule of consensus led to a paralysis that inhibited any major reform. Local school autonomy, an overhaul of the assessment of educational performance with a system of 'end terms' and other major reforms quickly became a reality on the Flemish side after regionalisation. On the Francophone side, educational policy has been more in a state of deadlock since the regional reform. The government has to screen every budgetary item in its search for spending cuts and is consequently at odds with the unions of students and teachers, resulting in major protests during the last few years, which have put educational policy on the Francophone side in a state of deadlock for some time now. In public transport, vocational training for unemployed and equal opportunities for women, quantitative indicators demonstrate the greater effectiveness in delivering policy promises on the Flemish side. Comparing the reference years, the offer of training courses, the amount of kilometres supplied by public transport and the number of women recruited or promoted inside their own administration have increased more, or in the case of public transport, slightly more in the Flemish case than in the Walloon case. Finally, the Flemish region is more advanced and stricter in its environmental policy compared to its Walloon counterpart. This becomes especially clear at times when the two sides meet to prepare a common Belgian position and reaction to draft legislation from the European Commission that was submitted to the Council of Ministers.

As far as the process of governing is concerned, different issues should be looked at. In his research on the Italian regions, Putnam attaches importance to cabinet stability, budget promptness and the statistical and information facilities at the disposal of the administration. For the latter aspect the Flemish government is better equipped with a centralised system of policy and societal indicators that are not only used for internal purposes, but that are also widely distributed to the general public. From my own experience while doing this research it became clear that the Walloon government is less advanced in this domain. As far as cabinet stability and budget promptness are concerned, no differences occur between the regions. But other evidence related to the process of governing points in the direction of a better Flemish performance. A regional ombudsman has been established on the Flemish level in 1992, a bit earlier than in the Walloon region. The ombudsman allows citizens to file complaints against administrative actions and is thus an important instrument for exerting external control on government and administration. Finally, embryonic differences can be seen in the role of the regional parliaments. According to the tradition of Belgian politics, parliaments are put aside as much as possible in the decision-making process. The dominance of the executive branch has always been a fundamental pillar of the system of elite accommodation to keep a political system with multiple cleavages manageable. The regions copied the traditional model of a strong executive branch and a weak parliament. But the Flemish Parliament is slowly recovering ground, more than other parliaments in the Belgian system. Already from consulting parliamentary documents in both regions it becomes clear that the Flemish assembly (and the citizens who consult the parliamentary documents) is better informed. 'Green Papers' from each Minister explain the envisaged policies for the coming years and give the elected some tools for assessing policies. Press interviews with MPs from different assemblies confirm the dynamics that started at the Flemish level.

The third aspect of institutional performance is the responsiveness of a political institution to the demands of its population. There are no available data to allow us to measure the above data on effectiveness and on the process of governing to discover whether that is what the citizens expect. Approximate information on whether the region performs well in the eyes of the citizens can be found in the question whether the citizens think that the region ought to get more powers or not. Flemish and Walloon citizens have more or less the same opinion on that, with a somewhat higher percentage of the Flemish citizens in favour of further regionalisation: 37 per cent of the Flemish citizens and 31 per cent of the Walloons tend to agree 'that the region should decide on everything' [ISPO, 1993], as opposed to the statement that the 'national government should decide on everything'.

The fourth and final aspect that was stated earlier as an important element in judging the institutional performance of the regions is the evaluation made by the regional elites themselves of the regional performance. While Flemish citizens score only slightly higher than Walloons on the issue of whether a further regionalisation of powers should occur, the elites have more divergent views. A greater part of the Flemish elite wants to go still further in the process of regionalisation, which could show that they find the regional institutions more responsive to their demands than the Walloon elite do. As far as politicians are concerned, moderate nationalists such as the Christian Democrats have their list of powers 'to be regionalised' ready: the child care and health care parts of the social security system, the research and development tasks that remained at federal level, the national railway company as the missing piece for a coherent Flemish public transport policy, the basic legislation on provincial and local governments. On the Walloon side, the argument goes more that the last reform of the state has not been digested yet. There is no similar willingness to go further with regionalisation at this stage. This view of the political elites converges with the viewpoints expressed by the social, economic and cultural elite. Based on in-depth interviews with ninety-four top people in the Flemish and Walloon society, half of whom were entrepreneurs, Van Dam concludes that the Flemish elite is almost totally in favour of the federal structure, while the Walloon elite is split into equal halves of people with a positive view and people with a negative or intermediate position. When specifically asked about one policy sector, three-quarters of the Flemish elite expressed a positive appreciation of the actions taken by the regional investment company, as opposed to one-third of the Walloon elite [Van Dam, 1995, pp. 284, 472).

Three out of the four components point consistently to the better institutional performance of the Flemish region. It has a greater capacity to deliver policies; it has made some changes in the process of collective decision-making that enhance the role of Parliament and the opportunities of citizens to act against its government, it administers an elaborated system of policy and societal indicators, and finally, its elite is more anxious to take on new responsibilities compared to their Francophone counterpart and expresses more satisfaction with the way things work at present. Apparently, regionalisation has triggered off more dynamics on the Flemish side compared to the Walloon side. How can this be explained? This question is of importance, both theoretically for political science and public policy analysis and practically for predicting the future of Belgian federalism: is it likely that this divergence will increase, or could the situation reverse relatively quickly to put the Walloon region in the more advantageous position?

THE 'CIVIC CULTURE' THESIS TO EXPLAIN POLICY PERFORMANCE

Putnam's research attempts to show that the institutional performance of the Italian regions is determined by the 'civicness' of their societies, which is in turn shaped by a long historical tradition. On the basis of indicators related to the quality of the decision-making apparatus, the amount of legislative innovation, the production of policy outputs and the responsiveness of the bureaucracy to societal demands, he constructs a single index that expresses the global performance of each region. As a result of this, all the regions of the North are shown to perform better than the ones of the South, but there are also differences in performance inside the group of the Southern and the Northern regions. Two possible explanations for the differences in performance are looked at, both situated in the general context that surrounds the policy process: socio-economic development and 'civicness'. Putnam contends that socio-economic modernity is not the reason for the worse performance of the Southern regions. According to him, the key to explain regional performance and good democratic governance lies in the 'civicness' of society. The relationship between economic development and performance proves to be a spurious one in light of the evidence from the civic community. 'In other words, economically advanced regions appear to have more successful regional governments merely because they happen to be more civic' [1993,pp. 98–9]. On top of that, Putnam takes a quick look at the institutional performance of local governments and concludes that 'good government regionally and good government locally go together, precisely as we should expect if government performance is determined by civic traditions and social capital' [1993, p. 203].

How does Putnam define the concept of 'civicness'? In a civic community citizens actively participate in public affairs and they are more interested in public issues. They define their self-interest more in the context of broader public needs and are not so eager to reap short-term benefits than the members of a less civic community. Relationships between individuals in a highly civic society are more horizontal and characterised by reciprocity than in a less civic society, where interactions tend to be hierarchical between a patron and dependent clients. A civic society has also a higher membership rate of civil and political organisations than a less civic society. Such membership is important, both for internal effects towards the members itself and for external effects. Almond and Verba [1963] showed that members of associations have more political trust, participate more in politics and have a higher 'subjective civic competence'. The external effect consists of the potential for interest articulation and aggregation that is enhanced by the presence of a dense network of civil and political associations. Association membership increases the potential for collective action, as it provides a structure for social co-operation.

A final question of theoretical importance is then where such a civic culture could come from. How can it be explained that the North is more civic than the South, and that Emilia-Romagna is more civic than most other Northern regions? The degree of 'civicness' can be traced back to the individual history of each region. Putnam goes back as far as medieval Italy to explain the emergence of trust, reciprocity and networks of civic engagement. He contends that there has been a gradual accumulation of 'social capital' in regions that were characterised early on by a republican government, while regions that remained under a feudal regime were never able to generate the slow process of gathering social capital, often despite their economic prosperity at different times in history.

MEASURING CIVIC CULTURE IN THE BELGIAN CONTEXT

Putnam constructs a 'civic community index' on the basis of four indicators. Two indicators are related to broader aspects of society, namely the membership of associations and newspaper readership as an expression of interest for public life. The other two indicators are more concerned with purely political participation: they relate to elections (proportion of preference votes of the total votes as opposed to party votes, which illustrates the amount of personal clientelism) and to referendums (turn-out).

As far as civil organisations in the Belgian regions are concerned, there is clearly a denser network of associations with a higher membership level on the Flemish side. Asked whether they have been an active member in the last year of organisations such as parent–teacher organisations, environmental groups, sports clubs, cultural societies, and so on, 38.5 per cent of Flemish citizens replied positively as opposed to 31.1 per cent of the Walloons [ISPO, 1993]. Similar results came out of the European Value Study [Kerkhofs, 1992]. Specifically for economic associations (trade unions, organisations of employers or self-employed) 41 per cent of the Flemish reported that they were members as opposed to 33 per cent of the Walloons. The higher involvement of Flemish citizens in 'public life' could also be detected in more temporary commitments. Peace protest marches of the 1980s, for instance, mobilised more Flemish than Francophone citizens, which is in line with the general observation that 'new social movements' mobilise a greater part of the Flemish than the Francophone population [Hellemans and Kitschelt, 1990].[3] A final illustration of the higher degree of civil organisation in Flanders is provided by the presence of what is called 'pillar organisations' (*zuilorganisaties*). Such organisations form part of the broader Catholic or Socialist family or 'pillar', and to a lesser extent of the Liberal family. They created an important function for themselves in policy delivery at times when the multiple cleavages in Belgian society were deep, as they allowed co-existence between the different groups by granting each the monopoly of policy delivery in their own 'families'. Despite the weakening of societal cleavages, the pillar organisations have survived and continue to monopolise or occupy an important part in the delivery of certain policies. Education, health care, unemployment and child benefits, assistance for farmers and small firms, homes for the elderly and the handicapped are all examples of sectors in which 'public' policy delivery is dominated by these organisations. The phenomenon of 'pillarisation', however, is more pervasive in Flanders than in Wallonia [Billiet, 1990, pp. 99–100]. In Wallonia it is much less present in the sectors of education, health and welfare, where the public administration plays a stronger role. This means that the process of policy-making is more state-dependent in Wallonia as it relies less on organisations that form part of the civil society. As for newspaper readership, figures show a more or less equal readership on both sides of the language border.

Political participation in the Belgian context cannot be measured in the way that Putnam does it for Italy. Voting is compulsory, so that turn-outs are not very revealing. Neither can the amount of preference votes be seen as an indicator for clientelism: many more factors intervene in the choice of the voter for a person or for a party.[4] Available evidence from other sources suggests a higher political participation of the Flemish citizen compared to the Walloons. In more non-conventional ways of political participation the Flemish region scores higher than its Walloon counterpart. Both Smits [1984; 1995] and Collinge [1990] come to the conclusion that Flemings participate more in political demonstrations. However, the regional differences in protest behaviour are not so outspoken. More striking differences come from the European Values Study, which contains some questions that try to detect the political interest of the citizens. In general, Belgian citizens score very low for the importance attached to politics and for political interest compared to other countries in the survey. Three questions of the EVS [Kerkhofs *et al.*, 1992] are worth considering regarding political interest and the importance attached to politics. A first question (Q1) asks the degree of importance the respondent attaches to politics, as part of a whole list of issues (religion, work, family, leisure, friends). A second question (Q2) asks the respondent, 'To what extent are you interested in politics? (very, rather, rather not, not at all, don't know)'. Finally, a third question (Q3) asks, 'Do you talk about politics to friends? (regularly, occasionally, never)'. Table 12.1 presents the results for these questions for Belgium, with the regional breakdown for Flanders, Wallonia and Brussels. For Q1 and Q2 the categories 'very (important)' and 'rather important ' are grouped here. For Q3 the table groups the respondents who declared that they discuss politics on a regular or occasional basis with friends.

The context in which the first question is asked, where politics figures amongst a wider range of issues, lowers the percentage a bit compared to Q2, except for the Walloon region. In Wallonia the results on all questions are remarkably lower compared to the Belgian and the Flemish results. Political interest varies of course according to other variables, such as sex, age, and profession. But regional differences persist also for each of these classes. Flemish women are more interested in politics and find politics more important than Walloon women. The same is true for the several age categories, where the Flemish have a

Table 12.1 National and regional averages for importance attached to politics (Q1), taking an interest in politics (Q2) and talking to friends about politics (Q3) (%)

	Belgium	*Flanders*	*Wallonia*	*Brussels*
Q1	25	29	19	26
Q2	29	34	19	36
Q3	52	59	38	61

consistently higher score than the Walloons. It is well known that political interest and finding politics varies greatly according to the level of education. Also here, the regional differences are remarkable, as Table 12.2 illustrates. The table reports on the answers given by persons who finished their studies at 21 years or older.

Table 12.2 Importance attached to politics (Q1) and political interest (Q2) of citizens with a higher education (%)

	Belgium	*Flanders*	*Wallonia*	*Brussels*
Q1	40	44	29	38
Q2	51	57	31	51

In terms of the dichotomy 'horizontal vs. vertical relationships' some data on the contacts between the citizens and the regional political elites are revealing. De Winter [1992] shows that MPs from Walloon political parties are in general more active in delivering individual services to their constituents (such as arranging pension and fiscal files, obtaining number plates for cars obtaining licences for construction works). This system of delivery of personal services is essentially clientelistic: it implies that a politician interferes in the bureaucratic process to claim individual rights or grant favours, which leads to a different treatment of those citizens with and those without access to a politician. Whether this system is effective or not for obtaining personal votes, it produces a hierarchical relationship between the politician and 'his or her' citizens. The ISPO survey data at the level of the individual citizens confirm the data that De Winter obtained by surveying MP backbenchers: 27 per cent of the Walloon citizens state that they called upon the personal service of a politician to obtain something from the government, as opposed to 17.7 per cent of the Flemish. The fact that the regional elite in Wallonia operates more in accordance with a pattern of dependence in its interaction with 'subordinates' is confirmed by the persistent amount of political nominations inside the public administration. Political support has long been necessary to get recruited or promoted in the Belgian public administrations, even at the lowest operational levels. Recently, the federal and Flemish governments have confined this practice to top-level nominations to maintain an ideological balance inside the top layer of the administration. The practice of individual ministers or ministerial advisers interfering in the personnel policy of the administration to put clients from their own constituency in the desired position has been reduced drastically in recent years. The latest available report shows that this practice has almost entirely disappeared inside the Flemish administration, but that it still exists extensively in the Walloon administration. On top of that, the Walloon political leaders state they have no intention of changing this practice, as shown by a recent discussion in the Walloon Parliament where the Prime Minister defended the politicisation of his administration.

From the first evidence gathered for this chapter it becomes clear that the Flemish 'civicness' is higher than the Walloon one. The evidence on various phenomena points consistently in this direction. Additional evidence comes from the fact that Flemish people report a higher happiness and a higher life satisfaction than the people in Wallonia [Kerkhofs *et al.*, 1992]. As shown by Inglehart [1990; see also Putnam, 1993] there is a strong correlation between civic culture and the general satisfaction with life.

EXPLAINING THE 'CIVICNESS' AND THE INSTITUTIONAL PERFORMANCE OF THE FLEMISH AND WALLOON REGIONS

The higher score of Flanders on the civic community indicators cannot be the outcome of a long historical process during which 'social capital' was accumulated, as Putnam contends for the Italian regions. The Belgian regions are relatively new social constructs dating only from the end of the nineteenth century, a period during which language became a nation-building factor throughout Europe. 'Wallonia' as a concept was invented at that time, and 'Flanders' took on its present meaning to denote the whole region.[5] Only from then onwards did the horizontal line that divides Belgium in its Germanic and Roman part have a salient political and social meaning. In the margin of this historical excursion it is important to note that Belgium as a single entity pre-dates the creation of the independent state in 1830 and that it existed longer as a political and social space than the recent regions. This long existence leaves its traces still today, at a moment when Belgium as an institutional entity is under great pressure. Data show clearly that, despite this pressure, Belgium still survives as a cultural entity. So although the above evidence shows marked differences in civic culture between both regions, the importance of these differences should not be overestimated when seen in an international perspective. In terms of cultural patterns of both regions, the European Value Study concludes that a Flemish citizen is closer to a Walloon than to a Dutch person, with whom he shares the same language but not the same religious history. Similarly, a Walloon citizen is closer to a Flemish person in cultural patterns than to a Frenchman [Kerkhofs, p. 270]. Based on totally different research material, Hofstede [1984] argues that the two language areas in Belgium are culturally very similar, unlike the language areas in Switzerland. The cultural similarity of Flemings and Walloons as well as the attachment to Belgium as a political entity is also revealed by different questions in surveys, which show a preference of the respondents for the Belgian level compared to the regional level. This sentiment is a bit stronger with the Francophones, but it is also an attitude held by the Flemish majority. Even on the question whether the social security system should be regionalised or remain national, almost 50 per cent of the Flemish replied that it should remain at the Belgian level, compared to 36 per cent who chose the regional option, despite the material gains that would result from a separation for the wealthier Flanders [ISPO, 1993].

Although differences between Flanders and Wallonia should not be exaggerated in an international context, where it is shown that there exists such a thing as 'Belgian-ness' and a typical Belgian culture, intra-Belgian differences remain, as the above figures and explanations have shown. These differences cannot be attributed to a different historical path that started in remote times. Alternatively, and more as hypotheses than as firm conclusions, three sets of interrelated explanations could be put forward. First, there are structural differences between the two societies in demographic and economic terms. Wallonia has relatively more elderly people and has a much higher unemployment rate. The elderly and the unemployed tend to be less integrated into civil and political life. Second, the two regions are characterised by a different kind of nationalism, which is linked to the origins of their nationalist movement. Flemish nationalism was born inside the civil society, as a positive movement to gain full rights and recognition as a specific group. The Francophones were put in a defensive position towards this new Flemish agenda and reacted to it mainly from inside the political system, at first to defend established power positions in the existing unitary Belgium. Even today, the constellation of actors who 'carry' the movements reflects this. There are multiple civil associations that fight for the Flemish cause and that keep a certain distance from the political system. Such associations are less seen on the Francophone side, where the reaction is mainly shown by regional parties and politicians [Fonteyn, 1996]. Third, the elite-guided mobilisation of the 'regional interest' happens in a more straightforward way on the Flemish side. As explained in the first section of this chapter, the Walloon movement that stresses the positive importance of autonomy to regenerate social and economic life in an endogenous way, often finds itself in a difficult position in the discussions on the reform of the national state. A Francophone elite competes with the Walloon regionalists to shape the political agenda in the direction of defending French-speaking group rights against the Flemish, which should unite Walloon French-speakers with the Francophone elite in Brussels. The Brussels establishment is exactly what the Walloon regionalists want to differentiate themselves from, as it is largely seen as the external centre of investment that reaped the benefits in Wallonia during the boom of industrial capitalism without preparing for a diversified economy that would meet the challenges of the post-industrial period. Such a divide does not exist on the Flemish side, where identification and mobilisation of both elite and citizens on the concept of regional interest are more straightforward. This is reflected in the fact that Flemish citizens identify themselves more with their region than the Walloon citizens do: almost 40 per cent of the Flemish identify themselves with their region, as opposed to 22.5 per cent of the Walloons who identify themselves with the region or with the French-speaking Community. Some 67 per cent in Wallonia opt in the first place for the Belgian state, while this is only 42 per cent in Flanders ([Maddens, 1994], confirming the trend of numerous surveys). Specifically concerning the elite, Van Dam [1995] concluded that a large majority of the Flemish elite in her survey identifies itself with the region, while this feeling of identification is less outspoken and present to a lesser extent with the Walloon elite.

Thus, the structural differences in the Flemish and Walloon societies, the fact that the movement for autonomy in Flanders originated inside the civil society and is at present still more supported by civil associations as opposed to the more political nature of the movement on the Francophone and Walloon side, and the divide inside the Francophone–Walloon elite which diminishes the potential for mobilisation could all account for the observed differences in civic culture.

This explanation is less deterministic than the one that attributes a determinant role to 'history' to explain civic culture.

Whatever the underlying cause of 'civicness' may be, a second question arises from Putnam's research. Does the higher 'civicness' of the Flemish explain why their government performs better? No doubt Putnam has a convincing point in showing the impact of the cultural context on institutional and policy performance. But there are problems in the deterministic way in which he presents this thesis and in the way he tests his hypothesis. On the basis of co-variance between two fundamentally different variables, civic culture and performance of political institutions, he concludes on a causal link between these two. Therefore, he concentrates in particular on the contending hypotheses of 'civic culture' versus 'economic development' to explain the observed patterns of governance. At no point does he recognise that policy outputs are in the end produced by political and social actors, who are of course influenced by the context in which they have to operate, but who are at the same time able to define and shape that context. The dismissal of the role of actors in the policy process leads to a fallacy in the conclusion. It is not because two variables occur at the same time in a society that they are also linked to each other in a causal way. The analysis has to be enriched here to show at a more micro-level how political and social actors try to influence policy outputs and institutional performance within the constraints of a political structure and a cultural context, and how in turn they try to influence the context and structures in which they operate. This analysis of the process inside the region is indispensable for any conclusion on the causal relation between 'civicness' and the performance.

Thus, pointing to the higher network of organisations in the areas of the environment and women's rights in the Flemish region would already be one step forward in the analysis, as it starts to look at sector-specific variables to explain the higher performance of the region on both of these policies. But the importance of these associations should not only be looked at as an expression of 'civicness' and a potential for collective action in specific sectors. Their role in the policy process itself should be explained. In the Belgian case, an in-depth analysis of the 'black box' process would reveal that these societal groups are more policy-oriented on the Flemish side. They make more 'noise' at the political level, where there is apparently also a higher receptiveness to the input given by some of these groups. The structure of the policy networks in both regions in terms of openness or being closed is crucial here: in general, Flemish policy networks tend to be more open than Walloon policy networks. Environmental groups were co-opted into the advisory team of the Flemish Minister for the Environment, for instance. There is a delicate interaction here between the civicness of the society in terms of having more environmentalist movements compared to the Walloon side, and the mobilisation of these groups by the political elites themselves. Thus, there is more to it than civicness alone. The political constellation has to be relatively open to the input that is provided by civil associations, and no doubt the political elite does have a decisive impact on the structure in which these groups gain access.

Further evidence on the more closed nature of the policy-making process at the Walloon side is given by Hooghe, who contends that the process concerning the EU Structural Funds is different in both regions. On the Flemish side, 'local private and public organisations are active in initiating programme applications, and in the negotiations with the EC Commission in the different stages of a programme execution'. This bottom-up activity is co-ordinated by the Flemish government. On the Walloon side, however, 'the administration of the Structural Funds is deconcentrated to a special-purpose bureau. Bottom-up input by other actors is limited' [1995b, p. 160]. Hooghe additionally notes that the governments of the Walloon region and the Francophone Community tend to be more irritated by the EU Commission negotiating directly with social groups and local authorities. Other evidence for the more closed nature of the policy process in Wallonia was given above. First, a more politicised public administration depends more on a political patron than an administration in which merit and career patterns play a greater role in recruitment and promotion. In the latter case, the potential for a more pluralist policy process is greater. Second, it was shown above that policy delivery on the Flemish side is more in the hands of a 'pillar organisation' than on the Walloon side, which could also be seen as an element that accounts for the greater dispersion of influence in the Flemish policy process. The same dispersion of influence can be seen in the denser network of functionally decentralised agencies at the disposal of the Flemish government.

CONCLUSION

Putnam's research on Italian regions argues that their civic culture determines their institutional performance, and that civic culture itself is a result of a long historical process during which social capital has been accumulated. Although the amount of cases in Belgium is too small to draw affirmative conclusions on causal relations, the observations of this chapter cast doubts on the universal pretensions that Putnam attaches to his findings in the Italian peninsula.

A detailed analysis inside Belgium reveals first of all that the Flemish region has at present consistently higher scores on civic community indicators and, second, that the Walloon political elite operates more in accordance with a hierarchical patron–client pattern than the Flemish elite does. These differences cannot be attributed to remote history, but should rather be linked to a blend of factors: there are structural differences between the two societies partly related to their recent economic fate, the developments and present nature of the movements for autonomy differ, as well as the capacity for elite-guided mobilisation. Thus, to explain the divergence in civic culture the interaction of economic factors, strategies and actions of the elite and the cultural context should be analysed, rather than focusing on one of these as the single predictor for variations. Similarly, Inglehart asserts that the impact of the cultural context is closely related to economic, social, technological and political factors [1990, p. 14], and Verba confirms that culture is but one aspect of politics [1965, p. 513].

Thus, the current position of both Belgian regions is not a stable equilibrium that is determined by their history, but it is contingent on the present conditions of economy, society and politics. As a result, and contrary to what Putnam seems to suggest for the Italian case, the present trend is reversible. A Walloon regionalist elite could stand up more unambiguously, and civil movements in Wallonia could gather pace around the theme of regenerating the economy. Certainly, some effect of this would be found in institutional performance, which in turn could mould the civic culture in a positive way. An interesting topic for further analysis would be why this is only happening to a more moderate extent than in Flanders at the moment. In this chapter, the division between the Francophone–Walloon elite was indicated as a power struggle that inhibits the generation of a higher dynamics on the Walloon side. Under the hypothesis that not much would change on the Walloon–Francophone side, differences in Flemish–Walloon 'civicness' would probably widen. Under these conditions, the dynamics that occurred at the early stage of regional autonomy and the first steps taken by political actors inside the Flemish and Walloon regional institutions should be taken into account to explain the 'persistently' higher civic culture.

Second, the thesis that institutional performance would be determined by civic culture underestimates the fact that policy outputs and the process of governing depends ultimately on actions that are taken by political and social actors who operate within the constraints and opportunities offered by the structures of policy networks. Putnam deserves great credit for his attempt to incorporate the cultural dimension into public policy analysis. However, there is no automatic institutional return on social capital. An analysis that remains at the macro-level can never trace the actor-related phenomena that function in between the civic culture and the production of concrete policy outputs and institutional performance.

These theoretical considerations have important consequences for the functioning of Belgian federalism. At present, the Flemish region finds itself in a stronger position due to its greater dynamics and its resulting financial basis. This is clearly echoed in the call for still more powers and for at least a partial split of the social security system. The party leader of the biggest Flemish party, the centrist Christian Democrats, stated at the end of 1995 that 'Flanders can no longer be the cow that is milked by Wallonia'. Our analysis shows that the stronger position of the Flemish region might well be temporary. Once upon a time, when Flanders was a helpless calf, mother Wallonia was a pioneer in exporting its industrial goods to the world market.

NOTES

1 I would like to thank Lieven De Winter (Université Catholique de Louvain) and Theo Jans (Vrije Universiteit Brussel) for their comments on an earlier version of this chapter.

2 Throughout this chapter 'Flemish' will be used to denote the language spoken in the Northern part of Belgium. To avoid confusion it should be stressed that Flemish is the same as Dutch.

3 This could confirm Inglehart's [1990] thesis, which contends that post-materialist values flourish better when people are economically secure.

4 Some commentators doubt the validity of using this indicator in the Italian case to measure clientelism, as was done by Putnam [Oberti, 1994].

5 Before the County of Flanders denoted a much smaller area than the present Flanders. It comprised the modern provinces of West and East Flanders, and part of what is now France.

13 Britain

The rise of the regional agenda to combat increased fragmentation?

John Mawson

INTRODUCTION

In recent months the issue of regionalism in England has been the subject of increasing interest and political debate, particularly since the Prime Minister launched his attacks on the Labour Party's proposal for the English regions at the beginning of 1995. The purpose of this chapter is not to consider this political debate but, rather, to explore some of the background forces underlying the re-emergence of the regional agenda in the English regions and the organisational and managerial issues which it raises. The chapter presents a brief chronological account of post-war regionalism focusing in particular on the past fifteen years. It then goes on to explore the government's response to the mounting pressures on its urban and regional programmes and regional administration leading to the 1992 Conservative Party manifesto [Conservative Party, 1992] commitments and the November 1993 announcements [Department of the Environment, 1993] to establish a new strengthened regional administrative machinery. The next section considers, in more detail, the economic and longer-term structural trends, which have impacted on the regions and the manner in which this is leading to new forms of urban and regional working. Then we discuss the political, administrative and managerial trends in recent years in the group of organisations that operate beyond the confines of Whitehall and Westminster, the majority of which deploy regional administrative structures of one form or another. Grey [1994] has referred to this group of organisations as sub-national government (SNG) namely, local government, the National Health Service (NHS), regional and local outputs of the centre (including public corporations) and a collection of quangos. The chapter concludes with an overview of current trends in urban and regional governance and the longer-term policy implications.

Interest in the decentralisation of decision-making through territorial management and the creation of elected regional structures has fluctuated over time [Garside and Hebbert, 1989]. The past fifteen years is regarded as a period in which the regional dimension of government became an unfashionable concept, nevertheless, it is during this period that the seeds of a revival of interest can be identified. A number of (not necessarily related) trends and events brought the issue to a head at the end of the 1980s which are explored in more detail in the following section.

DEVELOPMENTS UNDERLYING THE REVIVAL OF INTEREST IN THE REGIONAL ADMINISTRATIVE TIER

While an elected regional structure has been strongly opposed by the present government, nevertheless, it has remained in the political background as an issue which cannot be ignored by any British political party. The rise of Scottish and Welsh nationalism in the 1970s prompted the Wilson and Callaghan governments to engage in active consideration of devolution. Over the past fifteen years both major opposition political parties have retained a commitment to a move to some form of elected regional institutions for the English regions, either in the form of a federal structure as per the Liberal Democrats or regional assemblies in the case of the Labour Party.

The continuing significance of the Nationalist vote in Scotland and the use of the concept of the 'Europe of the Regions' to justify the case of an independent Scotland, have certainly maintained pressure on the Labour Party to support a Scottish Assembly, and in turn elected assemblies in the English regions [Coulson, 1990]. Some commentators take the view that the present government is seeking to enhance its presence at this level by administrative decentralisation in order to forestall pressures for an elected regional tier. Of perhaps more immediate relevance for the purposes of this chapter, developments within the European Community and now the European Union have been seen as a significant contributory factor behind the government's decision to establish strengthened regional offices. During the course of the 1980s the mechanisms for allocating ERDF and subsequently Structural Fund monies through the 'programme approach' resulted in tensions surrounding the degree of EC participation in what was regarded as essentially a domestic policy matter [Martins and Mawson, 1982]. The Commission's continuing insistence on the production of detailed regional programmes, based on a 'partnership' model with local actors, has reinforced the message of the importance of a strong co-ordinated regional administrative presence, not least in Treasury circles [Stewart, 1994a].

In the realm of business and trade, the launching of the Single European Market, the European Economic Area and further enlargement of the Union has heightened awareness of the opportunities and competitive threats of a trading bloc of over 380 million people. Business leaders have become increasingly concerned about the weakness of the present business support infrastructure in the English regions compared with that of some of our European competitors [Coopers and Lybrand, BITC, 1992]. Related concerns have also been expressed about the organisation of inward investment, the lobbying for, and management of European funds, and the future of regional strategic planning against the background of uncertainties arising from local government reorganisation. The management of these functions and the division of responsibilities between various agencies has resulted in further complications at the sub-regional level as Chambers of Commerce, Training and Enterprise Councils, and local authorities and their regional associations/forums have vied for leading roles [Bennett *et al.*, 1994]. To this complex institutional map at the regional and sub-regional levels must be added the role of statutory bodies such as the New Towns Commission, the Rural Development Commission, English Partnerships and the development agencies established by the former nationalised industries – British Coal Enterprises and British Steel Industries. Given the increasingly complex and multifaceted nature of the regeneration task and the need to co-ordinate the overlapping programmes and roles of a myriad of agencies, many of which are funded by central government, directly or indirectly, it has been recognised that organisational capacity at the regional level needs to be strengthened in areas such as partnership and network development [Lewis, 1992; House of Commons, Trade and Industry Committee, 1995].

Such arguments surrounding the question of co-ordination could equally be applied in other realms. Water, waste, electricity, gas, telecommunications, and radio, television and cable have all experienced a decade of liberalisation and privatisation leading to a patchwork of private utility companies, often with a strong regional organisational framework [Marvin and Cornford, 1993]. Given the significance of these services for economic development, physical planning and social policy some critics have argued for a regional as well as a national regulatory framework perhaps along the lines of the US State Utility Commissions. Elsewhere in the public service the move to establish 'arm's length' Next Step agencies namely, the Benefits

Agency, the Highways Agency, Hospital Trusts raises similar questions about the strategic dimensions of public service delivery in cities and regions, against the background of an increasingly fragmented public domain.

This problem has perhaps been most striking in the field of urban regeneration and it is, perhaps, not surprising that it is from this direction that some of the greatest pressure has come for change. By the end of the 1980s, it was becoming evident that the 'patchwork quilt' of government programmes, alongside a panoply of agencies engaged in economic and urban regeneration, often with no formal relationship with either government offices or local authorities, was causing confusion and leading to duplication and wasted effort [Audit Commission, 1989a]. Criticisms along these lines by the Audit Commission and the National Audit Office were further strengthened by the personal experience of business leaders asked to head various government initiatives and by Ministers who were given responsibility for the co-ordination of government policies in specific cities [House of Commons, Committee of Public Accounts, 1990; National Audit Office, 1990].

It was against the background of these pressures that the 1992 Conservative Party manifesto made a commitment to the introduction of Integrated Regional Offices (IROs) in the English regions and the creation of a Single Regeneration Budget (SRB) alongside other mechanisms to improve co-ordination such as One Stop Shops/Business Links and the Urban Regeneration Agency subsequently retitled English Partnerships [Conservative Party, 1992]. Such proposed changes, however, must also be considered alongside reforms in the internal management of the civil service. These have included the launch of the Efficiency Unit and the Financial Management initiative in the early 1980s followed by the Citizens Charter (1987), the Next Steps initiative (1988), market testing (1991) and finally the establishment of the Office of Public Service and Science (OPSS) headed by a cabinet minister after the last election [Her Majesty's Government, 1994].

The underlying philosophy behind such developments is the delegated provision of public services in which control and responsibility are pushed down and out of the central government machinery, wherever possible through the use of market or quasi-market mechanisms. In policy terms this fragmentation of the public domain inevitably leads to tensions. Freedom to manage results in demands that the centre yields power. However, the increasingly federated character of the civil service, and the absence of an integrating and coherent strategy for public service provision at central government level, also raise the question of what compensating co-ordination mechanisms are required. It is in this context that the issue of the territorial dimension of public policy becomes particularly important.

The Secretary of State for the Environment, for example, when launching the IROs in November 1993, commented that they would 'provide their customers with a more comprehensive and accessible service . . . meet the widespread demand for a single point of contact . . . bring services closer to the people they serve, simplify the government machine and improve value for money' [Gummer, 1993]. However, in this regard the centralised and compartmentalised character of decision-making in the civil service has historically presented considerable difficulties for the co-ordination of central government policies at the regional level [Morran, 1993]. With no single civil servant clearly responsible for government policies, not all government departments present in the regions and only limited interdepartmental co-ordination machinery through the Planning Boards, it is not surprising that problems should surface in various policy areas such as European funding and urban regeneration [Stewart, 1994b].

The 6th Report of the Treasury and Civil Service Committee 1988–89 highlighted some of the difficulties when it pointed out that there was no disaggregation on a consistent basis of public expenditure information for the English regions nor were there adequate attempts to examine or plan the inter-relationships between programmes and their impacts. This situation was contrasted with the position in Scotland, Wales and Northern Ireland which had the benefit of co-ordinated political management, devolved territorial departments, block budgets and expenditure switching discretion between programmes within these blocks. The committee noted that this discretion was valued by the Secretaries of State concerned since 'it assists policy co-ordination and financial management . . . moreover it permits substantive policy differences and adjustment of UK policy measures in the light of different traditions and circumstances' [Treasury and Civil Service Committee, 1989].

THE GOVERNMENT OFFICES FOR THE REGIONS

In April 1994 the government established a network of ten new integrated regional offices (subsequently referred to as Government Offices for the Regions (GORs) which were introduced alongside the announcement of a major reform of the government's regeneration programmes [Mawson *et al.*, 1994]. These changes have been seen by a number of commentators as a potentially very significant development in the evolution of public policy in this field [Hogwood, 1994]. For the first time civil servants in the Training and Enterprise Division (TEED) of the Department of Employment (DE) and the Departments of the Environment (DOE), Transport (DT) and Industry (DTI) were made accountable to one Senior Regional Director (SRD). Subsequently in 1995 the Department of Education was merged with the Department of Employment (DFEE) adding a further significant dimension to the work of the Government Offices [DOE, 1993]. Reporting to the four Secretaries of State, each SRD is responsible for all staff and expenditure routed through the offices and for ensuring that the necessary co-ordination and links are established between their main programmes and also other public monies. In addition, the GORs are to ensure close links with those Departments without a regional presence. To facilitate part of the work of the GORs, a Single Regeneration Budget (SRB) was established drawing together twenty separate programmes from five departments: DOE, DTI, DE, HO, DES, totalling some £1.4 billion. Its purpose is to provide flexible support for regeneration and economic development and is available throughout each region. A proportion of the SRB is allocated on the basis of annual local bids (in the short term the sum available is relatively small).

Drawing on the City Challenge experience, the bids are led by local authorities and/or Training and Enterprise Councils (TECs) or other appropriate bodies such as those from the private or voluntary sectors. The SRB is the responsibility of the Secretary of State of the Environment and in making decisions about funding he is to be guided by a Ministerial Committee for Regeneration (EDR). It considers regeneration policies and their co-ordination, sets the guidelines for the single budget and selects the bids. To facilitate the process, a network of seventeen sponsor ministers covering thirteen areas advise EDR ministerial colleagues on regeneration issues related to their own particular city or area.

A final innovation announced in November 1993 was a pilot programme, City Pride, in which local authorities in three cities (London, Birmingham and Manchester) were invited to prepare, in partnership with other public and private sector bodies, a City Prospectus setting out a vision for their city over a 10-year period and the actions each participant would take to achieve that outcome [DOE, 1993]. This document is intended to provide a framework for public and private sector investment.

In order to implement the GOR policy initiative centrally, a Deputy Secretaries' Management Board was established responsible to the four

Permanent Secretaries [Mawson and Spencer, 1996]. It is serviced by an inter-departmental group headed by an Under-Secretary in the DOE which deals with administrative and overall policy direction and meets the Senior Regional Directors on a regular basis. A set of overall objectives has been established for the GORs and within this framework each SRD has been given a degree of local autonomy to develop structures and processes appropriate to the local situation. The overall objectives may be summarised as:

1 to achieve operational requirements of each department;
2 to promote a coherent approach to competitiveness, sustainable economic development and regeneration, using public and private resources;
3 to develop the skills and methods of working of staff to achieve these objectives;
4 to develop local partnerships;
5 to provide a single point of access and deliver high-quality services on Citizens Charter principles [ibid.].

While the GORs all have a broadly similar range of functions, management structures and relationships with Whitehall there are, nevertheless, some important differences worthy of note. Undoubtedly the most significant relates to the Government Office for London (GOL) which services a Cabinet Sub-Committee and consequently has direct access to ministers from all the key government departments which impact on the Capital. Both GOL and the Government Office for Merseyside (GOM), as urban-focused regions, have large-scale regeneration programmes including responsibility for the two highest spending Urban Development Corporations [Hogwood, 1994]. GOM also oversees the Objective 1 European Programme for Merseyside. In contrast, the South East and Eastern regions have comparatively few economic development or regeneration programmes of any significance nor do they have access to sponsor ministers. Reflecting the size of the regions, they have inherited a number of physically separate office buildings in different locations established by the former departmental government offices. The South-West region is the only GOR which has a full sub-office, for Devon and Cornwall.

It is important to note that the GORs do not encompass a number of government departments which may have significant policy and operational relationships with the four parent departments at the regional level, e.g., the Department of National Heritage, the Ministry of Agriculture, the Home Office, and the Department of Education (although in the latter two cases special co-ordination arrangements were set in place and more recently the Departments of Employment and Education have merged). It is evident that a focus of the work of the GORs, arising from the programmes of their parent departments, is that of environment, infrastructure, regeneration and economic development. Another interesting feature of the new GORs structure is that there is no direct line management relationship between the SRDs and the Next Step agencies of the four parent departments or other departments even where such agencies have a significant regional presence and impact in policy terms, e.g., the Highways Agency, the Employment Service, the Benefits Agency. Likewise, the GORs have no line management relationship with the various non-departmental public bodies such as the Rural Development Commission, the Housing Corporation, and the National Rivers Authority which, moreover, have their own regional structures and boundaries. English Partnerships which was established during the same time frame as the GORs also has a different regional framework, despite having an operational relationship with the GORs in the field of economic development and regeneration.

HOW REGIONS REACT TO STRUCTURAL TRENDS

Any explanation for the resurrection of the regional agenda, and the associated administrative issues and problems which it raises, requires not merely an empirical investigation of the developments themselves but also an understanding of the more deep-seated economic, social, political and organisational forces at work, but they are not addressed as such in this chapter. It is also necessary within this analysis to take account of the important historical differences between Scotland, Wales, Northern Ireland and the English regions as well as the importance of Britain's position within a wider Europe.

New models of local and regional development are beginning to emerge based on strengthening local organisational capacity and developing a shared agenda between all the key actors. In this approach it is recognised that all areas are now faced with rapid and complex economic and technological change in an increasingly interdependent international economy. How change affects cities and regions is dependent on the interaction between these broader forces and the unique combination of circumstances in each locality in particular – geography; the structure of the local economy; the character of the labour market; cultural and educational facilities; the size, structure, and ownership pattern of local industry, and the strength and competence of its local institutions, sometimes termed organisational capacity. Organisational capacity may be defined as the ability of an area as a whole, its key institutions, public, private, voluntary, and its business, professional, trades unions and political leaders and citizens to work together in coping with rapid change in the modern European economy. There is ample research evidence to show that a favourable combination of local circumstances may not be sufficient to secure economic growth [Parkinson *et al.*, 1992; Cheshire, 1990].

In this context Parkinson argues that effective management of local resource and political leadership has been the key to success – through the building up of local organisational capacity – based on collaboration and partnership between key local decision-makers and institutions. In this respect the United Kingdom and particularly the English regions are seen as being at a disadvantage because of the centralising tendencies of UK central government, the historically unco-ordinated nature of regional structures and the comparatively weakly developed business support networks. In contrast, regions elsewhere in Europe such as Catalonia, Nord Pas-de-Calais and North Rhine-Westphalia have long realised that they need to co-ordinate, direct and market their own resources. These regions have been able to develop successful development plans through their ability to achieve a 'critical mass' – the necessary scale of economic activity governed by new forms of pro-active institutional and political management. Significantly, some researchers have emphasised not merely administrative but also political devolution as put forward in the case of the German *Länder* such as Baden-Württemburg [Cooke and Morgan, 1990a, b].

In contrast, the elements of what might be termed a technocratic rather than the democratic devolved model above are being widely diffused in Britain by researchers, consultants, business organisations, etc. [Le Galès and Mawson, 1995]. The approach is evident in the 1991 Sunningdale agreement between TECs, Chambers and enterprise agencies and in the recommendations of the Audit Commission to local authorities regarding the preparation of local regeneration strategies [Audit Commission, 1989a]. The approach is also clearly present in the advice provided by the CBI and Business in the Community to Business Leadership Teams as to the process they should follow in their attempts to regenerate cities and regions [Business in the Community, 1990]. The City Challenge initiative, the Single Regeneration bid and City Pride strategies of the Department of the Environment are based on this framework as are those of the DTI's new Business Link programme. Finally, the model is also utilised by the TEC National Training Taskforce report on the role of TECs in network and partnership development.

Drawing on various papers and reports, we can summarise this orthodoxy as follows – there is no simple formula which areas should follow in building up their organisational capacity, since much is dependent on the presence, or absence, of organisations, the strengths and competencies of local institutions and decision-makers.

This consensus partnership model is increasingly being deployed to resolve the fragmented institutional structures of regions in Britain. Within it are very positive features as evident from the success of some regions elsewhere in Europe. Equally, however, there are weaknesses and hidden dangers in areas such as the degree of political accountability, the dominance of a private sector ethos which ignores a community perspective, taking into account wider cost and benefits, and the exclusion of disadvantaged groups and areas.

POLITICAL, ADMINISTRATIVE AND MANAGERIAL TRENDS AND THEIR IMPACT ON REGIONS

To understand the issues surrounding the contemporary regional agenda also requires an appreciation of the British constitutional tradition which is unusual for a large modern state in not having a written constitution [Sharpe, 1993b]. Parliamentary sovereignty means that a majority in the legislature is the supreme constitutional arbiter. In theory, therefore, there is no legal impediment to Parliament abolishing local authorities, the only elected tier below Whitehall or reducing the freedom of action of authorities as, indeed, has been the case in the past fifteen years. The United Kingdom is also unusual for a large Western unitary state in that it has no comprehensive and uniform level of decentralised territorial administration between local and central government. It could be argued that because of this high degree of centralisation, government is fundamentally concerned with a national public and policy agenda rather than with regional and local publics and policies, and public accountability tends to focus on national rather than local political institutions.

This in turn means that policy tends to be devised overwhelmingly in nationwide terms rather than in relation to the effectiveness of policies in respect of regional and local diversity of problems and opportunities. Stewart highlights the emphasis in Whitehall upon functional division at the expense of territorial integration and co-ordination which he traces back to the Haldane Report (1918) [Stewart, 1994a]. The exception to this situation arises in the case of the three Offices of State for Scotland, Wales, and Northern Ireland which have emerged over the past 100 years for various pragmatic political reasons associated with their historic national identities and political pressures for decentralisation. Each office is under the control of a Secretary of State who sits in the Cabinet.

While power has been highly centralised in Britain, central government historically has shown little interest in direct service delivery, rather, it has deployed various institutions to undertake the task. A number of writers [Rhodes, 1988] have referred to the group of organisations that operate beyond the confines of Whitehall and Westminster as sub-national government (SNG). Grey groups them into four families of organisation: local government; the NHS; regional and local outposts of the centre (including public corporations); and a collection of quangos [Grey, 1994]. All four categories deploy regional frameworks in the case of some, or all of the organisations concerned, namely, regional forums/association of local authorities, Regional Health Authorities, government regional offices, Regional Tourist Boards.

Up to the 1970s this group of institutions was given a reasonable degree of freedom in terms of operational activities while the centre retained ultimate control over finance and policy. There were periods of significant reorganisation (e.g., local government reorganisation) but fundamentally the overall framework remained in place. We can broadly summarise the first three decades of the post-war period as one in which a series of government agencies and organisations delivered services directly to the public, with the key role in local community government being played by the local authority. Within this framework the local authority played a key role. It was characterised by: the undertaking of a wide range of services; being under the control of locally elected representatives; having, therefore, the political legitimacy to speak on behalf of the area and its electorate; having rights to determine local tax and an ability to determine priorities and levels of expenditure. Unlike the other agencies involved the local authority was, in the words of Clarke and Stewart thus constituted for local 'choice' and local 'voice' [Clarke and Stewart, 1991]. However, there have been significant changes in recent years particularly following the election of a Conservative government and as a consequence a new pattern of local and regional governance has begun to emerge. These changes have been not just in the role and nature of local government but in the disposition of the other players in the SNG system.

The so-called 'dual polity' between central government and SNG began to break down during the 1970s and 1980s under the increasing pressures on public finance, political and ideological shifts, and a new public service management agenda [Bulpitt, 1983]. As Grey points out, the prevailing SNG was out of tune with a radical Conservative agenda given its focus primarily on the public sector, emphasising collective provision of goods and services, and operating in a non-market fashion. Just as significant was that, at a time of financial stringency, a major proportion of public expenditure was handled by the sector. As the delivery of SNG was not the direct responsibility of the centre, this enabled the government to engage in radical new approaches in organisation structure and management and yet still be in the position to deny responsibility for the consequences of policy change when they went adrift.

During the course of the 1980s central government encouraged organisations within SNG to move in a broadly similar direction, although the speed and precise direction reflected the particular characteristics of the sector concerned. It was a period of trial and error leading to a variety of outcomes. Nevertheless, Stewart and Stoker [1992] summarise the major themes as: fragmentation, competition, user charges, choice, 'business-like' management and a separation of accountability and responsibility from service provision. Much of this agenda has impacted at the regional and sub-regional levels and the following section illustrates some of the dimensions of this development.

Executive Agencies, the NHS and TECs

The general trend of government policy is epitomised in the creation of executive agencies to discharge an increasing proportion of central government business within an overall policy framework set by Whitehall but outside the direct control of central departments [Greer, 1994]. The Chief Executives of Next Steps agencies through service agreements were given the freedom to develop their management and some with nationwide operations have developed a regional tier, namely, the Benefits Agency, and the Employment Service. Unfortunately where there are clear policy relationships across agency boundaries this has not always been manifested in terms of common geographical boundaries and management structures and a willingness between the agencies to engage in a policy dialogue and co-ordination.

Other important areas of restructuring of government activity affecting the regional agenda which have arisen from decentralisation but without the deployment of the 'Next Steps' model, include training and health. In 1988 the government launched a radical reform of the training system which ultimately devolved the administration of national training schemes to eighty-two Training and Enterprise Councils (TECs) in England and Wales and twenty-two Local Enterprise Companies (LECs) in Scotland. They are companies limited by guarantee with directors, at least two-thirds of whom are local businessmen. Each TEC has an operating contract with the Department of Employment, or equivalent in Scotland and Wales, to deliver primarily national YTS and adult training schemes (in the case of England) together with a small proportion of their income set aside for broader economic development initiatives.

The TECs were initially regarded with some suspicion by both local authorities and Chambers of Commerce as duplicating their own roles in education, training and economic development [Emmerich and Peck, 1992]. This suspicion was quickly confirmed as surveys of TEC chairpersons showed that their view of the role was much broader in terms of engaging in economic development and providing a leadership role in this respect at the local level. However, there was criticism of their inexperienced staff and a lack of a coherent framework for their work either at regional or national levels. The Chambers of Commerce, faced with this threat, have launched a restructuring of their own network nationwide, with the aim of reducing their number from over 200 to 40, providing high-quality business advice, and support services [Bennett and McCoshan, 1993].

This competitive environment led to a meeting at Sunningdale in 1991 in which Chambers, TECs and Enterprise Agencies agreed to develop collaborative and co-ordinated strategies at the local level in partnership with local authorities. Since that date the government has launched the Business Link initiative which provides financial assistance to encourage the establishment of co-ordinated business support services between all the various local actors on a 'One Stop Shop' basis. A further development is the recent announcement of two pilot mergers between Chambers and TECs. In the longer term this may well be the direction which reorganisation takes. However, the situation remains highly fluid with continuing mutual suspicion in many areas between the main players against a background of increasing financial constraint which is forcing them to, nevertheless, consider collaboration. A further element in this dynamic situation is the threat that local government reorganisation will break up existing organisational capacity on economic development and European work. In anticipation of this development, partnerships often formally constituted between local authorities, TECs, Chambers and other bodies are increasingly being established, sometimes to deal with business service delivery issues and/or more strategic questions such as inward investment, lobbying and European funding at a regional/sub-regional level.

There is evidence that TECs are now establishing collaborative forums at the regional level to develop common strategies and address the above strategic issues. They mirror the emergence/reconstitution of a network of regional local authority forums/associations in the English regions which are now beginning to act on a collective basis to address issues of common concern. Initially established in the 1960s to address regional planning issues, they have added to their agenda economic development and European questions. The overall picture is thus one of continuing change against a background of financial constraint and competition for roles which is taking place in the territorial policy vacuum between central and local government. The TECs themselves are increasingly looking to a regional presence and some would like to see an intermediate body in England and Wales rather than negotiate directly with the Department of Employment. A representative body comprising TEC chairpersons has been established with representatives from the regions to represent the views of these agencies to central government.

In Scotland the picture is slightly clearer with the merger of the Scottish Development Agency and the Highlands and Islands Development Board to form Scottish Enterprise, and Highlands and Islands Enterprise, each with a network of local enterprise companies (LECS). They have a broader economic development remit than their English counterparts (drawing on previous SDA functions) and also enter into a contract with their parent agency. In Wales, the Welsh office is the sponsoring department but their activities have not been merged with those of the WDA.

Turning to the health service, this has also gone through a radical restructuring in recent years in which the regional dimension has figured to a great extent. The introduction of the purchaser–provider split with the development of 'self-governing trusts' having to enter into contracts with District Health Authorities has introduced a managed market into the NHS [Ham, 1992]. Initially there was speculation that a regional tier providing a strategic role would no longer be required. However, in 1993 the Secretary of State announced the abolition of the Regional Health Authorities which had previously administered the NHS through a Board of nominated representatives. They were replaced by eight regional offices headed by a director responsible to the Chief Executive of the NHS executive which has remained within the NHS. The NHS board has been restructured to include non-executive representatives from each of the eight regions. Regional Health Authorities are assuming a greater role in market management, while the day-to-day management of health purchasing and provision is the job of purchasers and providers acting under national guidance. It is not yet fully clear how the new regional offices will operate but they may move to encourage systems of accreditation and performance review of both sides of the market, encouraging effective public participation in decision-making, and acting in situations where market arbitration is needed.

Accountability and quangos

One of the effects of the fragmentation of the public domain has been to increase the number of cases where appointee members, rather than elected representatives, control local and regional affairs [Davis and Stewart, 1993]. This is most obviously the case in the creation of special purpose agencies. In other cases – joint boards, arm's length companies and governing bodies – councillors have a role, but at one stage removed, i.e. appointed from the councils. This process has been referred to by John Stewart, Professor of Local Government at Birmingham University, as the creation of a 'new magistracy'. In many cases there has been a tendency to appoint people with a business or commercial background, as has been shown in a study of the West Midlands. However, irrespective of their background, such appointees cannot be regarded as representatives of the public in the same way as someone who is elected [Davies and Stewart, 1993].

In the case of the North East region, Robinson and Shaw [1994] in a study for UNISON, have shown how a comparatively small number of individuals drawn from specific political, institutional and family backgrounds have been able to control the major regional development institutions and regional policy agenda. A similar picture has emerged in Wales. In the case of the WDA, the lack of accountability, mismanagement of funds and allocation of resources to rural areas beyond the agency's geographical remit has resulted in censure from the National Audit Office and the Public Accounts Committee. A similar story can be told in respect of other SNG institutions such as the Regional Health Authorities.

Local government

Clarke and Stewart [1994] have pointed out that as fragmentation has increased in the SNG with the creation of a series of new special purpose agencies, this has often gone alongside the removal of, or competition and overlap with, responsibilities from one or other parts of local government. This trend is exemplified in the establishment of the Manpower Services Commission and its successor bodies through to the creation of the TECs (and LECs in Scotland), Task Forces, Urban Development Corporations, Housing Action Trusts, Health Service Trusts, Grant Maintained Schools and autonomous Higher and Further Education institutions. Subsequently, in a number of these cases pressure has emerged for some form of regional co-ordination. For example, following the granting of university status to the former polytechnics, the PCFC and University Funding Councils were wound up and separate Funding Councils were established for Scotland, Wales and England. In the case of further education, nine Regional Councils have been established. In relation to 'opted out' schools, the 1992 Education Act provides for Funding Agencies for Schools in England and Wales. It is widely held that given the likely scale of the work a regional structure will be necessary.

The structural changes to local government itself, arising from the abolition of the metropolitan countries and the GLC have resulted in the creation of a series of inter-authority joint committees and Boards to handle strategic conurbation-wide sub-regional and regional issues. In policy fields such as economic development, transportation and planning, the outcome of these new organisational mechanisms has been less than convincing as has been revealed in the work of Leach *et al.* [1992] on the metropolitan areas, and Begg and Whyatt [1994] and others in the case of London. There has been no ostensible government for the Capital since the abolition of the GLC at which point a variety of powers and functions were vested in thirty-three boroughs. This was followed in the early 1990s by a number of changes of power and transfer of functions to a network of agencies and organisations, some of which cross borough boundaries, some of which operate on a pan-London basis. Various private and public sector partnerships have also been created. The result is a complex matrix of activity, some of which Begg and Whyatt conclude operates well, some of which fails to carry out intended functions or objectives, and a further group still which are frustrated in their activities because of the absence of any national or regional framework within which to operate. The latter point applies particularly to transport but also to other strategic issues. This gives rise to particular difficulties in the sense that the major resourcing of programmes and major strategic decisions are often based in, or arise from, the structures which have been formed rather than the needs and requirements of the Capital and those who reside within it. Faced with these difficulties the government has established a Cabinet Subcommittee with a Minister – the Secretary of State for the Environment – given a lead responsibility. Acting through the Government Office for London there has been an increasing effort to foster co-ordination and collaboration between the myriad of agencies through the establishment of networks and partnerships and more formally through the framework established to produce the London Pride document. The process of preparing the document has succeeded to some degree in bringing public and private sectors together in a way which has not previously been possible in London.

The current Local Government Review undertaken by the Audit Commission which is considering the two-tier system outside the metropolitan areas also highlights the increasing problems of securing co-ordination of policies in an increasingly fragmented public domain [Leach, 1994]. The Commission has paid relatively little attention to the issue of economic development and European issues despite the fact that representatives of industry and commerce and the voluntary sector, in most of the areas studied, have argued for wider 'authorities' with a combination of strategic planning and economic development powers. The CBI in its evidence to the Commission argued that land use planning, infrastructure planning and other strategic services delivered by local government, need to be carried out over a relatively large geographic area. Indeed, there needs to be the basis of sufficient economies of scale to develop staff expertise, mobilise adequate resources, and develop organisational capacity as evidenced in a study of the role of Durham County Council in its planning, economic development and European roles [Mawson, 1993].

The Commission has taken the view that under a unitary system this issue can be adequately accommodated by voluntary joint machinery. However, given that these functions entail political choices which may benefit one part of a wider area rather than others, joint arrangements involving executive powers are probably more often than not necessary. Leach argues that if this is the case, then with three formal joint bodies – structure planning, police, and fire – the unitary principle looks fragile [Leach, 1994]. When the arguments about the need for executive joint arrangements is extended to cover waste disposal, highways, transportation and economic development, then the arguments for a unitary structure look very threadbare. The Commission itself has acknowledged the weaknesses of joint arrangements in some of the metropolitan areas. If, as seems inevitable, there will be a growth of such bodies post-reorganisation, it will be interesting to see whether the GORs feel the need to strengthen or adapt their regional role.

CONCLUSIONS

In conclusion, it is evident from the trends set out in previous sections that the fragmentation of public services and their marketisation has, amongst other things, led to a process of decentralisation which has had a noticeable impact on regional and sub-regional levels. Broader economic, political and structural forces emphasising powerful trends of globalisation, on the one hand, and decentralisation to the locality, on the other, have increasingly emphasised the role of regional and local institutions, within a wider international framework. In this context the existing pattern of national–regional and central–local relations has become increasingly outmoded. Against this overall background the United Kingdom has embarked upon a radical reform of its public sector involving decentralisation through marketisation, whilst at the same time strengthening the grip of the central state over local democratic institutions.

There are some strengths within this emerging system of urban and regional governance. As Clarke and Stewart point out, creation of units limited to specific purposes allows for a concentration of effort. There are strengths in institutional innovation as assumptions that have dominated the working of the traditional system have been challenged, opening up new possibilities, most notably the challenge to the assumption of self-sufficiency – that any part of government given a task has to carry out that task directly. The greatest challenge has perhaps come from the development of government by contract and the acceptance of a plurality of provision. Government, by contrast, provides a basis on which the performance of different agencies can be judged managerially and made accountable, if not always politically [Clarke and Stewart, 1994].

The strengths of this approach are greatest in the delivery of narrow specific services. The weaknesses are most evident when the overall system is judged. Clarke and Stewart question whether the needs to be met by community government can all be reduced to such a series of precise and separately defined functions and activities or whether, in the definitions and the separation, key needs are lost and emerging problems ignored. In the development of public policy it needs to be recognised that the changing needs of society demand a flexible and continually changing pattern of response. Special purpose agencies with clearly determined tasks assume a certainty which may often be inappropriate in a rapidly changing urban and rural environment. As exemplified by the experience of TECs, there is a danger of imposing national standards which secure a uniformity of practice areas across the country but which impose a strait-jacket making it difficult to adjust to local needs and circumstances. This tension between national uniformity and local choice and diversity is one which is not easily resolved irrespective of the form of government.

It is clear that the centre is searching for new ways to resolve these tensions and issues of inter-dependency of public policy, through improved territorial co-ordination as, for example, in the establishment of GORs. Another response is the recent commitment of government to facilitate networks and partnership mechanisms in various areas of public policy at the regional and sub-regional levels. Yet within these initiatives there remain inherent tensions and contradictions. For example, how far will the government be willing to allow decentralisation of decision-making and budgets from Whitehall to the new GORs, in comparison with the degree of policy discretion available to the Secretaries of State in Scotland and Wales? How sustainable are the various partnership structures currently being propagated at regional and sub-regional levels in the longer term, given that they comprise partners often with quite different perspectives and sets of interest? There are dilemmas about public accountability in the new agencies and quangos which have been established. In the case of the proliferation of privatised utilities with a variety of overlapping regional structures, how will the planning of new development schemes be managed, i.e. overspill estates, complex large-scale urban regenerations, and facilities provided for major inward investments? What are the implications of the telecommunications and cabling for regional development or the provision of social services in remote rural areas?

It is evident that the pressures of co-ordination face all the various actors in sub-national government not just central government. Faced with financial constraints, local authorities and other agencies are being drawn together to share resources and expertise at regional level, i.e. collaborations between TECs, Chambers and local authorities. They are also seeking to operate across regions (i.e. local authority associations) and even in some cases across national boundaries through European networks to facilitate lobbying, accessing finance, exchange of experience, technology transfer and trade.

These issues seem likely to be of increasing concern given the persistence of the trends described in the regional sphere in Britain and more generally in the EU. Certainly, given some political scenarios based on the present commitments of the Liberal Democrats and Labour Parties [Coulson, 1990] for elected regional structures, and the nationalist parties' perspectives on the future of an independent Scotland and Wales in a 'Europe of the Regions', the regional agenda will take on even greater significance than at present.

14 Conclusion – government and governance of regions*

Structural weaknesses and new mobilisations

Patrick Le Galès

Once upon a time there were regions in Europe. Carried by the thrusts of democratisation, local economic development, state reorganisation and regionalist pressures, they seemed to have everything going for them. They were supposed to be democratic, legitimate, efficient, functional, they highlighted different identities and they seemed to be moving with the tide of history, that is towards European integration. Reforms implemented in several European countries during the 1970s and 1980s enabled us to have a glimpse of the possibility of a Europe of Regions or at least of a Europe within which regions, that is elected regional governments, were to play a major political role (see M. Keating's chapter in this book).

With a view to critically examining this view, we decided at the beginning of this book to look at regions, first in the classical and institutional sense of the term, before going on to a reflection in terms of governance and political capacity. In standardised European terms, we began with regions which are classified in the NUTS 2 category (Italian, French and German regions, Dutch and Belgian provinces and Spanish Autonomous Communities), that is to say, on a level higher than that of the co-ordination of municipalities. As mentioned in the Introduction, we wished to avoid the flaw of studies on the regions which deadlock on conflicts and co-operation between different 'Meso' levels [Sharpe, 1993b] including the groupings in the different NUTS categories (see table 14.1)

As V. Wright observes somewhat regretfully in his chapter, this dynamic is cumulative in the European political space. It is self-sustaining and propagates itself. The genie appears to be out of the bottle, but, paradoxically, the regions are not necessarily the beneficiaries. The idea of a more homogeneous model of sub-national territorial

* Translation Uttam Bharthare and Claire O'Neal

Table 14.1 NUTS 1, 2 and 3 categories

	NUTS 1	*NUTS 2*	*NUTS 3*
Belgium	Regions	Provinces	*Arrondissements*/ districts
Fed. Rep. Germany	*Länder*	*Regierungsbezirke*	*Kreise*
Spain	NUTS 2 groupings	Autonomous Communities	Provinces
France	ZEAT (*Zones étendus d'aménagement du territoire*)	Regions	*Départements*
Ireland			Planning regions
Italy	NUTS 2 groupings	Regions	Provinces
Netherlands	*Landsdelen*	Provinces	COROP-*regios*
Portugal	NUTS 2 groupings	NUTS 3 groupings	Groupings of *concethos*
U.K. regions	Standard regions	NUTS 3 groupings	Counties, Scottish

Source: Commission of the European Communities, 1987

organisation of states does not correspond to empirical reality. Whereas fifteen years ago, there was every reason to believe that regions were going to become an essential level of government, this evolution did not take place. Why do regions (elected regional government) not constitute a more homogeneous level of government in Europe?

Economic globalisation processes and the reorganisation of capitalism are two variables which are systematically put forward to explain the development of regions in Europe. Although this question has not been dealt with systematically in this book (this is because the link between regions and economic development has been the subject of numerous studies and publications),[1] its impact on regions and the political reorganisation of sub-national territories is decisive. The 'Europe of the Regions' thesis drew support particularly from the rediscovery of regional economies and the successes of Silicon Valley, on the one hand, and Italian industrial districts and certain German *Länder*, on the other. It launched a fully fledged debate among regional economy specialists. An ample account of this debate is given in the work of

Benko and Lipietz [1992]. Several points from these different works have been emphasised and used more or less directly in this chapter:

- Globalisation processes do not make the question of territories uninteresting. While the proliferation of networks can destructure certain sub-national territories, it increases the importance of others for economic development [Harvey, 1989; Veltz, 1996].
- Regions of economic development are practically never regions in the institutional sense. Regions are primarily either territories which regroup several communes, or urban regions because European cities are the main beneficiaries of capital concentration and they serve as nodes for technical networks [Harding *et al.*, 1993; Veltz, 1996]. In centralised European countries, economic growth in national capitals is disconnected from growth in regional capitals and regions either stagnate or decline. Consequently, most (but not all) of the arguments in favour of regional economic development and the pertinence of regions as places for politics and interest organisation concern, in fact, either cities or diverse more or less institutionalised intra-national territories.
- The same is true for public policy. Economic development policies (institutions) (see Brusco, 1994, for example; Cooke *et al.*, 1995, and chapter by Dunford) are often implemented at sub-regional level. In Germany, training and technological innovation/transfer policies are generally considered to be exceptions. In the absence of highly structured economic interests at regional level (cf. supra), it is difficult for regional policies not to fall into clientelism or symbolism.
- Due to the reorganisation/withdrawal of nation–states, sub-national territories, and notably regions (but especially cities), are pulled into the competition game in order to attract social groups and public and private investments [Cheshire and Gordon, 1995].
- Even though this point is debatable, the idea that European integration would bring about a homogenisation of regional wealth levels seems inexact [Leonardi, 1993a]. If there was a relative decrease in the wealth gap during the post-war period, it has nothing to do, even indirectly, with European integration. All European countries (barring exception), witnessed a decrease in spatial and social inequalities during this period, which refers us back to economic growth and redistribution carried out in the framework of the welfare state. The logic was national [Oddo and Poinat, 1989]. By contrast, most studies of the late 1980s report either a stagnation or a reinforcement of inequalities which are once again spatial and social (see Cheshire, 1990, and Dunford's chapter, and Fagerberg

> and Verspagen, 1996). Several authors anticipated an increase in these inequalities [Beggs and Mayes, 1993]. Without denying the importance of the Structural Funds policy (especially its financial impact), it is very premature to consider it the main tool for reducing economic inequalities [Nanetti, 1996]. Territorial development issues are complicated and real effects in terms of economic development are at least uncertain, not to mention inequalities among regions. Economic and monetary integration was realised according to a predominantly liberal logic which favours the free movement of capital. The emphasis on economic competition and the competitiveness of national, regional or local economies risks significantly increasing sub-regional and inter-regional, social and spatial inequalities and states may not wish to or be able to react. New forms of spatial and social marginalities are developing in Europe [Mingione, 1995]. Undoubtedly this contradiction between the effects of the large European market and the desirable vision of economic homogenisation within European territory [Smith, 1995] could have led to social cohesion policies, but there must be solid bureaucratic optimism to expect significant short- or medium-term effects. The present form of these policies will not be able to counterbalance the effects of increased competition which will reinforce the most powerful economic zones in Europe and some other regions or cities [Amin, 1992]. Given the initial wealth gaps which are quite considerable, numerous European regions are justifiably worried [Eskelinen and Snickars, 1995; Hadjimichalis and Sadler, 1995], even though some of them in *a priori* unfavourable conditions, manage to enjoy forms of sustained economic growth whether they are tied or not to public policies.
>
> [Rhodes, 1995a]

Hence, the impact of globalisation seems above all to strengthen territorial sub-regional mobilisation to resist or adapt, that is, it reinforces the political process at this level [Le Galès, 1996].

While there has been a general reinforcement of intermediary levels of government in EU countries and of inter-relations, developments observed in different European countries remain very different. There is no or little convergence in the emergence of a level of elected regional government, which is the subject of the first part of this chapter. Developments are rather slow and severely constrained by initial politico-administrative systems and political circumstances. This is not surprising since all European nation–state building processes also took extremely varied forms and rhythms. Thus all the good reasons which led to the emergence of a regional (or meso) level should not be overestimated.

Taking into account the structural weaknesses of the constitution of regions in the framework of nation–states, it can be hypothesised that original forms of regional governance are likely to emerge. In the classical framework of public policy studies, the state is defined by the domination and the power which it exercises over society and economy. In governance we find ideas of leading, guidance, and direction, but the sovereign state is not given primacy. Stating the question of governance suggests understanding the articulation of different types of regulation on a territory, both in terms of political and social integration and in terms of capacity for action. Jessop proposes the following definition:

> one could define the general field of governance studies as concerned with the resolution of (para-) political problems (in the sense of problems of collective goal-attainment or the realisation of collective purposes) in and through specific configurations of governmental (hierarchical) and extra-governmental (non-hierarchical) institutions, organisations and practices.
>
> [Jessop, 1995, p. 317]

Governance is hence defined as a process of co-ordination of public and private actors, social groups and institutions in order to attain clear aims, which are debated and defined collectively, in uncertain and fragmented environments. The second part of this chapter examines the factors which are likely to facilitate the emergence of governance regimes in regions.

To put it somewhat simplistically, this book has basically mobilised political scientists and sociologists to deconstruct a uniform view of European regions beginning with two theoretical options: first, the dynamics of relations between different levels of government (*bottom up* as well as *top down*) and second, a 'new political economy' perspective to highlight the problems of governance and regional political capacity beginning with the reorganisation of the state, civil society and capitalism. This last chapter aims to characterise the various forms of regional governance and to explain the relatively weak institutionalisation of regions.

THE SLOW AND UNEQUAL PROCESS OF INSTITUTIONALISATION OF REGIONS DOES NOT MARK THE ADVENT OF A REGIONAL LEVEL OF GOVERNMENT

The works of Mény [1982b], Hebbert and Machin [1984], Keating [1988], Mény and Wright [1985] and others explained the development of regions in Europe through regionalist movements and pressures on states that, in a number of countries, led to reforms which strengthened regions or at least a meso-level of government. In the chapter on regional government in Europe, M. Keating illustrates the different political, socio-economic and cultural factors which facilitate the understanding of the development of regions in Europe, especially the role of the regionalist movements (which is not covered in this work). Challenging neither the dynamics of decentralisation nor devolution, of which there are now traces in almost all European countries, nor the support of the EU, he found that regions, meaning elected regional government, still remain a minority and are fragile.

Despite the notable exceptions of Germany, Spain, Belgium and the historical nations of Wales and Scotland, regions as a level of elected government have generally remained relatively weak. They have weak autonomy, weak resources, weak political capacity and weak legitimacy. The exceptions are more than exceptions, and they are not disappearing. In the Belgian, German and Spanish cases, the financial and institutional resources of the federated or almost federated states are considerable and they demonstrate strong dynamism in Europe. In European polycentric governance, it becomes difficult, indeed almost impossible, to reason in terms of competence levels.

The weak institutionalisation of the regions

Thus, in the relatively small centralised countries of Europe, such as the Scandinavian countries, Portugal, Ireland and Greece, regions exist only in an embryonic state of co-ordination or implementation of programmes. Without predicting the future, and particularly the impact of European integration, it can be asserted that these countries are not examples of triumphant regionalisation. In the Scandinavian countries, and in particular Sweden, a functional, regional level has emerged. This manages scarcity, that is to say it manages health and social service expenditure in particular. Its development, however, is quite modest. The modernisation reforms of local structures in Norway, Finland, Denmark and Sweden have already contributed to dealing with management problems which could emerge given the degree of urban development, for example with the creation of counties (NUTS 3). Taking the organisation of civil society and diverse interests or a more political dimension of action, the regional level remains noticeably absent. Scandinavian countries in particular have centralised states with a strong municipal tradition in which the state and the communes remain powerful and have large bureaucratic and political resources at their disposal. An intermediary level for management, co-ordination, and implementation of programmes was progressively created in a perspective which Sharpe [1993b] calls rational–functional.

In relation to other unitary countries, the analyses presented in this book bring to light not the triumphant march of the regions but the slow and difficult pace of reforms moving in this direction. The cases of the Netherlands, Italy, France and the United Kingdom are particularly revealing. They demonstrate that there is no inevitability of regions, and that rationality and functionality arguments, despite their presence in discourse, have increasingly less weight in the dynamics of inter-institutional processes. Other modes of organisation, (for example the pillars of Dutch society, the proliferation of loosely co-ordinated and not necessarily territorialised agencies, or the recourse to markets or quasi-markets) can thus help to accomplish relatively similar functions.

In his enlightening chapter, Toonen gives an account of the vicissitudes of Dutch reformers for several decades. Nothing is lacking in this exciting *exposé* (see also Toonen, 1993), neither rational–functional arguments, nor coalitions, nor the dramatic turn of events, nor political reversals. Toonen demonstrates in particular how the pillar organisation of Dutch society facilitated the management of diversity, which undoubtedly led to the absence of regionalist claims, given the fact that each of these pillars had a marked territorial dimension. Provincial administration and powerful municipalities (notably Rotterdam, Amsterdam, The Hague and Utrecht) have left no room for regions to emerge. The recent vague desires of reformers have above all shown the electoral opposition in Rotterdam to the division of the municipality. Holland is not characterised by the absence of regions but by an excessive number of meso-level organisations. For France, Balme has illustrated the slow development of regions and the weakness of the institution, whereas paradoxically it seems that the French state is in the process of regionalisation [Faure, 1994]. This appraisal of French regions and their development clearly differs from previously observed success [CURAPP, 1993]. This is explained by the conditions in which French regions were created [John and Le Galès, 1996], and by weak regional capacity for political action. On the other hand, if fresh initiatives or fields of intervention are stressed, appraisals may differ. Whereas during the 1980s the United Kingdom appeared to be an exception, this is no longer the case. As J. Mawson demonstrates, the manifold increase in the number of all kinds of agencies and organisations leads to a need for co-ordination, and the creation of an embryonic, somewhat dynamic regional governance. This dynamic could well continue. Drawing lessons from the Scottish and Welsh cases, the government is likely to strengthen its administrative presence at regional level (to the extent of creating a sort of regional prefect, is Napoleon's influence crossing the English Channel?), to attempt to guard against the demands for elected regions. Finally, in Italy the situation is a little more complicated due to the well-known territorial variations, thus a political situation of reorganisation is added. However, the localism characteristic of Italian society and its communal organisation are not threatened by the creation of regions as A. Bagnasco and M. Oberti demonstrate. The new generation of elected mayors in Italian cities, since the beginning of the 1990s, notably in Turin, Venice, Rome or Naples (not to mention the classical case of Bologna), demonstrate an increased political capacity to develop local policies and to mobilise different actors for a collective project. The collapse of the First Italian Republic and the pressure from the Northern League put the question of federalism and increased regionalisation on the political agenda. This political dynamic also strengthens the neo-fascists of the National Alliance who act as guarantors of Italian unity and defend a strong state. However, the Italian region as an institution, barring exceptions, remains fragile [Cassese and Torchia, 1993]. In Holland, France and Italy, transformation processes are relatively slow in strongly rooted politico-administrative systems.

Federal states or states on the path of federalisation: Germany, Spain and Belgium

The Belgian and Spanish cases take us back to the logic of federated or almost federated states. The evolution of the Belgian state towards federalism (the last stage before disintegration?) constitutes one of the most intriguing transformation (cf. De Rynck's chapter and also [Hooghe, 1995b]). According to S. De Rynck's stimulating research, it seems to lead to an increasingly greater differentiation between the Walloon and Flemish political systems. In Spain, the dynamic process reinforcing the Autonomous Communities was built on the renewal of democratic Spain, the demands of historical communities and their diffusion (see the chapters by Genieys and Ritaine), as well as the political situation which provided the Catalans with national influence. The political change of 1996 was successful only because the conservative prime minister gave in to the Catalans despite a hostile campaign rhetoric. In both of these cases, and in contrast to the preceding ones, the dynamics that lead to the reinforcement of regions which become federal states are remarkably diverse. With every compromise, central state leaders think that they have managed to stabilise territorial organisation.

In Spain the two major political parties are trying to slow down this process. Thus, several Autonomous Communities frequently change presidents and national political parties ensure that new baronies are not being created. Moreover, a number of Autonomous Communities have no forceful strategy for political reinforcement. In their chapters, W. Genieys and E. Ritaine clearly stress the considerable gap between different Autonomous Communities. The Basque Country and Catalonia are cases of a different nature and they are supported by very distinct societies, territorial mobilisation, organisations and parties. The major parties have become aware of the fact that it is now difficult for them to obtain a majority without the support of nationalist parties irrespective of their rhetoric. As a result, they are somewhat helpless in the face of repeated demands, all the more so, since for example, the Pujol government has proved to be remarkably durable. Despite regular pressure to homogenise the powers of the Autonomous Communities (a dynamic which W. Genieys outlines), the fact that gaps between Communities will increase is to be expected. In the Spanish case, while making the distinction between historical Communities and others (with some exceptions in the others), we note that the processes of institutionalisation are weak in a number of Communities.

In both the Belgian and Spanish cases, the dynamic is forging ahead. The genie has escaped from the bottle and we may witness the process, yet not foresee how it will all end. In these particular cases, there is no doubt that these developments lead to a considerable weakening of the state.

The German *Länder* (along with Catalonia) are generally thought to be the reference point for all supporters of a Europe of the regions. Their institutional, political and economic successes, despite their initial, to say the least, artificial delimitation, except in the case for example of Bavaria, make them the inevitable models for any European regional political leader. As A. Benz rightly points out in his chapter, the institutional power of the *Länder* masks a significant diversity between meso institutions, and in particular, a process of reinforcement of German (sub-*Länder*) regions that attempt to develop their autonomy and political capacity, especially with regard to the Länder and are supported by Brussels and the opportunities opened up by multilevel governance. According to A. Benz, this is the reason why German *Länder* have been cautiously observing the increase of regional representation in Brussels.

This brief overview brings to the fore the relative weakness of regions as elected institutions and the importance of interdependencies/competition among levels of government which, even today, become meaningful only in a national context. This is what makes the comparisons of powers and competencies at a particular government level in different European countries[2] risky and sometimes quite pointless.

The structural weaknesses of regional governments in Europe

Three types of factors emerge to explain the absence of homogeneous regional government in Europe: (1) the diversity of realities regrouped under the term region; (2) the rivalry between levels of government and (3) the reorganisation of states in relation with European integration.

The creation of nation–states as a collective project has historically been quite successful in Europe. One of the differentiating factors that the creation of the nation kept was the diversity of base material that national elites used in their compositions. The formidable Jacobin centralising will is partially explained in the light of the diversity of French provinces. Since Europe is also historically characterised by a mosaic of local and regional societies, cities, empires, and principalities which were progressively integrated into nation–states, the term region necessarily refers to a very large diversity. If we accept the idea that the political construction of territories passes through conflicts whose outcome is uncertain, the creation of a regional level of government cannot but proceed in an irregular fashion. Given the entrenchment of the territorial organisation of certain states as well as the antiquity of their cities and certain historical regions, any process of homogenisation would also demand tremendous energy in an extremely wilful collective project. Neither the European integration process, the functional logic of state reorganisation, nor globalisation processes seem to correspond to this process.

As expected, the fact that the term 'region' is a blanket term which refers to different realities according to country and historical diversity [Anderson, 1994] is confirmed. Even the useful categories NUTS 1, 2 and 3 find it difficult to describe this diversity. In the field of institutions and levels of government the term meso is better, especially in Sharpe's [1993b] sense. This is what is suggested by several authors in this book. Meso refers to a whole group of institutions between the central state and communes. This diversity is, without a doubt, one of the signs of the increasing complexity of our societies. There is no point in conjuring up grand reforms to rationalise all this, because comparisons teach us that we will have to live with this complexity. On this point, the Germans have taken a lead in explaining the subtleties of horizontal and vertical networks and forms of governance [Lehmbruch, 1995; Mayntz, 1993; Héritier, 1993].

Competition between institutions and levels of government is one of the main reasons why regions find it difficult to emerge as a level of government. The development of regional institutions goes hand in hand with the opposition of existing levels. Although it is not a zero-sum game, it is rare that everyone emerges as a winner. In centralised countries, the political and administrative organisation of relatively small states and powerful municipalities (or counties) has left little scope for regions. In part, this is also true for Portugal (which has followed a very different path to that of Spain) or Ireland. In Holland, France, Italy and the United Kingdom, real or potential regions have to face a whole group of institutions, that generally have no desire to find themselves under the tutelage of a level rather close to government and they are hostile to any kind of regional centralisation.

In many regards, these regions have only two possibilities. They are either a level of co-ordination which is accepted and defined as such by the much older local authorities, especially by cities, or they are condemned to remain a relatively underdeveloped level of government, with prospects of a slow evolution, which is surrounded and contested by other institutions. By contrast, the relatively rapid development of regions or federated states in Germany and Spain is partially explained by the opportunities created by reconstruction, or transition to democracy after periods in which the state lost legitimacy. Nevertheless, inter-institutional competition is not absent. The role of city–states and regions in Germany, on the one hand, and the rivalry between Catalonia and Barcelona, on the other [Morata, 1995], amply demonstrate this. The Belgian case remains exceptional. This competition between institutions which structures or serves as competition between leaders and political parties does not prevent co-operation. However, it is rare to see a regional institution with the political clout of Catalonia that enabled it to break up the metropolitan government of Barcelona. Consequently, in this competition, regions act as one mobilisation space among others, as M.C. Smouts emphasised.

Following the example of M. Keating (see his chapter), for example, the role of cities (or urban regions) which seem to benefit more from economic and technological transformations, on the one hand, and political ones, on the other, can be stressed [Harding *et al.*, 1993; Castells, 1985, 1989; Veltz, 1996]. This is not surprising. After all, modern Europe was in part invented in the cities of the Middle Ages. With the exception of nineteenth-century industrial cities, a large majority of European cities have been in existence for several centuries, since the first communes. European urban structures proved to be quite stable throughout European history despite the upheaval of the Industrial Revolution (especially in England). For example, when he examines century-old relations among trade unions, employers' unions and states in Western Europe, Crouch [1993] demonstrates the importance of the heritage of guilds and urban interest organisations in Holland, Germany and Austria, a little less in Scandinavian and Mediterranean countries (not in France where the Revolution had done its work). In the face of fragile identities and regional social structures, cities often appeared as places for structuring political and social games. They also constituted a place for the accumulation of infrastructure which gives them a physical consistency. Given their economic and social dynamism, European cities are not really ill-equipped to compete with regions. The chapters in this book have in part shown that clearly.

This dynamic of competition (and co-operation) between government levels is one of the aspects which certainly needs some further illustration. The formation of polycentric European governance is certainly not a zero-sum game. A part of the discourse on partnership, co-operation, contracts and multilevel governance can also be interpreted as a cover which veils the more direct stakes in terms of power redistribution. It is possible that certain processes lead to positive sum games . . . but not for everyone everywhere in Europe.

In order to explain the relative absence of regions as institutions in most European countries, we may also draw attention to the fact that the past fifteen years have not been especially favourable for political representation authorities. Everywhere in Europe the problems of governance, legitimacy of leading elites and the difficulties of democracy have been discussed. Whereas earlier, in the 1960s and 1970s, regions appeared as possible answers to tensions, as a democratisation factor for states, this idea has now disappeared. When cities or communes can experiment with direct forms of democracy, have more often the capacity to implement visible policies and to be credited with the results and have the capacity to play the democracy card in everyday life (in a more or less real fashion), regions hang somewhere in between the two. The development of elected political regions was undoubtedly not helped by the suspicion which developed in relation to representative authorities who are somewhat remote or are perceived as such by the citizens.

Nation–states reorganise according to logics which seem more comparable, even though their political capacities vary considerably. Without going so far as to identify a model of the state of the *Schumpeterian workfare* type as is suggested by Jessop,[3] V. Wright in his chapter reveals the pressures on states. These pressures are related to globalisation processes, the extension of market boundaries (including ideological ones) and increased economic competition between states. In this context, relations between states and regions (regional institutions) change. It is true that the state is no longer so central, which opens up possibilities for regions, but also allows the state to reorganise and concentrate its efforts on tasks which it considers to be more fundamental, even though it means leaving to regions and EU social cohesion policy the task of managing regions in crisis. As Mény and Wright already noted in 1985, as did urban sociologists such as Préteceille [1991], giving regions the responsibility of managing scarcity and shortage, particularly in the field of welfare, always introduces a powerful dynamic for change (or makes recourse to market mechanisms as in the United Kingdom). In Scandinavian countries and especially Sweden, a level of regional management has emerged basically to manage social and health services, and in particular to manage stagnating or decreasing funds. The case of France is exemplary in this regard. Subsequent to handing over the management of social services to *départements* with the decentralisation laws, the state along with regional elected representatives, is transferring to the regional level the responsibility of 'rationalising' the hospital set-up. Thus in France a two-speed state is being designed. On the one hand, the French state is becoming more regionalised in its organisation and particularly in its structures, in order to manage territorial inequalities, culture, environment as well as social and health expenditure, on the other, in their outline of the strategist state, *Commissariat Général au Plan* experts defend the new role of the post-interventionist state in terms of the development of national economic competitiveness and the defence of its international interests [Blanc, 1992]. Meanwhile the management of scarcity could, in the medium term, considerably fortify regions by giving them budgets as well as expertise, arbitration and regulation capacities.

In this process of reorganisation, states (or more precisely a core of senior civil servants and politicians), do not hesitate to defend more clearly their interests at the expense of local and regional authorities. Moreover, this phenomenon is accentuated in a single currency and monetary union perspective. In order to meet the famous convergence criteria, EU Member States are in the phase of budgetary reorganisation in order to conform to the criteria fixed in Maastricht. That this reorganisation is partly artificial and corresponds to an externalisation of budgetary pressures (to para-public organisms or local authorities) is of little importance. States are tightening the budgetary belt to 'be in'. The finance laws voted in Autumn 1996 in Germany, France, Belgium, Italy and Spain are proof of this state mobilisation. One of the most convenient and rapid means for states to shed their responsibilities is to transfer them elsewhere. Germany has made powerful use of this means to make Western *Länder* finance reconstruction in the Eastern part (former East Germany), but Italy and France are transferring responsibilities to local authorities, and especially regions and cities which provokes strong protest from them.

This point needs some further elaboration. In times of economic growth, meso government levels as well as regions are capable of demonstrating greater dynamism and innovation, seizing opportunities, and witnessing a perhaps rapid evolution in their tax system. They benefit from the legitimacy tied to economic success, whatever the cultural basis of the carving out which presided over the creation of these institutions, may be. In this regard, the case of the German *Länder* is exemplary in the context of state reconstruction and post-war German society. To a lesser extent, Spanish Autonomous Communities benefited from similar circumstances in the framework of democratisation and subsequently strong economic growth in the 1980s. On the contrary, difficult economic and budgetary periods tend to exacerbate rivalries among institutions and levels of government. This situation is thus relatively more favourable for states which have resources and legitimacy to impose the sharing of sacrifices. In these complex national games of relations between levels of government, regions can increase their political capacity if they are given a role in arbitration, in serving as a forum for negotiations and in taking the lead in managing scarcity. If this role is not given to them, they are rendered fragile with regard to the older institutions which are their rivals and are more deeply rooted in society. French and Italian regions are today caught somewhere in the middle, and it is still a little early to know which way they will turn.

If European regions are weak levels of government, an analysis in terms of governance and capacity for political action is likely to do more justice to their role. As regards the analysis of the dimensions of this political capacity, we shall not repeat the analyses presented in the M. Keating and E. Ritaine's chapters, in particular the presentation of the different dimensions of regional power. In a complementary fashion, here we reflect on the perspective of regional governance.

REGIONAL GOVERNANCE: CAN REGIONS CONSTITUTE POLITICAL ACTORS?

Governance as co-ordination of public policy

Given the various transformations of the state, markets and society, an analysis in terms of governance has come to be favoured. The arguments are too well known to be taken up here [Mayntz, 1993; Peters and Savoie, 1995; Leca, 1996]. This approach is mobilised at national, local, regional, European and international levels.

From the examples of European cities, a definition of the governance of sub-national territories was proposed and it remains to be completed, particularly in connection with problems of organisation and interest regulation:

> regional or urban governance: the capacity to integrate and shape local interests, organisations and social groups, on the one hand and on the other, the capacity to represent them outside and develop more or less unified strategies with private actors, the state, other cities and levels of government.
>
> [Le Galès, 1995, p.90; 1996]

This meaning of the term refers to that which happens beyond an organisation, to the capacity to organise collective action and to construct coalitions and public and private partnerships which are oriented towards specific goals. In this case, we go beyond the simple problem of efficiency and co-ordination and it is necessary to introduce different types of legitimacy, power struggles and identity creation. Knowing what good governance is, is not the issue here. What is important is to highlight the mechanisms and processes that enable (or do not enable) a governance which is more or less important and more or less structured.

To this question of regional governance (meaning co-ordination), Wright's answer is unambiguous:

> Today regional government is increasingly a prisoner of the traditional demands of the nation–state: to manage contradictions and

> elaborate legitimate forms of governance. Governance requires the co-ordination of multiple levels of interdependencies in a complex framework, and includes not only official politico-administrative actors, but also a vast series of economic and social actors, both public and private, that manage, control . . . and are members of networks which in some cases, exceed official political boundaries.

All this goes well beyond the capacity of regions . . . and to some extent even that of states. Streeck and Schmitter [1992, p.220] also negatively defined regions as: 'a territorial society without control of its borders'. They also added that European integration was likely to transform tomorrow's nation–states into the regions of today.

Keeping in mind these observations, we can try to see if in certain circumstances, certain regions are capable of regulating different networks, developing new forms of governance and reinforcing their political capacity (see Keating, 1992b; and Ritaine's chapter).

The co-ordination of different forms of public action is one of the main problems in all European countries, and it goes hand in hand with fragmentation tendencies that have been described. Several distinct responses have emerged such as making recourse to the market and agencies, which again leads to problems of co-ordination (Mawson's chapter). All of the studies on polycentric governance and public policies in Europe illustrate a multitude of sectoral networks which are often dominated by experts, as well as all kinds of communities which extend beyond borders. A large part of these networks cross regions. A classical analysis illustrates the scarcity of resources of European regional institutions, in particular their weak capability for sanction. Y. Papadopoulos [1995] and others, however, suggest that in complex societies, information-based strategies (negotiation, delegation, co-ordination and knowledge) are likely to help the regulation of this complexity, and perhaps its governance.

From this perspective, European regions, or rather some of them, seem to have assets, especially in the form of information in European governance. Thus, in an institutional context which is marked by interdependencies and institutionalised negotiation, A. Benz points out the possibilities of German regions, especially in view of their flexibility. In the French case, R. Balme notes the development of regions as a political arena which allows certain regional presidents to behave as political entrepreneurs and to aggregate different networks. There are plenty of examples demonstrating that regions are present in a number of networks, are learning new rules of the political game and in some cases, incertain sectors and certain countries, we can see the structuring of regionalised forms of governance, not only in Scotland, Baden-Württemberg or Catalonia. One could point out that these forms are still extraordinarily limited or that, on the contrary, the pressure from market forces is compelling different actors to demand horizontal co-ordination, indeed political structuring, in order to protect themselves from the destructuring caused by markets. In many regards, these points partially outline a field of research. We have absolutely no empirical or comparative data regarding these points, except perhaps with regard to the European Structural Funds policy, and to a lesser degree, economic development [Rhodes, 1995a]. One can also presume that the creation of regionalised forms may become an objective for different actors and interest groups.

In other words, examples of regionalised governance and networks co-ordinated at regional level (not necessarily by the institution) are not often present. There are some examples: P. Cooke, K. Morgan and their collaborators, have long since brought to light the development of networks mobilised and activated in favour of economic development in Wales [Cooke *et al.*, 1995; Cooke, 1995]; R. Leonardi and R. Nanetti have done the same for Emilia-Romagna and Tuscany [1990]. In certain sectors such as culture or the environment, there are examples of regulation which is becoming regionalised. For training we have no examples, except the German *Länder* which have been analysed by W. Streeck [1992], but there are some attempts in France and England, which moreover are often encouraged by the state.

Finally, as we noted earlier, forms of regionalised regulation seem to be emerging in the territorialised management of the welfare state, the management of scarcity and reorganisation. In this example, regions have or could have the capacity to arbitrate. They become a forum for discussion and negotiations with a sanction capacity.

V. Wright's observation is not without foundation. However, it needs to be qualifed by including interest groups and regional governance, this time conceived as an articulation of different forms of regulation.

Which regional governance?

Beginning with studies of economic transformation, globalisation (cf. supra) and European integration, we hypothesise that certain regions and cities are likely to organise themselves as political actors and fragmentation processes are likely to be arrested by stabilised regulations, as well as by the planning and implementation of collective projects which will help to guide different actors. These processes can take very different forms such as: arrangements between organised interests; a strong civil society; structuring of political parties; multiple office holding; forming of coalitions and different partnerships; and creation of institutions and interaction of social groups. The list is not yet over. As there is no systematic enquiry into these points, the following paragraphs attempt to highlight some factors which are likely to favour forms of regional governance, in particular, organised interest groups, the formation of social groups and identity which is examined separately.

Organised interests

Keeping in mind the points made earlier in relation to the relatively weak institutionalisation of regions in Europe (with the exception of Belgium, Spain, Germany and some others) as well as their weak capacity for co-ordination, the structuring of regional governance should depend on organised interests, with presumably different forms of organisation and relations with regional institutions. The idea of the development of regionalised regulation of interests and regionalised political exchange was one of the hypotheses envisaged in the research of the 1980s (particularly in projects co-ordinated by Schmitter and Streeck, see also Marin, 1990b). A large part of the literature on corporatism and neo-corporatism studied interest group formation in a national framework, with a view to later developing forms of political exchange (see especially Crouch, 1993). When corporatist or national neo-corporatist models became weak, the hypothesis that similar forms would develop either at a supranational level, especially the European level [Streeck and Schmitter, 1992; Greenwood *et al.*, 1992; Mazey and Richardson, 1993], or at a sub-national territorial level, was advanced. If regions were to become an important level of government, it was normal that the employer interest organisations should adapt to better defend their interests.

Moreover, this dimension was not ignored by the main authors of these works because territory constitutes one of the dimensions of the structuring of organised interests [Streeck, 1992]; (see also Cawson, 1986 and his analysis of meso-corporatism). However, in the latter half of the 1980s, these territorial issues appeared to be more important than previously, hence the search for territorialised forms of political exchange [Parri, 1990] and regionalised organisation of interests. At first two aspects were underlined in the studies collected in Coleman and Jacek [1989]: (1) the sub-national territorial dimension is indeed an important dimension of the structuring of employer organisations in several European countries and (2) employer organisations tend to copy the structures of the state and sectors (except the construction and farm produce sectors, [Van Waarden, 1989]). In other words, when regional institutions are strong and, even more so when they are supported by regionalist movements with strong identity components (as in Scotland or in the Basque Country), then employer organisations play a significant role (and sometimes historically this has been the case) in regional dynamics.

On the contrary, it also appears that if employer organisations adapt to the structuring of the state, and to a certain extent, to the organisation of society, they do not have any specific reasons, as in the majority of European cases, to be important at a regional level, except for reasons related to the organisation of their sector of activity [Schmitter and Lanzalaco, 1989]. Thus, in Scandinavian countries, Ireland, Portugal, but also France, the Netherlands and the United Kingdom, most often in Spain and Italy (for Italy see Trigilia, 1991; Grote, 1992), regional employer associations are remarkably weak, and less likely to engage in the logic of exchange. One can, of course, often put forward the existence of forums of representation (such as Economic and Social Councils in France). However, it remains a fact that these organisations are not very obvious or structured at this level, barring notable exceptions for example in Germany (see the analysis of Streeck, 1992), Scotland [Grant, 1989] or Catalonia, the Basque Country and some others, where the identity dimension gives rise to regional mobilisation. Otherwise, we find indications, sometimes in Italy, indeed in the United Kingdom [Shaw, 1993], for the case of the north-east England which J. Mawson mentions in his chapter, which point in that direction.

Consequently, in most European countries, on the one hand, interests are relatively weakly organised at a regional level and, on the other hand, there is no significant empirical proof of the reorganisation of interest organisations at regional level unlike at European level. As a consequence, apart from the cases cited previously, employer organisations do not play a supporting role for the development of regions, contrary to what was suggested by Coleman and Jacek [1989]. This point is not developed for trade unions, for which the regional level is even less important, barring rare exceptions.

An indicator of the consistency of regional governance (or power) consists in the capacity to obtain a modification in the behaviour of other actors, who could be external (for example, big firms), but who are likely to modify their behaviour in a more durable way in order to take into account the strategies of a region or city. The emphasis on regional strategic planning and elaboration of developmental projects aims to constitute the external dimension of governance mentioned earlier. These regional plans and strategies have gained importance, especially due to EU pressure. This constitutes one of the blind spots of our work. Considering, on the one hand, the weakness of organised interests in most European countries at the regional level, and on the other, the weak institutionalisation of regions, we suppose (based on the Italian and French cases) that the exercise of regional planning is likely to have little impact in terms of governance.

Conversely, the considerable body of research on public–private partnerships, the formation of growth-coalitions or of European-style urban regimes, suggest that a number of more or less organised private actors adapt their behaviour to the strategies of cities.

Social groups

In the absence of organised interests, regions could be a level of structuring for social groups. Bagnasco and Oberti's chapter facilitates reflection on the restructuring of western societies and on the reorganisation of social formations on territories. In view of the erosion of (more or less) integrated national societies and major institutions which structure national societies (parties, unions, churches), it could be assumed that other levels of structuring of social groups are likely to have a greater importance. Thus, studies on the lower middle classes in the United Kingdom or in France have clearly shown that these *classes moyennes* do not organise like classical classes at central level but rather, they are structured in localities. Research on localities in Italy, France and the United Kingdom have shown how social groups can be formed in the framework of conflicts or local collective action, because all social groups obviously do not have the same type of attachment or interests in a locality. Progressively in the United Kingdom (it was always more the case in Italy), the sociology of social groups and classes took local and regional dynamics into account of the creation of these social groups. Following Esping-Andersen [1993] and others, several attempts were made to formalise the social structuring of capitalist societies. A. Bagnasco and M. Oberti take a new political economy perspective. Rather than taking the regional level as given and attempting to find indications to prove that certain Italian regions play a role in structuring the social game, they tackle the problem back to front. They propose drawing the main lines of the restructuring of Italian capitalism and social groups and, in a second phase, they question the pertinence of Italian regions as a level for structuring social groups and their games. Their answer is negative and they contrast the economic and social dynamism of Italian localities with regions which continue to constitute a purely institutional level. Using other methods, they thus confirm the analyses of Trigilia [1991], Cammelli [1990], Grote [1992] and E. Ritaine (her chapter) on the weakness of Italian regions with regard to civil society. They also very clearly take a view which is completely the opposite of that of other studies which have instead insisted on the importance of some Italian regions.

Apart from the Italian case (the conclusions would be fairly similar for France), it would be interesting to use the same method for other European countries. *A priori*, one could imagine that the regionalisation of social structures would be more marked for example in the United Kingdom, given the concentration of economic activity in the south-east, or in Belgium, as is suggested by De Rynck.

Research on social groups is usefully complemented by research on European values and regional differences, even though these inquiries encounter the difficult problem of defining pertinent regions. From the results of two inquiries on European values, Chauvel [1995] has pointed out important regional disparities within states, in particular in Ireland, Belgium and Spain. Conversely, by devising a synthetic indicator of sub-national disparities, Chauvel illustrates the relative national cultural homogeneity of the United Kingdom (despite the Scots and Welsh who are distinct only in relation to their attachment to their region), Germany and the Netherlands – three countries characterised by a mixed religious tradition – and to a lesser degree, Northern European countries. This relative homogeneity is superior to that of Jacobin France and the remarkably fragmented Mediterranean countries (Portugal, Italy, Spain). It also highlights significant differences between the economically advanced main cities/regions (Berlin, Amsterdam/Rotterdam, Ile-de-France, Greater London, Brussels) and others, in particular regions which are very much anchored in traditional Catholicism. This undoubtedly brings us back to the effects of social organisation and the influence of large cities. The lessons on cities of Simmel and Weber could recover a renewed validity in the context of the accelerated metropolisation of European cities.

Identity and economic development in regional mobilisation

These analyses lead us to the dimensions of identity, belonging, values and culture. These questions are obviously fundamental when dealing with European regions, or at least certain European regions or governance, even though regions in the institutional sense, assemble clearly distinct localities in terms of values or identity. In several texts, local or regional identity (historical, present, invented or reinvented) serves as a rallying point to justify or explain local political mobilisation and regionalism. Identity is supposed to play a very important role even when definition elements are not very clear. In the perspective outlined here, we concur with Arnaldo Bagnasco who suggests that regional identity (or that of a city) consists of an implicit or explicit project developed by certain local actors who consider it advantageous or appropriate to continue orienting their actions reciprocally. This neither excludes conflicts nor rivalries, but instead implies a certain, relatively stabilised framework of interaction, with projects elaborated by several actors, investments in local society producing results differing in time and the production of collective goods which serve as common resources. The civicness to which Putnam refers [1993b] or Coleman's [1990] social capital are concepts which express the cultural component active in this case. Identity defined in this way, however, refers to a strategy and an economic and political structure centred on a local society which relates to cities [Bagnasco and Le Galès, 1997].

This original conception of identity facilitates explaining 'economic and identity' regionalist mobilisation. One of the paradoxes of the current situation in Europe lies in the fact that some regionalist movements the revival of which was celebrated in the 1970s, have now declined. For example in Brittany, Alto-Adige and Val d'Aosta, regional identities have not disappeared, but autonomy or decentralisation claims were satisfied, and thus regionalist movements became dormant.

Let us suggest a hypothesis. In certain cases, mobilisation against the state has been one of the *raisons d'être* of regionalist movements, but this is now rarely the case. A part of the dynamics associated with top-down regionalism was made obsolete by changes of scale. In cases where communities and territories were very different (as in Scandinavian countries in the second half of the nineteenth century), in Germany or the Mediterranean countries (including France), national elites mobilised more or less successfully in order to reduce disparities, and create a nation. Local and regional societies did not remain passive in the face of this process. Some of them integrated, others disappeared, and some invented strategies (for example by reinventing traditions) to maintain, sustain and fortify their real or imagined social, political and cultural uniqueness. Opposing the state was one of the mainsprings of collective action in different regions. Can they still mobilise against the state? In the Basque Country and

Corsica, yes. Yes also for the Northern League in Northern Italy that struggles against the state which absorbs too many resources.

However, certain states have granted, on the one hand, a certain political autonomy and, on the other, they have modified their priorities in order to facilitate mobilisation in international economic competition. By political choice (the effect, for example, of the neo-liberal turning point [Jobert, 1994]) and/or in the face of (rarely admitted) public impotence, certain states have noted that their economic development mainly depends on certain regions (Ile-de-France and Rhône-Alpes in France, the South East in the United Kingdom, Lisbon and Porto in Portugal and the urban regions of the capitals in Scandinavian countries). In other words, the mobilisation of the periphery and equality among sub-national territories are no longer state priorities (irrespective of grand debates and symbolic measures meant to prove the contrary). This withdrawal of the state which corresponds to a reorientation towards more strategic tasks, is evident in most European countries [Wright and Cassese, 1996]. Therefore identity-seeking regional mobilisation partly structured against centralised states loses some of its spirit. If it is not linked to economic development forms and does not participate in a greater collective project in Bagnasco's sense, as is the case in Flanders or Catalonia, then in the present context, it appears to be either dormant or regressing. This does not explain everything. In fact, in certain cases they become radical (the Basque Country and Corsica). Thus, the Scots had to fight against a brutal and centralising Conservative Government in the 1980s. In other words, in the framework of the hypothesis outlined above, Mrs Thatcher played an essential role in the remobilisation of Scottish identity in a political direction by, for example, turning Scotland into a laboratory for experimenting with new policies such as the poll tax. Conversely, one could imagine that in the case of an elected Scottish assembly and with a government less hostile to London, the Scottish national movement would mobilise less, at least for a certain period of time, unless it were to succeed in giving more substance to a collective project and in drawing support from dynamic forms of economic development. Pushing this hypothesis a little bit further, it could be presumed that certain historical regions which are not facing economic crisis and are not benefiting from private economic development, would make constant their dependence *vis-à-vis* the state. Therefore, one can imagine that certain regions that feel threatened by economic restructuring and market logics, (discreetly) become fervent supporters of the centralised state which protects them. Several French regions are in this situation, including Brittany, which would make for an interesting reversal. It is true also for southern Italian regions. In other words, on the condition of a little political autonomy, regions could become faithful supporters of nation–states, especially if they have a more important role, in terms of influence, on public policies. As suggested above, it is not certain that the elites at the heart of the state are so very enthusiastic with regard to this reversal. In other words, in more centralised countries, regional mobilisation based solely on cultural identities could lose a part of their dynamic.

Conversely, and this is the second hypothesis which we wish to suggest, when this identity is defined or articulated along territorialised social formations (in Bagnasco and Oberti as well as Ritaine's sense, see their chapters), and/or structured and dynamic forms of economic development are expressed in a collective project, then this mobilisation is likely to be stronger (on this point see also Keating's chapter). It seems to us that the cases of Wales, Catalonia, Flanders, Scotland and the Northern League (which draws support from small entrepreneurs) correspond quite well to these cases. On the other hand, in studies of globalisation, it has been indicated that territorialised mobilisation of actors in favour of economic development was becoming more and more central in Europe, notably in cities [Harvey, 1989; Mayer, 1995; Harding and Le Galès, 1997], but also in certain regions and is one of the driving forces in the formation of governance regimes in certain territories. Therefore one can imagine that the case of the *Lega* in Italy is not an isolated one and that comparable forms (to a certain extent) of regionalist movements and/or regional mobilisation are developing in other countries. In Bavaria and Alsace, relative economic prosperity and identity could sustain a new regionalism.

As a consequence, today, it is undoubtedly this articulation of identity (in Bagnasco's sense), and the constitution of political actors to adapt to and resist the destructuring pressure on local and regional societies, which makes up the main driving force in the development of regions. From this, one could formulate the hypothesis in a different way to the one suggested by Badie [1995a]. The revival of identity-seeking claims (in the classical, ethnic sense of the term) perhaps count less in Western Europe to explain regional and local mobilisation and claims, than the (offensive and defensive) reaction to globalisation processes. We have mentioned elsewhere [Le Galès, 1996, see also Bagnasco and Le Galès, 1997] the prospect of a reinforcement of sub-national, territorial, political mobilisation to face the destructuring of local and regional societies, keeping in mind, on the one hand, globalisation processes and on the other, rivalries between sub-national territories. As Ritaine asserts, 'competition produces politics'. From a 'new political economy' perspective the hypothesis is made that social groups, organised interests and institutions mobilise collective projects, reinvent local identities and organise in governance regimes, in order to resist politically, culturally and economically or in order to adapt to globalisation processes. We would thus witness the reappearance of forms of sub-national 'return of the politics', not politics classically defined in terms of domination and monopoly of violence, but politics in terms of mobilisation and collective projects, including undoubtedly a strong cultural/identity dimension (which [Majone, 1990], considers to be a structural element in the constitution of Europe). In this framework, certain regions could become political actors.

All that has been identified earlier relating to governance (social groups, interests, identities, but also the impact of globalisation processes) also applies to cities and regions. If identity and culture were the dominant factors of sub-regional territorial mobilisation, European regions would most often be the place for the expression and structuring (more or less complete or successful) of governance regimes (in the sense of articulation of market regulations, communities and hierarchies). Conversely, if globalisation processes and social and political reactions are dominant, especially in terms of economic development (but not exclusively), then (some) cities are likely to be the main area for the structuring of political and social games, organisation of different interests and planning of collective strategies in many European countries [Le Galès and Harding, 1996]. Adhering to the theoretical current of new political economy, we emphasise the political game and social and economic groups, rather than cultural and identity factors considered in isolation.

CONCLUSION: REGIONS CONTRIBUTE TO THE ORGANISATION OF THE TERRAIN OF THE EUROPEAN GOVERNANCE, BUT THEY ARE NOT OFTEN THE PLAYERS

This book and, in particular, this chapter have stressed the structural weakness of regions and their link with nation–states. Too often, the dynamics of particular regions and the discourse of Europe of the regions, have led one to overlook the fact that regions are structurally weak in terms of government and governance. There are important exceptions and the medium-term impact of European integration could modify the deal. In the framework of polycentric European governance, we shall perhaps witness the increase of all kinds of networks. Few regions will, however, be capable of organising regional regulations and modes of governance (see also [Streeck and Schmitter, 1992], for a similar argument).

Consequently, a small number of regions (and cities) are on their way to becoming collective political actors in European governance and this undoubtedly merits our attention in the future. In a different way from Keating in his chapter and other authors (for example Négrier, 1995) suggest, European regions are not often involved in this process. At best, and this is one of the main conclusions of this work, European regions become rather weakly organised passageways for all kinds of networks and they constitute one of the political forums of governance and one of the many possible areas for mobilisation. Moreover, this dimension of forum is important in democracies. Except in the case of strong institutionalisation (Germany and certain Spanish Autonomous Communities), and/or in rare cases of structured regimes of governance (certain Italian regions), regions do not constitute European governance actors. They are rarely a place for political exchanges and have a feeble political capacity in Ritaine's sense. Therefore, at best, to borrow an image suggested by Bagnasco, regions help in preparing the ground for the European governance game at a sub-national level, but often, cities constitute the real actors.

Most often regions are functional spaces (either for the state or the European Union) for some policies. They are weakly institutionalised, endowed with a weak political capacity, and are destined to manage scarcity or economic decline, as well as to protect culture, the environment and identities. All this could constitute a very important role and turn out to be a resource. The national top-down, bottom-up dynamics that sustained the regionalisation movement of the 1970s (see Keating's chapter), partially dissolved due to the effects of globalisation and European integration, as well as the unstable reorganisation of inter-governmental relations. In this sense, Mény was no doubt right in qualifying the 1970s as the decade of regionalisation, in so far as the pressures for change partly strengthened regions. Beginning with the analysis of technological change in order to understand mechanisms of territorial differentiation of the formation of employer organisations, Schmitter and Lanzalaco, however, clearly saw the limits of this argument [1989, p. 215] when they stressed the fact that regions in the 1970s appeared as the optimum level for solutions to problems. Apart from technological change, changes of scale (globalisation and European integration versus nation–states) have unquestionably caused regions to lose their appeal.

Previously, it was explained that regionalisation and European integration went hand in hand, which meant the advent of a new European political order and a European governance characterised by the term 'Europe of the Regions'. Following several other authors from Anderson [1992], Borras-Alomar *et al.* [1994] to Hooghe [1996b], we have attempted to demonstrate in this book that this 'Europe of the Regions' is more mythical than anything else. Of course the myth has to be taken seriously, all the more so as it produces territorial mobilisation, including attempts to create new inter-regional areas such as the Atlantic Arc [Balme, 1995]. However, irrespective of its capacities for mobilisation, its importance should not be exaggerated. In her chapter which poses the question in a more general way, Smouts demonstrates clearly the attractiveness of this myth but also the limits of this 'regional fantasy'. We sometimes come across the view that a Europe of the regions is for the moment a myth, but the success of this mobilising slogan will contribute to the social construction of European governance. The success of the discourse is of course going to lure the effects of reality. This determinist constructivism seems to overlook the fact that from time to time, the performative efficiency of the discourse can come across serious difficulties. The chapters of this book and particularly the national studies have amply demonstrated this. However, the question remains open and the medium- and long-term impact of the EU on the sub-national political organisation of Europe remains to be seen. If we begin in Brussels and analyse the effects of EU programmes as well as the strategies of regions in Brussels [Christiansen, 1996], we are led to recognise the EU as the main force of relative homogeneous restructuring and change. If, as was the case in this book, we start with the existing systems and take into account cities, regions, states and Europe as well as economic and social changes, the weight of the variable 'European integration' in explaining ongoing reorganisation appears to be remarkably modest, although quite considerable in certain cases. Perhaps it is a question of time and cumulative dynamics. Thus, when Christiansen examines the regions of the Baltic Sea, he identifies a 'regional policy' scenario in which EU regional policy programmes lead to the creation of a 'Baltic Sea Euro-region' [1997, forthcoming]. It is clear that by comparison, the Atlantic Arc had to face stronger resistance.

The analysis of polycentric governance in Europe stresses actors, their strategies and interactions. Ultimately, following the work of the deconstruction of the state as a collective actor, we may end up studying only individual actors. One of the possible diversions consists in attributing too much importance to the constitution of a collective actor and the development of institutions, favouring the games of individual actors and forgetting the weight of structures. Forced in this direction this model leads to a kind of European chaos where a multitude of public and private, individual and collective actors act and interact. This is the reason why instead of using the term polycentric governance, Wright prefers to talk of a mosaic or a kaleidoscope. In fact the whole game is not open. Political and social actors organise in networks and in exchange relations from which they try to exclude others and enter into competition with others. As Weber has shown for social groups, the dynamics of 'social closure', and exclusion of others is part of the political and social game. Certain sectors are monopolised by structured and closed networks. Certain domains remain under state control. The problem is to underline the lines of reorganisation and restructuring of the political in a 'European polity' in which nation–states have lost their central position, but not their importance. This requires studying the reorganisation of the state, the European Commission or regions and cities.

The supporters of the top-down approach sometimes tend to study this territorial reorganisation in Europe in terms of all that is new, all that moves, to discover the European Union and public policies to which it is linked. Thus, the term region serves as a blanket term for all sub-national actors. For example, the regions are vigorously analysed *vis-à-vis* their offices in Brussels [Marks *et al.*, 1996], the Committee of the Regions [Christiansen 1996], and in terms of social cohesion and Structural Funds policy. The impact of these policies enables illustrating differential territorial mobilisation (see Hooghe, 1996b on all these points), the diversity of institutional contexts and facilitates speculation on the transformation of regions and European states with the effects of European integration [Nanetti, 1996]. Without denying the considerable indirect impact of European integration on intergovernmental relations and territorial restructuring, in this volume we have attempted to emphasise the fact that the economic and social effects of globalisation processes and the reorganisation of capitalism in Europe, are for the moment at least as important. Following the example of Smith [1995] or Dunford (his chapter), it is understandable to think that on regional 'losers', the European Union is likely to have a greater impact by helping a major market to emerge, than through its policies of social cohesion or the creation of a Committee of Regions.

However, the objective of the book was not to show that regions do not count in Europe because the exceptions to which we referred weigh heavily and can serve as reference models for others. In the face of fragmentation, regions continue to appear as a level of co-ordination or regulation of multiple actors and networks, especially for those who do not have regions [John and Whitehead, 1996]. Our argument is that they do not often succeed. The thesis which is defended here is not the decline of regions in Europe, but the decline of causes that logically converge to reinforce regions. Reasoning less in terms of discourse and more in terms of collective actors (including the constructivist dimension) and economic and social structures in order to analyse inter-governmental relations, the role of regions is made relative.

This work follows other works that have strongly challenged the idea of a 'Europe of the Regions' as a new European political order. This idea has been replaced by the idea of a 'Europe with the regions'. Analysing in detail the effects of EU Structural Fund and Cohesion policy, Hooghe [1996b, p.121] demonstrates that a Europe of all the regions has not emerged. Instead there is a 'Europe with certain regions'. This book has attempted to reverse the perspective and suggest the view that European governance will be marked (more than anything else) by the strategies of collective political actors, that is, by 'some regions (and cities) in Europe'.

NOTES

1 See in particular Harvey, 1989; Stöhr, 1990; Amin and Dietrich, 1991; Dunford and Kafkalas, 1992b; Benko and Lipietz, 1992; Cooke, 1995; Rhodes, 1995b; Bagnasco and Sabel, 1994; Lash and Urry, 1993; Cheshire and Gordon, 1995; and on the effects of globalisation Veltz, 1996.

2 See, however, how G. Marks and his collaborators [1996], following Ersson and Lane [1991] have made an interesting attempt to define an index of regional autonomy. From the three aggregated indices (a federalism index from 0 to 4), one for territories with special autonomy (0–4) and another to measure the role of regions within the state (0–4), Marks gives a score of regional autonomy which varies from 0 to 8 for the European countries. The majority of countries under consideration (before the inclusion of Sweden, Austria and Finland) have a score of 0 or 1 (Denmark, France, Greece, Ireland, Italy, Luxemburg, Holland, Portugal, the United Kingdom) whereas Germany, Belgium and Spain have a score of 5 or 6.

3 Bob Jessop has theorised this post-Fordist transition for the state, that is passing from the Keynesian welfare state to the Schumpeterian workfare state [Jessop, 1994]. This new state which is characteristic of western countries has the following traits: (1) to promote innovation in terms of products, processes, organisation and markets in globalised economies in order to improve the competitiveness of countries. Thus it affects supply; and (2) to subordinate social policies to the needs of flexibility of the labour market and to the constraints of international economic competition. Evidently this means calling into question the welfare state as we know it in the sense of American and British policies, and for regions and cities a restructuring of local forms of the welfare-state to enhance economic competitiveness. Like Harvey, in this process of *hollowing out of the state*, he sees a victory of the market logic over the political.

Bibliography

Abéles M., *Jours tranquilles en 89. Ethnologie politique d'un département français*, Odile Jacob, Paris, 1989.

Abromeit H., *Der verkappte Einheitsstaat*, Leske und Budrich, Opladen, 1992.

Agnew J., *Place and Politics: The Geographical Mediation of State and Society*, Allen and Unwin, London, 1987.

Albrechts L., Moulaert F. and Roberts P., *Regional Policy at the Crossroads: European Perspectives*, Jessica Kingsley, London, 1989.

Allen J. and Massey D. (eds), *The Economy in Question*, Sage, London, 1988.

Allies P., 'Régions et utilisation de l'espace européen: la politique du sud de la France', *Sciences de la Société*, 25, 1992.

Almond G. and Verba S., *The Civic Culture: Political Attitudes and Democracy in Five Nations*, Princeton University Press, Princeton, 1963.

Amin A., 'Big firms versus the regions in the Single European Market', in M. Dunford and G. Kafkalas (eds), *Cities and Regions in a New Europe*, Belhaven Press, London, 1992.

Amin A. and Dietrich M. (eds), *Towards a New Europe?*, Aldershot, Edward Elgar, 1991.

Amin A. and Thrift N., 'Neo-marshallian modes in global networks', *International Journal of Urban and Regional Research*, 16, 1992.

—— 'Living in the Global', in A. Amin and N. Thrift (eds), *Globalization, Institutions, and Regional Development in Europe*, Oxford University Press, Oxford, 1994.

Andersen, S. S. and Eliassen K., 'European Community lobbying',*European Journal of Political Research*, 20, 1991.

Anderson J., 'Sceptical reflections on a Europe of Regions: Britain, Germany and the European Regional Development Fund', *Journal of European Public Policy*, 10(4), 1991.

—— *The Territorial Imperative: Pluralism, Corporatism and Economic Crisis*, Cambridge University Press, Cambridge, 1992.

Anderson, P., 'The invention of the region, 1945–1990', *EUI Working Paper EUF* 94(2), European University Institute, Florence, 1994.

Andeweg R. and Irwin G. A., *Dutch Government and Politics*, Macmillan, London, 1993.

Aquina, H., 'PGOs' in the Netherlands', in C. Hood and G. F. Schuppert (eds), *Delivering Public Services in Western Europe: Sharing Western European Experience of Para-Governmental Organization*, London, 1988.

Arrighi G. (ed), *Semiperipheral Development: The Politics of Southern Europe in the Twentieth Century*, Sage, London, 1985.

Audit Commission, *Regeneration Audit Guide*, HMSO, London, 1989a.

—— *Urban Regeneration and Economic Development: The Local Government Dimension*, HMSO, London, 1989b.

Aydalot P., *Milieux innovateurs en Europe*, GREMI, Paris, 1986.

Aymard M., 'Nation–states and interregional disparities of development', in G. Arrighi (ed.), *Semiperipheral Development: The Politics of Southern Europe in the Twentieth Century*, Sage, London, 1985.

Bach D., 'L'intégration en Afrique de l'Ouest: crise des institutions et crise des modèles', in R. Lavergne (ed.), *L'intégration économique en Afrique de l'Ouest*, CRDI-Karthala, Paris 1995a.

—— 'Les dynamiques paradoxales de l'intégration en Afrique subsaharienne', *Revue française de science politique*, 45(6), December 1995b.

Badie, B., *La fin des territoires. Essai sur le désordre international et sur l'utilité sociale du respect*, Fayard, Paris, 1995a.

—— Report presented to the conference on 'L'international sans territoire', Paris, 16–17 March 1995, forthcoming in *Cultures et conflits*, 1995b.

Bafoil F., 'Entre mémoire et attente: une approche sociologique de la frontière Neisse', *Cahiers du Roses*, Grenoble, 1, March 1995.

Bagnasco A., *Tre Italie. La problematica territoriale dello sviluppo italiano*, Il Mulino, Bologna, 1977.

—— *Torino. Un profilo sociologico*, Einaudi, Turin, 1986.

—— *La costruzione sociale del mercato*, Il Mulino, Bologna, 1988.

—— 'Regioni, tradizione civica, modernizzazione italiana: un commento alla ricerca di Putnam', *Stato e Mercato*, 1, 40, 1994.

Bagnasco A. and Le Galès P., 'Les villes comme acteurs et comme sociétés locales', in A. Bagnasco and P. Le Galès (eds) *Les villes en Europe*, La Découverte, Paris, 1997.

Bagnasco A. and Sabel C. F. (eds), *Small Firms and Economic Development in Europe*, London, Pinter, 1995.

Bagnasco A. and Trigilia C, *Società e politica nelle aree di piccola impresa. Il caso di Bassano*, Arsenale, Venice, 1984.

—— *Società e politica nelle aree di piccola impresa. Il caso della Val Delsa*, Franco Angeli, Milan, 1985.

—— *La construction sociale du marché*, Editions ENS Cachan, Cachan, 1993.

Balligand J. P. and Macquart, 'Aménagement du territoire: la mosaïque disloquée', *Revue politique et parlementaire*, 946, 1990.

Balme R., 'Les politiques de la subsidiarité: l "Europe des régions" comme catégorie générique du territoire européen', in R. Balme., P. Garraud., V. Hoffmann-Martinot and E. Ritaine (eds), *Le territoire pour politiques: variations européennes*, L'Harmattan, Paris, 1994.

Balme R. and Bonnet L., 'From regional to sectoral policies: the contractual relations between the state and the regions in France', in J. Loughlin and S. Mazey (eds), *The End of the French Unitary State?: Ten Years of Regionalization in France, 1982-1992*, Frank Cass, London, 1995.

Balme R., Brouard S. and Burbaud F., 'Coopération inter-régionale et genèse de l'espace public européen. Le cas de la façade atlantique', *Sciences de la Société* 34, February 1995.

Balme, R., Garraud, P., Hoffman-Martinot, V. and Ritaine, E. (eds) *Le territoire pour politiques: variations européennes*, L'Harmattan, Paris, 1994.

Balme R. and Jouve B., 'L'Europe en région: les fonds structurels et la régionalisation de l'action publique en France métropolitaine', *Politiques et Management Public*, 13(2): 1, June 1995.

—— 'Building the regional state: Europe and territorial organization in France', in Hooghe L. (ed.), *Cohesion Policy and European Integration*, Oxford University Press, Oxford, 1996.

Barbera A., '1970-85, como superare le insufficienze del decentramento', *Democrazia e diritto*, XXV(1), 1985.

Barbosa C., *L'enjeu linguistique en Catalogne*, report for the DEA local government, CERVL, Institut d'études politiques de Bordeaux, 1995.

Barr N. A., *The Economics of the Welfare State*, Weidenfeld and Nicolson, London, 1987.

Bayart J.-F., *L'illusion identitaire*, Fayard, Paris, 1996.

Bayart J.-F., Mbembe A. and Toulabor C., *Le politique par le bas en Afrique noire*, Karthala, Paris, 1992.

Becattini G. (ed.), *Mercato e forze locali: il distretto industriale*, Il Mulino, Bologna, 1987.

Begg I., 'European integration and regional policy', *Oxford Review of Economic Policy*, 2(5), 1989.

Begg I. and Whyatt A., *Economic Development in London in the Context of National Policy Priorities: Conceptual, Institutional and Practical Issues*, paper given at Ifresi-Pir Villes International Conference, Universities of Lille 1, 2, and 3, Cities, Enterprises, and Society at the eve of the 21st Century, Lille 1994.

Beggs I. and Mayes D., 'Cohesion, convergence and economic and monetary union in Europe', Regional Studies, 26(4), 1993.

Beltran M., *La elite burocratica espanola*, Ariel, Madrid, 1977.

Benet J., *El président Tarradellas en les seus textos 1954-1988*, Empuries, Barcelona, 1992.

Benko G. and Dunford M. (eds), *Industrial Change and Regional Development: The Transformation of New Industrial Space*, Belhaven Press, London, 1991.

Benko G. and Lipietz A. (eds), *Les régions qui gagnent: districts et réseaux: les nouveaux paradigmes de la géographie régionale*, PUF, Paris, 1992.

Benko G. and Strohmeyer U. (eds), *Space and Social Theory*, Blackwell, Oxford, 1996.

Bennett R. J. and McCoshan A., *Enterprise and Human Resource Development: Local Capacity Building*, Paul Chapman, London, 1993.

Bennett R., Wicks P. and McCoshan A., *Local Empowerment and Business Services: Britain's Experiment with Training and Enterprise Councils*, UCL Press, London, 1994.

Benz A., 'Mehr-Ebenen-Verflechtung. Verhandlungsprozesse in verbundenen Entscheidungsarenen', in A. Benz, F. W. Scharpf and R. Zintl (eds), *Horizontale Politikverflechtung*, Campus, Frankfurt, 1992a.

—— 'Redrawing the map? The question of territorial reform in the Federal Republic', *German Politics*, 1(3), 1992b.

—— 'Regionen als Machtfaktor in Europa', *Verwaltungsarchiv*, 84, 1993.

Bew P. and Meehan E., 'Regions and borders: controversies in Northern Ireland about the European Union', *Journal of European Public Policy*, 1(1), 1994.

Biarez S., *Le pouvoir local*, Economica, Paris, 1989

Biarez S. and Nevers, J-Y (eds), *Gouvernement local et politiques urbaines*, CERAT, Grenoble, 1993.

Bidegaray C., *L'Etat autonomique: forme nouvelle ou transitoire en Europe*, Economica, Paris, 1994.

Billiet J. *et al.*, *Rapport van de Club van Leuven. Vlaanderen op een kruispunt*, Lannoo, Leuven, 1990.

Biorcio R., 'La Lega come attore politico: dal federalismo al populismo regionalista', in R. Mannheimer (ed.), *La Lega Lombarda*, Feltrinelli, Milan, 1991.

Biorcio R., Corbetta P., Diamanti I., Parisi A., Riccamboni G. and Vassallo S., 'Voto 93: Fratture, regole, comportamenti', *Polis*, 1, 1994.

Bischof R., 'Debate: why German cycles give a better ride', *The Guardian*, Tuesday 27 December 1994.

Blanc C., *L'Etat stratège*, La Documentation française/Commissariat au Plan, Paris, 1992.

Blanc J., Bourdin J. and Paul H., *Les Finances régionales*, Economica, Paris, 1994.

Bodiguel M. and Buller H., 'Environmental policy and the regions in France', in J. Loughlin and S. Mazey (eds), *The End of the French Unitary State?: Ten Years of Regionalization in France, 1982-1992*, Frank Cass, London, 1995.

Bomberg E., *Green Parties and Politics in the European Community*, Routledge, London, 1995.

Bonachela Mesas M., *Las Elites Andaluzas*, Mezquita, Madrid, 1983.

Borkenhagen, F. H. U., 'Vom kooperativen Föderalismus zum "Europa der Regionen"', *Aus Politik und Zeitgeschichte*, B 42, 1992.

Borras S., 'The four motors of Europe and its promotion of R&D linkages: beyond geographical contiguity in interregional agreements', *Regional Politics and Policy*, 3(3), 1993.

Borras Alomar S., 'Inter-regional cooperation in Europe during the 1980's and 1990's', in N. A. Soerensen (ed.), *European Identities*, Odense University Press, Odense, 1995.

Borras-Alomar S., Christiansen T. and Rodriguez-Pose A., 'Towards a Europe of the regions', *Regional Politics and Policy*, 4, 1994.

Borzel. T., *Die Europafähigkeit des deutschen Bundesstaates*, (unpublished dissertation), University of Constance, 1995.

Botella J., 'The Spanish "new" regions: territorial and political pluralism', *International Political Science Review*, X(3), 1989.

—— 'Le format régional', conference on *Politiques du territoire*, Bordeaux, 19–22 October 1994.

—— 'L'élite gouvernementale espagnole', in E. Suleiman and H. Mendras (eds), *Le recrutement des élites en Europe*, La Découverte, Paris, 1995.

Bourdieu P., 'L'identité et la représentation. Eléments pour une réfléxion critique sur l'idée de région', *Actes de la recherche en sciences sociales*, 35, 1980.

Boyer, R. and Durand, J.-P., *L'après-Fordisme*, Syros, Paris, 1993

Bradbury J. and Mawson J. (eds), *British Regionalism and Devolution: The Challenges of State Reform and European Integration*, Jessica Kingsley, London, 1997.

Braudel, F., *L'identité de la France. Espace et Histoire*, Arthaud-Flammarion, Paris, 1986.

Brenac E., 'Néo-libéralisme et politiques industrielles: les conditions et les formes différenciées d'un changement de paradigme. L'exemple des télécommunications en Europe', in B. Jobert (ed.), *Le tournant néo-libéral en Europe*, L'Harmattan, Paris, 1994.

Brusco S., 'The Emilian model: productive decentralisation and social integration', *Cambridge Journal of Economics*, 6, 1982.

——'La leçon des districts et la nouvelle politique industrielle des régions', in A. Bagnasco and C. Sabel (eds), *PME et développement économique en Europe*, La Découverte, Paris, 1994.

Bullman U. (ed.), *Die Politik der dritten Ebene. Regionen im Europa der Union*, Nomos, Baden-Baden, 1994.

Bulpitt J., *Territory and Power in the United Kingdom*, Manchester University Press, Manchester, 1983.

Burch M. and Holliday I., 'Institutional emergence: the case of North West of England', *Regional Politics and Policy, 2(3), 1993.*

Business In The Community, *Leadership in the Community. A Blueprint for Business Involvement in the 1990s*, Business in the Community, London, 1992.

Caciagli M., 'Quante Italie? Persistanza e trasformazione delle culture politiche subnazionali', *Polis*, 3, 1988.

—— 'La destinée de la "subculture rouge" dans le centre-nord de l'Italie', *Politix*, 30, 1995.

Caisse Des Depots, *Economie et Territoire: vers une nouvelle dynamique du développement local*, Caisse des Dépôts et Consignations, 2 vols, Paris, 1986.

Calvi G. and Vanucci A., *L'elettore sconosciuto*, Il Mulino, Bologna, 1995.

Camilleri J. A. and Falk J., *The End of Sovereignty? The Politics of a Shrinking and Fragmenting World*, Edward Elgar, Aldershot, 1992.

Cammelli M., 'Regioni e rappresentanza degli interessi: il caso italiano', *Stato e mercato*, 29, 1990.

Caporaso J. A., 'The European Union and forms of state: Westphalian, regulatory or post-modern?', *Journal of Common Market Studies*, 1(34), 1996.

Cartocci R., *Fra Lega e chiesa. L'Italia in cerca di integrazione*, Il Mulino, Bologna, 1994.

Cassese, S. and Torchia L., 'The meso level in Italy', in L. J. Sharpe (ed.), *The Rise of Meso Government in Europe*, Sage, London, 1993.

Castells M., *High Technology, Space and Society*, Sage, Beverly Hills, California, 1985.

—— *The Informational City: Information Technology, Economic Restructuring and the Urban–Region Process*, Blackwell, Oxford, 1989.

Castles F. G. (ed.), *Families of Nations: Patterns of Policy Outcomes in Western Democracies*, Dartmouth, Aldershot, 1993.

Cawson A., *Corporatism and Political Theory*, Blackwell, Oxford, 1986.

Cazzola F., 'L'associazionismo istituzionalizzato', in M. Fedele (ed.), *Il sistema politico locale*, De Donato, Bari, 1983.

Cesare F. P. (ed.), *Dopo il familismo cosa?*, Angeli, Milan, 1992.

Charpentier J. and Engel C., *Les Régions de l'espace communautaire*, Presses Universitaires de Nancy, collection 'Cap Europe', Nancy, 1992.

Chauvel L., 'L'Europe des régions? Valeurs régionales et nationales en Europe', *Futuribles*, 54, 1995.

Cheshire P., 'Explaining the recent performance of the European Community's major urban areas', *Urban Studies*, 27(3), 1990.

Cheshire P. and Gordon I. (eds), *Territorial Competition in an Integrating Europe*, Aldershot, Avebury, 1995.

Chevallier J., 'Les compétences régionales', in Curapp, *Les Politiques Régionales*, Presses Universitaires de France, Paris, 1993.

Christiansen T., 'Second thoughts on Europe's third level: the European Union's committee of the regions', *Publius Journal of Federalism*, 2(26), 1996.

—— 'A European Meso-region? European perspectives on the Baltic Sea Region', in P. Joenniemi and B Lindström (eds), *The Restructuring of Political space around the Baltic Rim*, forthcoming, 1997.

—— 'Reconstructing space: from territorial politics to European multilevel governance', in K. E. Joergensen (ed.), *Reflective Approaches to European Governance*, Macmillan, London, 1997.

Clarke M. and Stewart J. D., *Choices for Local Government for the 1990s and Beyond*, Longman, London, 1991.

—— 'The local authority and the new community governance', *Regional Studies*, 28(2), 1994.

Clement, W., 'Der Regionalausschuß – mehr als ein Alibi', *Staatswissenschaften und Staatspraxis*, 3, 1993.

Clower R. W., 'Foundations of monetary theory', in R. W. Clower (ed.), *Monetary Theory*, Harmondsworth, Penguin, 1969a (first published 1967).

—— 'The Keynesian counter-revolution: a theoretical appraisal', in R. W. Clower (ed.), *Monetary Theory*, Harmondsworth, Penguin, 1969b.

Coleman D. and Jacek H. J. (eds), *Regionalism, Business Interests and Public Policy*, Sage, London, 1989.

Coleman J. S., *Foundations of Social Theory*, Harvard University Press, Cambridge, MA., 1990.

Colletis G. and Pecqueur B., *Les facteurs de la concurrence spatiale et la construction des territoires*, Documentation Française, Notes et Etudes Documentaires, no. 4769, 1993, 11.

Collinge M., 'La participation politique en Belgique', *Res publica*, 1990.

Conservative Party, *Manifesto 1992: The Best Future for Britain*, Conservative Council Central Office, London, 1992.

Cooke P. (ed.), *The Rise of the Rustbelt*, University College Press, London, 1995.

Cooke P. and Morgan K., *Learning Through Networking: Regional Innovation and the Lessons of Baden-Württemburg*, Regional Industrial Research Report 5, Department of City and Regional Planning, University of Wales College of Cardiff, Cardiff, 1990a.

—— *Industry, Training and Technology Transfer: The Baden-Württemburg System in Perspective*, Regional Industrial Research Report 6, Department of City and Regional Planning, University of Wales College of Cardiff, Cardiff, 1990b.

—— 'The network paradigm: new departures in corporate and regional development', *Environment and Planning*, 1993.

Cooke P., Moulaert F. and Swyngedouw E., *Towards Global Localization: The Computing and Communications Industries in Britain and France*, University College Press, London, 1992.

Cooke P., Price A. and Morgan K., 'Regulating regional economies: Wales and Baden-Württemberg in transition', in M. Rhodes (ed.), *The Regions and the New Europe*, Manchester University Press, Manchester, 1995.

Coopers and Lybrand, *Growing Business in the UK: Lessons from Continental Europe: Promoting Partnership for Local Economic Development and Business Support in the UK*, Business in the Community, London, 1992.

Corbetta P., Manheimer R. and Sani G., '5 aprile 1992: Italie ed Italiani', *Polis*, 2, 1993.

Cornford J. and Marwin S., 'Regional policy implications of utility regionalization', *Regional Politics and Policy*, 27, 1993.

Coulson A., *Devolving Power: The Case for Regional Government*, Fabian Society, London, 1990.

Courlet C. and Soulage B. (eds), *Industrie, territoires et politiques publiques*, L'Harmattan, Paris, 1994.

Coussy J., *Causes économiques et imaginaires économiques de la régionalisation*, Paper presented to the conference Pan-européen de relations internationales, Paris, 13–16 September 1995.

Croisat M. and Quermonne J.-L., *L'Europe et le fédéralisme*, Montchrestien, Paris, 1996.

Crouch C., *Industrial Relations and European State Traditions*, Clarendon Press, Oxford, 1993.

Crouch C. and Marquand D. (eds), *The New Centralism: Britain Out of Step with Europe?*, Blackwell, Oxford, 1989.

Crouch C. and Streeck W. (eds), *Les capitalismes en Europe*, La Découverte, Paris, 1995.

Crowther-Hunt L. and Peacock A., *Volume 11, Memorandum of Dissent*, Royal Commission on the Constitution, 1969–73, HMSO, London, 1973.

Cuadrado Roura, J., 'La política regional en los planes de desarollo', in R. Acosta España (ed.), *La España de las Autonomías*, vol.1, Espasa-Calpe, Madrid, 1981.

Curapp, *Les politiques régionales*, PUF, Paris, 1993.

Cutanda A. and Patricio J., 'Infrastructure and regional economic growth: the Spanish case', *Regional Studies*, 1(28), 1994.

Daalder H., 'On building consociational nations: the cases of the Netherlands and Switzerland', *International Social Science Journal*, 23, 1971.

—— 'Consociationalism, centre and periphery in the Netherlands', in P. Torsvic (ed.), *Mobilization, Centre–Periphery Structures and Nation-Building: A Volume in Commemoration of Stein Rokkan*, Oslo/Bergen, 1981.

—— 'English language sources for the study of Dutch politics', in *Compendium politiek en samenleving*, Alphen a/d Rijn, 1990a.

—— *Politiek en Historie, Opstellen over Nederlandse Politiek en Vergelijkende Politieke Wetenschap*, (eds). J. Th. J. van den Berg, B. A. G. M. Tromp, Amsterdam 1990b.

Daalder, H. and Irwin G. A. (eds), *Politics in the Netherlands: How Much Change?*, Pinter, London, 1989.

Darviche M. S., Genieys W., and Joana, J. 'Sociologie des élus régionaux en Languedoc-Roussillon et en Pays de Loire', *Pôle Sud*, 2, Spring, 1995.

Davis H. and Stewart J. D., *The Growth of Government by Appointment: Implications for Local Democracy*, Local Government Management Board, London, 1993.

Deaglio E., *La nuova borghesia e la sfida del capitalismo*, Laterza, Bari, 1991.

De Melo J. (ed.), *New Dimensions in Regional Integration*, Cambridge University Press, Cambridge, 1993.

De Miguel A., *Sociologia del franquismo. Analisis ideologico de los ministros del regimen*, (ed.) Euros, Barcelona, 1975.

Dente B., *Governare la frammentazione*, Il Mulino, Bologna, 1985.

—— 'Metropolitan governance reconsidered, or how to avoid errors of the third type', *Governance*, 3(1), January, 1990.

Department of the Environment, *New Regional Offices, Single Regeneration Budget, Cabinet Committee, Sponsor Ministers and City Pride*, Factsheets Nos 1–5, HMSO, London, 1993.

De Winter L., *The Belgian Legislator*, EUI, Florence, 1992.

Diamanti I., *La lega*, Donzelli, Rome, 1993.

Diamanti I. and Manheimer R. (eds), *Milano a Roma. Guida all'Italia elettorale del 1994*, Donzelli, Rome, 1994.

Doeringer P., Terkla D. and Topakian G., *Invisible Factors in Economic Development*, Oxford University Press, Oxford, 1988.

Douence J.C., 'The evolution of the 1982 regional reforms: an overview', in J. Loughlin and S. Mazey (eds), *The End of the French Unitary State?: Ten Years of Regionalization in France, 1982-1992*, Frank Cass, London, 1995.

Drevet J. F., Andre C. and Landaburu E., 'Regional consequences of the internal market', *Contemporary European Affairs*, 12(1), 1989.

Dulong R., *Les régions, l'Etat et la société locale*, PUF, Paris, 1978.

Duncan S. and Goodwin M., *The Local State and Uneven Development*, Polity, London, 1988.

Dunford, M., 'Winners and losers: the new map of economic inequality in the European Union', *European Urban and Regional Studies*, 1(2), 1994.

Dunford M. and Kafkalas G. (eds), *Cities and Regions in the New Europe*, Belhaven Press, London, 1992a.

—— 'The global–local interplay, corporate geographies and spatial development strategies in Europe', in M. Dunford and G. Kafkalas (eds), *Cities and Regions in the New Europe*, Belhaven Press, London, 1992b.

Durand J.-J., *L'Europe de la Démocratie chrétienne*, Editions Complexe, Paris, 1995.

Eissing R. and Kohler-Koch B., 'Inflation und Zerfaserung: Trends der Interessenvermittlung in der Europäischen Gemeinschaft', in W. Streeck (ed.), *Staat und Verbände*, Westdeutscher Verlag, Opladen, 1994.

Emmerich M. and Peck J., *Reforming the TECs*, Centre for Local Economic Strategies, Manchester, 1992.

Engel C., *Regionen in der EG. Rechtliche Vielfalt und integrationspolitische Rollensuche. Gutachten im Auftrag der Staats- und Senatskanzleien der Länder*, Bonn, 1993.

—— 'Regionen im Netzwerk europaïscher Politik', in U. Bullman (ed.), *Die*

Politik der dritten Ebene. Regionen im Europa der Union, Nomos, Baden-Baden, 1994.

Engel C. and Van Ginderachter J., *Le pouvoir régional et local dans la Communauté européenne*, Pédone, Paris, 1992.

English Regional Associations, *A Survey of the English Regional Associations*, 1 June, South East Regional Planning Conference, London, 1995.

Eskelinen H. and Snickars F. (eds), *Competitive European Periphery*, Springer, Berlin, 1995.

Esping Andersen G. (ed.), *Changing Classes*, Sage, London, 1993.

Esser J. and Hirsch J., 'The crisis of Fordism and the dimension of a "post-Fordist" regional and urban structure', *International Journal of Urban and Regional Studies*, 3(13), 1989.

Evans P. B., 'Building an integrative approach to international and domestic politics', in P. B. Evans., H. K. Jacobson and R. D. Putnam (eds), *Double-Edged Diplomacy: International Bargaining and Domestic Politics*, University of California Press, Berkeley, California, 1993.

Evans P. B, Jacobson H. K. and Putnam R. D. (eds), *Double-Edged Diplomacy: International Bargaining and Domestic Politics*, University of California Press, Berkeley, California, 1993.

Fagerberg J. and Verspagen B., 'Heading for divergence? Regional growth in Europe reconsidered', *Journal of Common Market Studies*, 34(3), 1996.

Faure A., 'Les élus locaux à l'épreuve de la décentralisation', *Revue française de la science politique*, 44(3), 1994.

Ferguson A., *An Essay on the History of Civil Society, 1767*, Edinburgh University Press, Edinburgh, 1966.

Fontaine J., *L'articulation des politiques nationales et locales: la décentralisation du système éducatif des collèges et lycées dans l'académie de Rennes*, report for the ministre de l'Intérieur DGCL, Rennes, CRAP, 1990.

—— 'Une région, des lycées, un rectorat. L'incidence politique de la décentralisation en Bretagne', *Savoir*, 4(4), Oct.–Dec. 1992.

Fonteyn G., 'De Waalse regionalisten zijn even weg', *De Standaard*, 18 January 1996.

Friedberg E., 'Generalized political exchange, organizational analysis and public policy', in B. Marin (ed.), *Generalized Political Exchange: Antagonistic Cooperation and Integrated Policy Circuits*, Westview Press, Boulder, Colorado, 1990.

—— *Le pouvoir et la règle*, Seuil, Paris, 1993.

Fua G. and Zacchia C. (eds), *Industrializzazione senza frattura*, Il Mulino, Bologna, 1993.

Fuhrmann-Mittlmaier D., *Die deutschen Länder im Prozeß der europäischen Einigung*, Ducker und Humblot, Berlin, 1991

Fürst D. *et al.*, *Regionalverbände im Vergleich,*, Nomos, Baden-Baden, 1990

Galasso G., *Passato e presente del meridionalismo*, Guida, Naples, 1978.

Gambetta D., *Trust: Making and Breaking Cooperative Relations*, Basil Blackwell, Oxford, 1988.

Garcia Barbancho A., *Disparidades Regionales y Ordenación del Territorio*, Ariel, Barcelona, 1979.

Garmise S., 'Economic development strategies in Emilia-Romagna', in M. Rhodes (ed.), *Regions in the New Europe*, Manchester University Press, Manchester, 1995.

Garraud P., 'Le processus autonomique et la fin de l'exception espagnole', in R. Balme, P. Garraud, V. Hoffman-Martinot and E. Ritaine (eds), *Le territoire pour politiques: variations européennes*, L'Harmattan, Paris, 1994.

Garside P. L. and Hebbert M., *British Regionalism 1900–2000*, Mansell, London, 1989.

Gemdev, *L'intégration régionale dans le monde*, Karthala, Paris, 1994.

Genieys W., *Les élites face à l'Etat. L'institutionnalisation des élites périphériques espagnoles*, PhD dissertation in political science, University of Paris I, 1994.

—— 'Les élites périphériques espagnoles face au changement de régime', *Revue française de science politique*, 4, 1996.

Gerbaux F. and Muller P., 'Les interventions économiques locales', *Pouvoirs*, 'La Décentralisation', 60, 1992.

Giblin-Delvallet, *La région: territoires politiques*, Fayard, Paris, 1990.

Gilbert G., 'The finances of the French Regions in retrospect', in J. Loughlin and S Mazey (eds), *The End of the French Unitary State? Ten Years of Regionalization in France, 1982-1992*, Frank Cass, London, 1995.

Giner S., 'Nationalismo etnico: centro y periferia en España', in F. Hernandez and F Mercade (eds), *Estruturas sociales y cuestión nacional en España*, Ariel, Barcelona, 1986.

Giner S. and Moreno L, 'Centro y periferia: la dimension étnica de la sociedad espanola', in S. Giner (ed.), *España. Sociedad y Política*, Espasa Calpe, Madrid, 1990.

Ginsborg P. (ed.), *Stato dell'Italia*, Il Saggiatore-Mondadori, Milan,1994.

—— *Storia d'Italia dal dopoguerra ad oggi. Società e política*, Einaudi, Turin, 1989.

Gipouloux F., *Regional Economic Strategies in East Asia: A Comparative Perspective*, Maison franco-japonaise, Tokyo, 1994.

Goetz K., 'National governance and European integration: intergovernmental relations in Germany', *Journal of Common Market Studies*, 1(33), 1995.

Gore C., *Regions in Question: Space, Development Theory and Regional Policy*, Mansell, London, 1984.

Grabherr G., *The Embedded Firm. On the Socioeconomics of Industrial Networks*, Routledge, London, 1993.

Grande E., *Vom Nationalstaat zur europäischen Politikverflechtung. Expansion und Transformation moderner Staatlichkeit – untersucht am Beispiel der Forschungs – und Technologiepolitik, Habilitationsschrift*, University of Constance, Constance, 1993.

Grant W., *Pressure Groups, Politics and Democracy in Britain*, Hemel Hempstead, Philip Allan, 1989.

Graziano L, *Clientelismo e sistema politico: il caso dell'Italia*, Franco Angeli, Milan, 1980.

Greenwood J., Grote J. and Ronit K. (eds), *Organized Interests and the European Community*, Sage, London, 1992.

Greer P., *Transforming Central Government: The Next Steps Initiative*, Open University Press, Milton Keynes, 1994.

Gremion P., *Le Pouvoir périphérique*, Editions du Seuil, Paris, 1976.

Grey C., *Government Beyond the Centre: Sub-National Politics in Britain*, Macmillan, London, 1994.

Gribaudi G., *Mediatori, antropologia del potere democristiano nel Mezzogiorno*, Rosenberg and Sellier, Turin, 1980.

—— *A Eboli. Il mondo meridionale in cent'anni di trasformazioni*, Marsilio Ed, Venice, 1990.

—— *Mediatori. Antropologia del potere democristiano nel Mezzogiorno*, Rosenberg/Sellier, Turin, 1991.

Grote J., 'Small firms in the European economy: modes of production, governance and territorial interest representation in Italy and Germany', in J. Greenwood, J. Grote and K. Ronit (eds), *Organized Interests and the European Community*, Sage, London, 1992.

—— 'Diseconomies in space: traditional sectoral policies of the EC, the European technology community and their effects of regional disparities', in R. Leonardi (ed.), *The Regions and the European Community*, Frank Cass, London, 1993.

Guellec A. (ed.), *La région, la marge de manœuvre européenne*, Presses Universitaires de Rennes, Rennes, 1995.

Guillorel H., 'The social bases of regionalism in France: the Breton case', in J. Coakley (ed.), *The Social Origins of Nationalist Movements: The Contemporary West European Experience*, Sage, London, 1991.

Gummer J., *John Gummer Announces Measures to Bring New Localism to Improved Government Services*, news release, 4 November, Department of the Environment, HMSO, London, 1993.

Gunlicks A., 'Introduction', *Publius*, 19 (no. 4, special issue on Federalism and Intergovernmental Relations in West Germany, ed. by A. Gunlicks), 1989.

Gunther R., 'Spain: the very model of the modern elite settlement', in J. Higley and R. Gunther (eds), *Elites and Democratic Consolidation in Latin America and Southern Europe*, Cambridge University Press, Cambridge, 1992.

Gunther R., Sani G. and Shabad G., *El sistema de partidos politicos en España. Genesis y evolución*, Centro de Investigaciones Sociológicas, Madrid, 1986.

Habert P., Perrineau P. and Ysmal C., *Le vote Eclaté. Les élections régionales et cantonales des 22 et 29 mars 1992*, Presses de la FNSP, Paris, 1992.

Hadjimichalis C. and Sadler D. (eds), *Europe at the Margins: New Mosaics of Inequality*, John Wiley, Chichester, 1995.

Hall P., 'Forces shaping urban Europe', *Urban Studies*, 30(6), 1993.

Ham C., *Health Policy in Britain: The Politics and Organisation of the National Health Service*, 3 edn, Macmillan, London, 1992.

Hambleton R., 'Future directions for urban government in Britain and America', *Journal of Urban Affairs*, 12(1), 1990.

Harding A., Dawson J. and Evans R.(eds), *European Cities Towards 2000*, Manchester University Press, Manchester, 1993.

Harding A. and Le Galès P., 'Globalization and urban politics', in A. Scott (ed.), *The Limits of Globalization*, Routledge, London, 1997.

Harvey D., *The Conditions of Postmodernity*, Blackwell, Oxford, 1989.

Harvie C., *The Rise of Regional Europe*, Routledge, London, 1994.

Hebbert M. and Machin H. (eds), *Regionalization in France, Italy and Spain*, London School of Economics, London, 1984.

Hechter M. and Brustein W., 'Regional modes of production and patterns of State formation in Europe', *American Journal of Sociology*, 85, 1980.

Heiberg M., 'Urban politics and rural culture: Basque nationalism', in S.

Rokkan and D. W. Urwin (eds), *The Politics of Territorial Identity: Studies in European Regionalism*, Sage, London, 1982.

Heinze R. G. and Schmid J., 'Mesokorporatistische Strategien im Vergleich: Industrieller Strukturwandel und die Kontingenz politischer Steuerung in drei Bundesländern', in W. Streeck (ed.), *Staat und Verbände*, Westdeutscher Verlag, Opladen, 1994.

Heinze R. G. and Voelzkow H., 'Regionalisierung der Strukturpolitik in Nordrhein-Westfalen', in B. Blanke (ed.), *Staat und Stadt. Systematische, vergleichende und problemorientierte Analysen 'dezentraler' Politik*, Westdeutscher Verlag, Opladen, 1991.

——(eds) *Die Regionalisierung der Strukturpolitik in Nordrhein-Westfalen*, Westdeutscher Verlag, Opladen, 1995.

Hellemans S. and Kitschelt H., 'Agalev en Ecolo als links-libertaire partijen, of de partijpolitisering van een nieuwe breuklijn', *Res Publica*, 1990.

Hendriks F., Raadschelders J. C. N. and Toonen T. A. J., 'Provincial repositioning in the Netherlands: some models and the impact of European integration', in U. Bullmann (ed.), *Die Politik der dritten Ebene: Regionen im Prozess der EG-Integration*, Nomos, 1994.

Heritier A., *Policy-Analyse, Kritik und Neuorientierung*, Westdeutscher Verlag, PVS Sonderheft 24, Opladen, 1993.

Heritier A. *et al.*, *Die Veränderung der Staatlichkeit in Europa*, Leske und Budrich, Opladen, 1994.

Her Majesty's Government, *The Civil Service: Continuity and Change*, CM 2627, HMSO, London, 1994.

Hernandez A., *Autonomía e integración en la segunda república*, Encuentro, Madrid, 1980.

Hernandez F. and Mercade F. (eds), *Estruturas sociales y cuestion nacional en Espana*, Ariel, Barcelona, 1986.

Hesse J. J. *et al.*, *Regionalisierte Wirtschaftspolitik*, Nomos, Baden-Baden, 1991.

Hesse J. J. and Benz A., *Die Modernisierung der Staatsorganisation*, Nomos, Baden-Baden, 1990.

Hessel B. and Mortelmans K., 'Decentralized government and Community law: conflicting institutional developments?', *Common Market Law Review*, 5(30), 1993.

Hettne B., 'The regional factor in the formation of a new world order', in Y. Sakamoto (ed.), *Global Transformation: Challenges to the State System*, United Nations University Press, New York, 1994.

Hirst P. and Zeitlin J. (eds), *Reversing Industrial Decline? Industrial Structure and Policy in Britain and her Competitors*, Berg, Oxford, 1989.

Hocking B., 'Regionalism: an international relations perspective', in M. Keating and J. Loughlin (eds), *The Political Economy of Regionalism*, Frank Cass, London, 1996.

Hofstede G., *Culture's Consequences: International Differences in Work-Related Values*, (abridged edition), Sage, London, 1984.

Hoggett P., 'A farewell to mass production? Decentralisation as an emergent private and public sector paradigm', in P. Hoggett and R. Hambleton (eds), *Decentralisation and Democracy: Localising Public Services*, School for Advanced Urban Studies, University of Bristol, Bristol, 1987.

Hogwood B., *The Integrated Regional Offices and the Single Regeneration*

Budget, Commission for Local Democracy, Research Report, no.15, London, 1994.

—— 'Developments in regional administration in England', *Journal of Regional and Federal Studies*, 1, 1995.

Hogwood B. and Keating M. (eds), *Regional Government in England*, Clarendon Press, Oxford, 1982.

Holmes M. and Reese N., 'Regions within a region: the paradox of the Republic of Ireland', in B. Jones and M. Keating. (eds), *The European Union and the Regions*, Clarendon Press, Oxford, 1995.

Hooghe L., *A Leap in the Dark: Nationalist Conflict and Federal Reform in Belgium*, Western Societies Program, occasional paper no. 27, Cornell University, Ithaca, New York, 1991.

—— 'Belgium: from regionalism to federalism', *Regional Politics and Policy*, 3(3), 1993.

—— 'Belgian federalism and the European Community', in J. Keating (ed.), *The European Union and the Regions*, Clarendon Press, Oxford, 1995.

—— 'Subnational mobilisation in the European Union', *West European Politics*, 18, 1995.

—— 'Belgium: a mission for European excellence. Federalization and European integration', in B. Dente and J. Sharpe (eds), *Policy-Making in Federal and Regional States*, Fondation Agnelli, Turin, 1996.

——(ed.) *Cohesion Policy and Subnational Mobilization*, Oxford University Press, Oxford, 1996.

Hooghe L. and Keating, M., 'The politics of European Union regional policy', *Journal of European Public Policy*, 1(3), 1994.

House of Commons, Committee Of Public Accounts, Thirty-third report. Regenerating the Inner Cities, House of Commons, Session 1989–90, vol. 216, HMSO, London, 1990.

House of Commons, Trade And Industry Committee, Fourth Report, Session 1994–95, HMSO, London, 1995.

House of Commons, Treasury And Civil Service Select Committee, Sixth Report, Session 1988–89, HMSO, London, 1989.

Hrbek R., 'Die doppelte Politikverflechtung', in R.Hrbek and U. Thaysen (eds), *Die deutschen Länder und die europäischen Gemeinschaften*, Nomos, Baden-Baden, 1986.

Hrbek R. and Weyand S., *Betrifft: Das Europa der Regionen*, Beck, München, 1994.

Humold C., 'Internationalization and the local state: democratic local governance reconsidered', report presented to the meeting of the ECPR, Bordeaux, May 1994.

Hutton W., 'The 30-30-40 society', *Regional Studies*, 29(8), 1995.

Huyse L., *De gewapende vrede. Politiek in België na 1945*, Kritak, Leuven, 1986.

Ignazi P and Katz R. (eds), *Politica in Italia. I fatti dell'anno e le interpretazioni*, Il Mulino, Bologna, 1995.

Igue J. O., 'Le Nigéria et ses périphéries frontalières', in D. Bach, J. Egg and J. Philippe. (eds), *Nigéria: un pouvoir en puissance*, Karthala, Paris, 1988.

Inglehart R., *Culture Shift in Advanced Industrial Society*, Princeton University Press, Princeton, 1990.

ISPO, 'Source book of the voters' study in connection with the 1991 general elections', *SOI*, Leuven, 1993.

Jerez Mir M., *Elites políticas y centros de extracción en España*, Centro de Investigaciones Sociológicas, Madrid, 1982.

Jessop B., 'Post-fordism and the State', in A. Amin (ed.), *Post-fordism*, Blackwell, Oxford, 1994.

—— 'The regulation approach, governance and post-fordism', *Economy and Society*, 3(24), 1995.

Jobert B. (ed.), *Le tournant néo-libéral*, L'Harmattan, Paris, 1994.

Jobert B. and Muller P., *L'Etat en Action*, PUF, Paris, 1987.

Jochimsen R., 'The regionalisation of structural policy: North Rhine-Westphalia in the Europe of the Regions', *German Politics* 1 (special issue on Federalism, Unification and European Integration), 1992.

John P., 'UK subnational offices in Brussels: diversification or regionalisation?', *Regional Studies*, 28(7), 1994.

John P. and Le Galès P., 'Is the grass greener on the other side? What went wrong with the French regions?', *Policy and Politics*, 4, 1996.

John P. and Whitehead A., 'English regionalism in the 1990's', *Policy and Politics*, 4, 1996.

Jones B., 'Wales. A developing political economy', in M. Keating and J. Loughlin (eds), *The Political Economy of Regionalism*, Frank Cass, London, 1996.

Jones B. and Keating M. (eds), *Regions in the European Community*, Oxford University Press, Oxford, 1995.

Kaldor N., 'The case for regional policies', *Scottish Journal of Political Economy*, 17, 1970.

Kantor, P., *The Dependent City Revisited: The Political Economy of Urban Development and Social Policy*, Westview Press, Boulder, Colorado, 1995.

Keating M., 'Is there a regional level of government in England?', *Studies in Public Policy*, 49, Centre for the Study of Public Policy, University of Strathclyde, Glasgow, 1979.

—— 'The rise and decline of micronationalism in mainland France', *Political Studies*, XXX111(1), 1985a.

—— 'Whatever happened to regional government?', *Local Government Studies*, 6(11), 1985b.

—— *State and Regional Nationalism: Territorial Politics and the European State*, Harvester Wheatsheaf, London, 1988.

—— *Comparative Urban Politics: Power and the City in the United States, Canada, Britain and France*, Edward Elgar, Aldershot, 1991.

—— 'Do the workers really have no country? Peripheral nationalism and socialism in the United Kingdom, France, Italy and Spain', in J. Coakley (ed.), *The Social Origins of Nationalist Movements*, Sage, London, 1992a

—— 'Regional autonomy in the changing state order: a framework of analysis', *Regional Politics and Policy*, II(3), 1992b.

—— 'Regions and regionalism in the European Community', *International Journal of Public Administration*, 3, 1993.

—— 'The political economy of regionalism', in M. Keating and J. Loughlin (eds), *The Political Economy of Regionalism*, Frank Cass, London, 1996a.

—— *Nations against the State: The New Politics of Nationalism in Quebec,*

Catalonia and Scotland, Macmillan, London, 1995; French edition, Presses de l'Université de Montréal, Montreal, 1996b.

Keating M. and Bleiman D., *Labour and Scottish Nationalism*, Macmillan, London, 1979.

Keating M. and Hooghe, L., 'By-passing the nation–state? Regions in the EU policy process', in J. J. Richardson (ed.), *Policy Making in the European Union*, Routledge, London, 1995.

Keating M. and Jones B. (eds), *Regions in the European Community*, Clarendon, Oxford, 1985.

Keohane R. O. and Hoffmann S., 'Institutional change in Europe in the 1980s', in R. O. Keohane and S. Hoffmann (eds), *The New European Community*, Westview Press, Boulder, Colorado, 1991.

Kerkhofs J. *et al.*, *De versnelde ommekeer. De waarden van Vlamingen, Walen en Brusselaars in de jaren negentig*, Lannoo & KBS, 1992.

Kickert W. J. M. and Van Vught F. A., *Public Policy and Administration Sciences in the Netherlands*, Harvester Wheatsheaf, Hemel Hempstead, 1995.

Kleinfeld R., *Mesokorporatismus in den Niederlanden*, Frankfurt/Main, 1990.

—— 'Strukturen und Prozesse der sozio-ökonomischen Interessenvermittlung in den Niederlanden', in, R. Kleinfeld and W. Luthardt (eds), *Interessenvermittlung und westliche Demokratien*, Marburg, 1993.

—— *Die Modernisierung des niederländischen Staates: Entwicklungen und Reformprozesse auf der mittleren Verwaltungsebene. Studie im Auftrage des IAT-Gelsenkirchen*, Hagen, 1994.

Kleinfeld R. and Hesse J. J., *Die Provinzen im politischen System der Niederlande*, Opladen, 1990.

Krafft A. and Ulrich G., *Chancen und Risiken regionaler Selbstorganisation*, Westdeutscher Verlag, Opladen, 1993.

Kriesi H., 'Federalism and pillarization: the Netherlands and Switzerland compared', *Acta Politica*, 4, 1990.

Kukawka P., 'Les interventions économiques des régions', in S. Wachter (ed.), *Politiques Publiques et Territoires*, L'Harmattan, Paris, 1989.

Kurth J. and Petras J. (eds), *Mediterranean Paradoxes: The Politics and Social Structure of Southern Europe*, Berg, Oxford, 1993.

Lafont R., *La révolution régionaliste*, Gallimard, Paris, 1967.

Laitin D. D., 'The civic culture at 30', *American Political Science Review*, 89(1), 1995.

Lane, J. E. and Ersson S. O., *Politics and Society in Western Europe*, Sage, London, 1991.

Lash S. and Urry J., *Economies of Signs and Space*, Sage, London, 1993.

Lax D. A. and Sebenius J. K., *The Manager as Negotiator: Bargaining for Cooperative and Competitive Gain*, The Free Press, New York, 1986.

Leach S. N., 'The missing regional dimension to the Local Government Review', *Regional Studies*, 28(8), 1994.

Leach S. N., Davis H., Game C. and Skelcher C., *After Abolition*, Institute of Local Government Studies, University of Birmingham, Birmingham, 1992

Le Bras H., *Les Trois France*, Odile Jacob, Paris, 1995.

Leca J., 'La gouvernance de la France sous la Vème République. Une perspective de sociologie comparative', in F. d'Arcy and L. Rouban, *De la*

Vème République à l'Europe, in honour of Jean-Louis Quermonne, Presses de Science Po, Paris, 1996.

Lecoq B. and Maillat D., 'New technologies and transformation of regional structures in Europe: the role of the milieu', *Entrepreneurship and Regional Development*, 4, 1992.

Le Galès P., 'Villes en compétition', in S. Biarez and J.-Y. Nevers (eds), *Politiques urbaines et gouvernement local*, Cerat, Grenoble, 1994.

—— 'Regional economic policies: an alternative to French economic dirigisme?', in J. Loughlin and S. Mazey (eds), *The End of the French Unitary State? Ten Years of Regionalization in France, 1982-1992*, Frank Cass, London, 1995.

—— 'Régulation, Gouvernance et Territoires', paper presented to the AFSP, Aix-en-Provence, April 1996, mimeo.

Le Galès P. and Harding A., 'Villes et Etats en Europe', in V. Wright and S. Cassese. (eds), *La restructuration de l'Etat en Europe*, La Découverte, Paris, 1996.

Le Galès P. and Mawson J., 'Contracts versus competitive bidding: rationalising urban policy programmes in England and France', *Journal of European Public Policy*, 2(2), 1995.

Le Galès P. and Thatcher M. (eds), *Les réseaux de politique publique. Débat autour des policy networks* L'Harmattan, Paris, 1995.

Leguil-Bayart J. F. (ed.), *La réinvention du capitalisme*, Karthala, Paris, 1994.

Lenoir R. and Lesourne J. (eds), *Où va l'Etat?*, Le Monde Editions, Paris, 1992.

Leonardi R. (ed.), *The Regions and the European Community*, Frank Cass, London, 1993.

—— 'Cohesion in the European Community: illusion or reality?', *West European Politics*, 4(16), 1993.

Leonardi R. and Nanetti R. Y. (eds), *The Regions and European Integration: The Case of Emilia-Romagna*, Pinter, London, 1990.

Leonardy U., 'Federation and Länder in German foreign relations: power-sharing in treaty-making and European affairs', *German Politics* 1 (special issue on Federalism, Unification and European Integration ed. by C. Jeffrey and R. Sturm), 1992.

Lequesne C., *Paris-Bruxelles. Comment de fait la politique européenne de la France*, FNSP, Paris, 1993.

—— 'La Commission européenne entre autonomie and dépendance', *Revue française de science politique*, 46(3), June 1996.

—— 'Les Etats membres de l'Union européenne: de la pertinence d'une approche institutionnelle', in J. Rideau (ed.), *Les Etats membres de l'Union européenne: adaptations, mutations, résistances*, Montchrestien, Paris, 1997.

Lewis N., *Inner City Regeneration: The Demise of Regional and Local Government*, Studies in Law and Politics, Open University Press, Milton Keynes, 1992.

Lijphart A., *The Politics of Accommodation: Pluralism and Democracy in the Netherlands*, Yale University Press, New Haven, Conn. (2nd rev. edn), 1975.

—— *Democracies, Patterns of Majoritarian and Consensus Government in Twenty-One Countries: A Reassessment*, Yale University Press, New Haven, Conn., 1984.

Linz J., 'Within-nation differences and comparisons: the eight Spains', in R. L.

Merrit and S. Rokkan (eds), *Comparing Nations*, Yale University Press, New Haven, Conn., 1966.

Linz J. J., 'State building and nation building', *European Review*, 1(4), 1993.

Linz J. L. and Montero J. R. (eds), *Crisis y cambio: electores y partidos en la España de los años ochenta*, Centro de Estudios Constitucionales, Madrid, 1986.

Lipietz A., 'De la régulation aux conventions: le grand bond en arrière?', *Actuel Marx*, 17, 1995.

Lipset S. M. and Rokkan S, 'Cleavage structure, party systems, and voter alignments: an introduction', in S. M. Lipset and S. Rokkan (eds), *Party Systems and Voter Alignments: Cross-National Perspectives*, Free Press, New York, 1967.

Llamares I., 'Estado y nacionalismo periféricos en la nueva política europea', *Sistema*, 124, 1995.

Lopez-Arangen E., *La Conciencia regional en el proceso autonómico español*, Centro Investigaciones Sociológicas, Madrid, 1983.

—— 'Nacionalismo, regionalismo y posnacionalismo en las Comunidades Autónomas del Estado español', *Razon y Fé*, 230, November 1994.

Lorca J. F., *El processo autónomico Andaluz*, Mezquita, Madrid, 1983.

Loughlin J., 'L'Etat-Nation et les Régions en Europe occidentale', *Revue de Science Administrative de la Méditerrannée*, April 1994.

—— 'Nation, state and region in Western Europe', in L. Beckemans (ed.), *Culture: the Building Stone of Europe 2002*, Presses Interuniversitaires d'Europe, Brussels, 1994.

Loughlin J. and Mazey S. (eds), *The End of the French Unitary State? Ten Years of Regionalization in France 1982-1992*, Frank Cass, London, 1994.

Lupo S., 'Usi e abusi del passato. Le radici dell'Italia di Putnam', *Meridiana*, 18, 1993.

Luyckx T. and Platel M., *Politieke geschiedenis van België*, Kluwer, Antwerpen, 1985.

Mabille X., *Histoire politique de la Belgique*, CRIPS, Bruxelles, 1986.

McAleavey P., 'The politics of European regional development policy: additionality in the Scottish coalfields', *Regional Politics and Policy*, 2(3), 1993.

—— 'European-funded strategies for regional economic development in Strathclyde and North Rhine-Westphalia', European Consortium of Political Research working paper, Madrid Sessions, 1994a.

—— 'The political logic of the EC structural funds budget: lobbying efforts by declining industrial regions', European University Institute working papers, Florence, 1994b.

Maddens B. *et al.*, *O dierbaar België? Het natiebewustzijn van Vlamingen en Walen*, SOI, Leuven, 1994.

Maddison A., *Dynamic Forces in Capitalist Development: A Long-Run Comparative View*, Oxford University Press, Oxford, 1991.

Majone G., 'Preservation of cultural diversity in a federal system: the role of the regions', in M. Tushnet, *Comparative Constitutional Federalism*, Greenwood Press, New York, 1990.

Marcet J., *Convergencia Democrática de Catalunya*, C.I.S, Madrid, 1987.

March J. and Olsen J. P. (eds), *Rediscovering Institutions: The Organizational Basis of Politics*, The Free Press, New York, 1988.

Marin B. (ed.), *Governance and General Exchange*, Westview Press, Boulder, Colorado, 1990a.

—— 'Generalized political exchange. Preliminary considerations', in B. Marin (ed.), *Governance and General Exchange*, Westview Press, Boulder, Colorado, 1990b.

Marks G., 'Structural policy in the European Community', in A. Sbragia (ed.), *Euro-Politics. Institutions and Policymaking in the 'New' European Community*, Brookings Institute, Washington, 1992.

Marks G., Hooghe L. and Blank K., 'European Integration since the 1980's: State-centric versus multi-level governance, *Journal of Common Market Studies*, 3(34), 1996.

Martin R., Sunley P. and Wills J., *Union Retreat and the Regions: The Shrinking Landscape of Organised Labour*, Jessica Kingsley/RSA, London, 1996.

Martins M. and Mawson J., 'The programming of regional development in the European Economic Community: supra-national or international decision-making?', *Journal of Common Market Studies*, 20(3), 1982.

Martins M., Mawson J. and Gibney J., 'The development of the European Community regional policy', in M. Keating and B. Jones (eds) *Regions in the European Community*, Clarendon, Oxford, 1985.

Marvin S. and Cornford J., 'Regional policy implications of utility regionalisation', *Regional Studies*, 27(2), 1993.

Mawson J., *Reorganisation and Regional Economic Policy: County, District and Region in North East England*, paper given at ESRC Regionalism and Devolution research seminar, 15 September, University of Strathclyde, Glasgow, 1993.

Mawson J., Beazley M., Burfitt A., Collinge C., Hall S., Loftman P., Nevin B., Srbljanim A. and Tilson B., *The Single Regeneration Budget: The Stocktake*, Association of County Councils, Association of District Councils, Association of Metropolitan Councils, by School of Public Policy, University of Birmingham, Birmingham, 1994.

Mawson J. and Skelcher C., 'Updating the West Midlands Regional Strategy', *Town Planning Review*, 51(2), 1980.

Mawson J. and Spencer K. M., 'Pillars of strength ? The government offices for the English regions', in S. Hardy, M. Hebbert and B. Malbon (eds), *Region-Building*, Regional Studies Association, Jessica Kingsley and RSA, London, 1996.

Mayer M., 'Urban governance in the post-fordist city', in P. Healey *et al.* (eds), *Managing Cities*, John Wiley, Chichester, 1995.

Mayntz R., 'Governing failures and the problem of governability: some comments on a theoretical paradigm', in J. Kooiman (ed.), *Modern Governance: New Government–Society Interactions*, Sage, London, 1993.

—— 'Föderalismus und die Gesellschaft der Gegenwart', in K.-H. Bentele, B. Reissert and R. Schettkat (eds), *Die Reformfähigkeit von Industriegesellschaften*, Campus, Frankfurt, 1995.

Mazey S., 'Regional lobbying in the New Europe', in M. Rhodes (ed.), *The Regions and the New Europe*, Manchester University Press, Manchester, 1995.

Mazey S. and Richardson J. (eds), *Lobbying in the European Community*, Oxford University Press, Oxford, 1993.

Mbembe A., 'Déflation de l'Etat, civilité et citoyenneté en Afrique noire', *Gemdev*, 1994.

Mény Y. (ed.), *Dix ans de régionalisation en Europe. Bilan et perspectives*, Cujas, Paris, 1982a.

—— 'Introduction', in Y. Mény (ed.), *Dix ans de régionalisation en Europe. Bilan et perspectives*, Cujas, Paris, 1982b.

—— 'Should the Community regional policy be scrapped?', *Common Market Law Review*, August 1982.

—— *Les politiques du mimétisme institutionnel*, L'Harmattan, Paris, 1993.

Mény Y. and Wright V. (eds), *Centre–Periphery Relations in Western Europe*, Allen and Unwin, London, 1985.

Meridiana, 'Melfi', special edition, 21, 1994.

Merloni F. 'Perché è in crisi il regionalismo', *Democrazia e Diritto*, 1, 1985.

Metcalfe L., 'Conviction politics and dynamic conservatism: Mrs Thatcher's managerial revolution', *International Political Science Review*, 14(4), October 1993.

Mingione E., 'Italy: the resurgence of regionalism', *International Affairs*, 3(69), 1993.

—— 'New aspects of marginality in Europe', in C. Hadjimichalis and D. Sadler (eds), *Europe at the Margins*, John Wiley, Chichester, 1995.

Ministère de l'intérieur et de l'aménagement du territoire, DGCL, *Guide des ratios des Régions 1992*, 7th edition, August 1994.

—— *Les Collectivités Locales en chiffres*, La documentation française, 1993.

—— *Les Collectivités Locales en chiffres*, La documentation française, 1994.

Ministro per gli Affari Regionali, *Rapporto 1982 sullo stato delle autonomie*, Istituto Poligrafico e Zecca dello Stato, Rome, 1982.

Molle W. and Cappelin R. (eds), *Regional Impact of Community Policies in Europe*, Gower, Aldershot, 1988.

Morass M., *Regionale Interessen auf dem Weg in die Europäische Union. Strukturelle Entwicklung und Perspektiven der Interessenvermittlung österreichischer und deutscher Landesakteure im Rahmen der Europäischen Integration*, (Schriften des Instituts für Föderalismusforschung Bd. 60), Braunmüller, Vienna, 1994.

Morata F., 'Regions and the European Community: a comparative analysis of four Spanish Regions', *Regional Politics and Policy*, 2(1/2), 1992.

—— 'La géométrie variable appliquée à "l'Etat des Autonomies": un bilan de la décentralisation politique en Espagne', in Forum européen 1994, *Régionalisation en Europe* (R. Dehousse and Y. Mény eds)., Institut universitaire européen, Florence, 1994.

—— 'L'Eurorégion et le réseau C6: l'émergence du suprarégionalisme en Europe du Sud?', *Pôle Sud*, 3, 1995.

Moravcsik A., 'Introduction: Integrating international and domestic theories of international bargaining', in P. B. Evans, H. K. Jacobson and R. D. Putnam (eds), *Double-Edged Diplomacy: International Bargaining and Domestic Politics*, University of California Press, Berkeley, 1993.

—— 'Preferences and power in the European Community: a liberal intergovernmentalist approach', *Journal of Common Market Studies*, 31, 1993.

Morawitz R. and Kaiser W., *Die Zusammenarbeit zwischen Bund und Ländern bei Vorhaben der Europäischen Union*, Europa Union Verlag, Bonn, 1994.

Morgan K., 'Innovating by networking: new models of corporate and regional development', in M. Dunford and G. Kafkalas (eds), *Cities and Regions in the New Europe*, Belhaven, London, 1992.

Morgan K.O., *Rebirth of a Nation. Wales, 1880-1980*, Oxford University Press, Oxford, 1980.

Morran G., 'Time for a dialogue on the regions', *Local Government Chronicle*, 19 February 1993.

Morvan Y. and Marchand M.-J., *L'intervention économique des régions*, Montchrestien, Paris, 1994.

Murray R., *Local Space: Europe and the New Regionalism*, CLES, Manchester, 1991.

Mutti A., 'La questione meridionale negli anni '90', in F. P. Cesare (ed.), *Dopo il familismo cosa?*, Angeli, Milan, 1992.

Myrdal G. *Economic Theory and Underdeveloped Regions*, Gerald Duckworth, London, 1957.

Nanetti R., *Growth and Territorial Politics: The Italian Model of Capitalism*, Frances Pinter, London, 1989.

—— 'EU cohesion and territorial restructuring in the Member States', in L. Hooghe (ed.), *Cohesion Policy and European Integration*, Oxford University Press, Oxford, 1996.

National Audit Office, *Regenerating the Inner Cities*, HMSO, London, 1990.

Negrier E., 'Intégration européenne et échanges politiques territorialisés', *Pôle Sud*, 3, 1995.

Nemery J.-C., 'Les institutions territoriales françaises à l'épreuve de l'Europe', in J.-C. Nemery and S. Wachter (eds), *Entre l'Europe et la décentralisation. Les institutions territoriales françaises*, DATAR/Editions de l'Aube, Paris, 1993a.

—— 'Les initiatives régionales. Un bilan de dix ans de décentralisation', in G. Gilbert and A. Delcamp (eds), La Décentralisation Dix Ans Après, *LGDJ, Paris, 1993b.*

Nemery J.-C. and Wachter S., *Entre l'Europe et la décentralisation. Les institutions territoriales françaises*, DATAR/Editions de l'Aube, Paris, 1993.

Nijkamp P., 'Towards a network of regions: the United States of Europe', *European Planning Studies*, 2(1), 1993.

Nordlinger E.A., 'Taking the State seriously', in S. N. Huntington and M. Weiner (eds), *Understanding Political Development*, Little Brown, Boston, 1987.

Northern Region Strategy Team, *Strategic Plan for the Northern Region*, Northern Regional Strategy Team, Newcastle, 1977.

Oberti M., 'Traditions démocratiques, développement économique et diversité régionale en Italie', *Revue française de science politique*, 44, 1994.

O'Brien R., *Global Financial Integration: The End of Geography*, Royal Institute of International Affairs, London, 1992.

Oddo B. and Poinat F., 'L'inégal développement des régions européennes: la prépondérance des effets nationaux', *Economie et Statistique*, 222, 1989.

Ollivaux J. P., *La Décentralisation - La région et l'aménagement du territoire*, Syros, Paris, 1985.

Oltra B., Mercade F. and Hernandez F., *La ideologia nacional catalana*, Anagrama, Barcelona, 1981.

Paci M., *Il mutamento della struttura sociale in Italia*, Il Mulino, Bologna, 1992.

—— (ed.), *Le dimensioni delle disuguaglianza*, Il Mulino, Bologna, 1993.

Palard J., *L'aménagement du territoire à l'épreuve de la décentralisation et de l'intégration européenne*, Librairies techniques/CNRS/GRAL, Annuaire des collectivités locales, Paris, 1993.

Pallida S., 'L'anamorphose de l'Etat-nation: le cas italien', *Cahiers internationaux de sociologie*, XCIII, 1992.

Palloix, C., *Les marchands et l'industrie. Un essai sur les rapports entre la société et l'économie*, ERSI, Amiens, 1993.

Papadopoulos Y., *Complexité sociale et politiques publiques*, Montchrestien, Paris, 1995.

Parkinson M., Bianchini F., Dawson J., Evans R. and Harding A., *Urban Change and the Function of Cities in Europe: A Report to the Commission of the European Communities*, John Moores University, Liverpool, 1992.

Parri L., 'Territorial politics and political exchange; American federalism and French unitarism reconsidered', in B. Marin (ed.), *Governance and General Exchange*, Campus Verlag, Frankfurt, 1990.

—— *Due regioni per la piccola impresa*, Franco Angeli, Milan, 1993.

Pasquino G., 'La politica al posto di comando: le fonti del mutamento in Italia', *Polis*, 3, 1988.

—— 'La politica ecclissata dalla tradizione civica', *Polis*, 2, 1994.

Pastori G., 'Le regioni senza regionalismo', *Il Mulino*, 268, 1980.

Pelletier F., 'La politique de l'environnement du Conseil Régional de Picardie', in Curapp, *Les Politiques Régionales*, Presses Universitaires de France, 1993.

Pennings P., *Verzuiling en ontzuiling: de locale verschillen. Opbouw, instandhouding en neergang van plaatselijke zuilen in verschillende delen van Nederland na 1880*, Kampen, 1991.

Perez-Agote A., 'Silence collectif et violence politique. La radicalisation sociale du nationalisme basque', *Espaces et Sociétés*, 70/71, 1992.

Perez-Diaz V., 'L'invention d'une tradition démocratique', in D. Schnapper and H. Mendras (eds), *Six manières d'être européen*, Gallimard, Paris, 1990.

—— 'Governability and the scale of governance: mesogovernments in Spain', in *Institut de Ciènces Politics i Socials-working papers*, 6, June 1990.

—— *The Return of Civil Society: The Emergence of a Democratic Spain*, Harvard University Press, Cambridge, (1st edn 1987), 1993.

—— *La primacia de la sociedad civil*, Alianza Editorial, Madrid, 1994.

Perrons D., 'The regions and the Single Market', in M. Dunford and G. Kafkalas (eds), *Cities and Regions in a New Europe*, Belhaven Press, London, 1992.

Peters B. G., 'Bureaucratic politics and the institutions of the European Community', in A. M. Sbragia (ed.), *Europolitics*, Washington, 1992.

Peters G. and Savoie D. J. (eds), *Governance in a Changing Environment*, McGill-Queen's Press, Montreal, 1995.

Petschen S., *La Europa de las regiones*, Generalitat de Catalunya, Barcelona, 1993.

Piattoni S., 'Local political classes and economic development. The cases of Abruzzo and Puglia in the 1970s and 1980s', in M. Keating and J. Loughlin (eds), *The Political Economy of Regionalism*, Frank Cass, London, 1996.

Pickvance C., 'Introduction: the institutional context of local economic development', in M. Harloe, C. Pickvance and J. Urry (eds), *Place, Policy and Politics: Do Localities Matter?*, Unwin Hyman, London, 1990.

Piore M. and Sabel C., *The Second Industrial Divide: Possibilities for Prosperity*, Basic Books, New York, 1984.

Pizzorno A., *I soggetti del pluralismo*, Il Mulino, Bologna, 1980.

—— 'Le difficoltà del consociativismo', *Le radici della politica assoluta*, Feltrinelli, Milan, 1993.

—— 'Dal consociativismo a nuovi scheriamenti di classe?', paper presented at the conference *50 ans d'histoire républicaine*, University of Pisa, Pisa, 1995.

Pole Sud, special edition, 'L'Europe du Sud', 3, 1995.

Politix, 'Incertitudes italiennes', 30 (Italy special), 1995.

Pongy M. and Saez G., *Politiques culturelles en Europe*, L'Harmattan, Paris, 1993.

Porla G., Marcou G. and Bosch N. (eds), *Investissements publics et régions*, L'Harmattan, Paris, 1994.

Postel-Vinay, K., *Japanese Actors and Transnational Relations in the Zone of the Sea of Japan,* Institut d'etudes politiques de Paris*, Paris, 1996.*

Pourtier R., 'Encadrement territorial et production de la nation', in E. Terray (ed.), L'Etat contemporain en Afrique*, L'Harmattan, Paris, 1987.*

Preteceille E., 'Social restructuring and French local government', in C. Pickvance and E. Preteceille (eds), *State Restructuring and Local Power*, Frances Pinter, London, 1991.

Putnam R. D., 'Diplomacy and domestic politics: the logic of two-level games', *International Organization*, 42, 1988a.

—— 'Rendimento istituzionale e cultura politica', *Polis*, 3, 1988b.

—— *Making Democracy Work: Civic Traditions in Modern Italy*, Princeton University Press, Princeton, NJ, 1993.

Putnam R. D., Leonardi R. and Nanetti R. Y., *La pianta e le radici. Il radicamento dell'istituto regionale nel sistema politico italiano*, Il Mulino, Bologna, 1985.

—— *Making Democracy Work: Civic Traditions in Modern Italy*, Princeton University Press, Princeton, NJ, 1993.

Putnam R. D., Pavoncello F., Leonardi R. and Nanetti R., 'L'évaluation de l'activité régionale: le cas italien', *Pouvoirs*, 19, 1981.

Pyke F., Beccatini G. and Sengenberger W., *International Districts and Inter-Firms Cooperation*, BIT, Geneva, 1990.

Quermonne J. L., 'Vers un régionalisme fonctionnel?', *Revue française de science Politique*, 13(4), 1963.

Quevit M. *et al.*, *L'impact régional de 1992. Les régions de tradition industrielle*, De Boeck-Wesmael, Brussels, 1991.

Rangeon F., 'Les politiques régionales: le cas de la Picardie', in Curapp, *Les Politiques Régionales*, Presses Universitaires de France, Paris,1993.

Rehfeld D., 'Disintegration and reintegration of production clusters in the Ruhr area', in Cooke P. (ed.), *The Rise of the Rustbelt*, ULC Press, London, 1995.

Rémond B., *La région*, Montchrestien, Paris, 1993.

Renzsch W., *Finanzverfassung und Finanzausgleich*, Dietz, Bonn, 1991.

Ress G., 'The constitution and the Maastricht Treaty: between co-operation and Conflict', in K. H. Goetz and P. J. Cullen (eds), *Constitutional Policy in Unified Germany*, Frank Cass, London, 1995.

Rhodes M. (ed.), *The Regions and the New Europe: Patterns in Core and Periphery Development*, Manchester University Press, Manchester, 1995a.

—— 'Regional development and employment in Europe's southern and western peripheries', in M. Rhodes (ed.), *Regions in the New Europe*, Manchester University Press, Manchester, 1995b.

Rhodes R. A. W., *Beyond Westminster and Whitehall: The Sub-Central Governments of Britain*, Routledge, London, 1988.

Ritaine E., 'La modernité localisée? Leçons italiennes sur le développement régional', *Revue française de science politique*, 2, 1989.

—— 'Territoire: espace du jeu politique', *Quaderni*, 13–14, 1991.

—— 'Italie: Territoires au bord de la crise politique', in R. Balme, P. Garraud, V. Hoffman-Martinot and E. Ritaine (eds), *Le territoire pour politiques: variations européennes*, L'Harmattan, Paris, 1994a.

—— 'Territoire et politique en Europe du Sud: actualisation', *Revue française de science politique*, 44(1), 1994b.

—— *Hypothèses pour le sud de l'Europe: territoires et médiations*, Working paper Centre R. Schuman, Institut universitaire européen, Paris, 1996.

Roberts P., 'Managing the strategic planning and development of regions: lessons from a European perspective', *Regional Studies*, 8(27), 1993.

Robins R.S., *Political Institutionalisation and the Integration of Elites*, Sage, London, 1976.

Robinson F. and Shaw K., *Who Runs the North?*, UNISON, Northern Region, Newcastle-upon-Tyne, 1994.

Rodriguez-Pose A., 'Struttura sociale et crescita regionale nell'Europa della ristrutturazione socio-economica', *Stato e mercato*, 1997.

Rokkan S. and Urwin D., *The Politics of Territorial Identity*, Beverly Hills, Sage, California, 1982.

Rondin J., *Le Sacre des Notables - La France en Décentralisation*, Fayard, Paris, 1985.

Roniger L. and Günes-Ayata A., *Democracy, Clientelism and Civil Society*, Lynne Rienner, Boulder, Colorado, 1994.

Rotelli E., 'Dal regionalismo alla regione', in E. Rotelli (ed.), *Dal regionalismo alla regione*, Il Mulino, Bologna, 1973.

Ruggie J., 'Territoriality and beyond: problematizing in international relations', *International Organisation*, 47, 1993.

Sack R., *Human Territoriality: Its Theory and History*, Cambridge University Press, Cambridge, 1986.

Saidj L. (ed.), *Les Finances régionales*, Economica, Paris, 1992.

Salvati M., 'La crisi politica 1992/1994: come uscirne?' (with contributions by M. Cammelli, M. Paci, G. Pasquino and C. Trigilia), *Stato e mercato*, 42, December 1994.

Sapir A., 'Le régionalisme et la nouvelle théorie du commerce international sonnent-ils le glas du GATT?', *Politique Etrangère*, 2, 1993.

Savelli G., *Che cose vuole la Lega*, Longanesi, Milan, 1992.

Savy M. and Veltz P., *Europe 2000: Outlook of the Development of the Community's Terrritory*, European Union, Luxemburg, 1991.

——(eds) *Economie globale et réinvention du local*, DATAR/Editions de l'Aube, La Tour d'Aigues, 1995.

Scharpf F. W., 'Die Politikverflechtungs-Falle: Europäische Integration und deutscher Föderalismus', *Politische Vierteljahresschrift*, 26, 1985.

—— 'Games real actors could play: the challenge of complexity', *Journal of Theoretical Politics*, 3, 1991.

—— 'Europäisches Demokratiedefizit und deutscher Föderalismus', *Staatswissenschaften und Staatspraxis*, 3, 1992.

——(ed.) *Games in Hierarchies and Networks: Analytical and Empirical Approaches to the Study of Governance Institutions*, Campus Verlag, Frankfurt, 1993.

Scharpf F. W., Reissert B. and Schnabel F., *Politikverflechtung. Theorie und Empirie des kooperativen Föderalismus in der Bundesrepublik*, Scriptor, Kronberg, 1976.

—— 'Policy effectiveness and conflict avoidance in intergovernmental policy formation', in K. Hanf and F. Scharpf (eds), *Inter-Organizational Policy-Making*, Sage, London, 1978.

Schmidtke O., 'The populist challenge to the Italian nation–state: the Lega Lombarda/Nord', *Regional Politics and Policy*, 3(3), 1993.

Schmitter C. P., *Democratic Theory and Neocorporatist Practice*, working paper, Institut universitaire européen, Florence, 1983.

Schmitter P. and Lanzalaco L., 'Regions and the organization of business interests', in W. Coleman and H. Jacek (eds), *Regionalism, Business Interest and Public Policy*, Sage, London, 1989.

Scott A., *Technopolis: High Technology Industry and Regional Development in Southern California*, University of California Press, California, 1993.

Scott A., Peterson J. and Millar D., 'Subsidiarity: a Europe of the Regions V. The British constitution', *Journal of Common Market Studies*, 1(32), 1994.

Sharpe L. J., (ed.), *The Rise of Meso-Government in Europe*, Sage, London, 1993a.

—— 'The United Kingdom: the disjointed meso', in L. J. Sharpe (ed.), *The Rise of Meso-Government in Europe*, Sage, London, 1993b.

—— 'The European Meso, an appraisal', in L. J. Sharpe (ed.), *The Rise of Meso-Government in Europe*, Sage, London, 1993c.

—— 'Regional planning and regional government: an understated link', *Workshop on The Political Economy of Regionalism, European Consortium for Political Research Joint Sessions*, Madrid, 1994.

Shaw K., 'The development of a new urban corporatism', *Regional Studies*, 3(27), 1993.

Shaw K., Robinson F. and Curran M. (forthcoming), 'Non-elected agencies and the new quangocrats: A profile of board membership in the North East of England', *Regional Studies*, 1996.

Sidjanski D. and Ayberg U. (eds), *L'Europe du sud dans la Communauté européenne. Analyse comparative des groupes d'intérêts et de leur insertion dans le réseau communautaire*, PUF, Paris, 1990.

Skelcher C. and Davis H., *The Membership of Local Appointed Bodies*, Local and Central Government Relations Research no. 35, Joseph Rowntree Foundation, York, 1995.

Smith A., *L'intégration communautaire face au territoire. Les fonds structurels en milieu rural en France, en Espagne et au Royaume Uni*, PhD in political science, IEP de Grenoble, March 1995.

—— *L'Europe au miroir du local. Les fonds structurels en France, en Espagne et au Royaume-Uni*, L'Harmattan, Paris, 1996.

Smith A. and Smyrl M., 'A la recherche d'interlocuteurs ... La Commission Européenne et le développement territorial en France', *Sciences de la Société*, 34, February 1995.

Smith N., 'Remaking scale: competition and cooperation postnational Europe', in H. Eskelinen and P. Snickars (eds), *Competitive European Periphery*, Springer, Berlin, 1995.

Smits J., 'Democratie op straat: een analyse van de betogingen in België', *Acco*, Leuven, 1984.

—— 'De spreiding van betogingen in België', *Res publica*, 1995.

Sorenson E., 'On the concept of governance', paper presented at the conference of tthe European Consortium of Political Research, Bordeaux, May 1995.

Stewart J. and Stoker G., 'Introduction', in J. Stewart and G. Stoker (eds), *The Future of Local Government*, Macmillan, London, 1989.

Stewart M., *Regionalism, Devolution and Economic Dynamism: The Shifting Institutional Framework?*, paper given at ESCR Regionalism and Devolution Research Seminar, 9 May, London School of Economics, London, 1994a.

—— 'Between Whitehall and town hall: the realignment of urban regeneration policy in England', *Policy and Politics*, 22(2), 1994b.

Stöhr W. B. (ed.), *Global Challenge and Local Response: Initiatives for Economic Regeneration in Contemporary Europe*, Mansell, London, 1990.

Stoker G., 'Creating a local government for a post-fordist society: the Thatcherite project', in J. Stewart and G. Stoker (eds), *The Future of Local Government*, Macmillan, Basingstoke, 1989.

—— 'Local governance, a conceptual challenge', paper presented at the conference of the European Consortium of Political Research, Bordeaux, May 1995.

Stoker G., Hogwood B. and Bullman U., *Regionalism*, Local Government Management Board, Luton, 1995.

Stone A, 'Le néo-institutionalisme, défis conceptuels et méthodologiques', *Politix*, 21, 1992.

Streeck W., 'Skills and the limits of neo-liberalism', paper presented at the conference on Mutamenti del lavoro e trasformazione sociale, Istituto Universitario di Studi Europei di Torino, Turin, 27–28 November 1987.

—— *Social Institutions and Economic Performance*, Sage, London, 1992.

Streeck W. and Schmitter P., 'From national corporatism to transnational pluralism', *Politics and Society*, 19, 1992.

Subirats J., *Un problema de estilo: la formación de políticas publicas en España*, Centro de Estudios Constitucionales, Madrid, 1992.

Swyngedouw E., 'The Mammon quest. "Glocalisation", interspatial competition and the monetary order: the construction of new scales', in M. Dunford and G. Kafkalis (eds), *Cities and Regions in the New Europe*, Belhaven Press, London, 1992.

Theret B., 'To have or to be: on the problem of the interaction between State and economy in its "solidarist" mode of regulation', *Economy and Society*, 23(1), February, 1994.

Thierstein A. and Leuenberger T., 'Der ProzeB der Internationalisierung: Handlungsspielraum für Regionen?', *AuBenwirtschaft*, 49, 1994.

Thoenig J.-C., 'De l'incertitude en gestion territoriale', *Politiques et management public*, 1995.

Thornley A., *Urban Planning Under Thatcherism: The Challenge of the Market*, 2nd edn, Routledge, London, 1993.

Tickell A., Peck J. and Dicken P., 'The fragmented region: business, the state and economic development in the North West England', in M. Rhodes (ed.), *Regions in the New Europe*, Manchester University Press, Manchester, 1995.

Tilly C., 'Stein Rokkan et les identités politiques', *Revue Internationale de Politique, 2(1), 1995.*

Todd E., *L'invention de l'Europe*, Seuil, Paris, 1990.

Toonen Th. A. J., 'The Netherlands: a decentralised unitary state in a welfare society', *West European Politics*, 4, 1987.

—— 'The unitary state as a system of co-governance, the case of the Netherlands', *Public Administration*, Autumn 1990.

—— 'Change in continuity: local government and urban affairs in the Netherlands', in J. J. Hesse (ed.), *Local Government and Urban Affairs in International Perspective*, Nomos, Baden-Baden, 1991.

—— 'Europe of the administrations: the challenges of '92 (and beyond)', *Public Administration Review*, 52(2), 1992.

—— 'Bestuur op niveau: regionalisatie in een ontzuild bestuur', *Acta Politica*, 3, 1993a.

—— 'Dutch provinces and the struggle for the meso', in L. J. Sharpe (ed.), *The Rise of Meso-Government in Europe*, Sage, London, 1993.

—— 'On the administrative condition of politics: an institutional conjecture on administrative transformation in the Netherlands', *West European Politics*, 19(3), July 1996.

Toonen Th. A. J., Hoetjes B. J. S., and Hendriks F., 'Federalism in the Netherlands. The federal approach to unitarism or the unitary approach to federalism?', in F. Knipping (ed.), Federal Conceptions in EU Member States: Traditions and Perspectives, Campus Verlag, Baden-Baden, 1994.

Toonen Th. A. J, Raadschelders J. C. N. and Hendriks F., *Meso-bestuur in Europees perspectief, De Randstadprovincies uit de pas? Deelrapport in opdracht van Regio Randstad Holland en Utrecht*, Rijkuniversiteit te Leiden, vakgroep Bestuurskunde, Leiden, november 1992.

Tornos-Mass J., 'Regioni e rappresentanza degli interessi: il caso catalano', *Stato e mercato*, 2, 1990.

Touraine, A., *Critique de la modernité*, Fayard, Paris, 1992a.

—— 'L'Etat et la question nationale', in R. Lenoir and J. Lesourne (eds), *Où va l'Etat?*, Le Monde Editions, Paris, 1992b.

Touraine, A., Dubet, F., Hegedus, Z. and Wieviorka, M., *Le pays contre l'Etat. Luttes occitanes*, Seuil, Paris, 1981.

Trigilia C., 'La regolazione localista: economia e politica nelle aree di piccola impresa', *Stato e mercato*, 14, 1985.

—— *Grandi partiti e piccole imprese*, Il Mulino, Bologna, 1986.

—— 'Il paradosso delle regione? Regolazione economica e rappresentanza degli interessi', *Meridiana*, 6, 1989.

—— 'The paradox of the region: economic regulation and the representation of interests', *Economy and Society*, 20(3), 1991.

—— *Sviluppo senza autonomia. Effeti perversi delle politiche nel Mezzogiorno*, Il Mulino, Bologna, 1992.

Turpin D., *La Région*, Economica, Paris, 1987.

Van Dam D., *Les représentations culturelles et politiques. Le cas des dirigeants en Flandre et en Wallonie*, PhD thesis, Université d'Etat de Liège, Liège, 1995.

Van Waarden F., 'Territorial differentiation of markets, states and business interest associations: a comparison of regional business associability in nine countries and seven economic sectors', in W. Coleman and H. Jacek (eds), *Regionalism, Business Interests and Public Policy*, Sage, London, 1989.

Veltz P., *Mondialisation, villes et territoires*, PUF, Paris, 1996.

Verba S., 'Comparative political culture', in L. W. Pye and S. Verba (eds), *Political Culture and Political Development*, Princeton University Press, Princeton, NJ, 1965.

Vicens Vives J., *Los catalanes en el siglo XIX*, Alianza, Madrid, 1986.

Viot P., 'Through regional planning towards regional administration', in E. Kalk (ed.), *Regional Planning and Regional Government in Europe*, IULA, The Hague, 1971.

Wallace H., 'Negotiations and coalition formation in the European Community', *Government and Opposition*, 20(4), autumn 1985.

Walton R. E. and McKersie R. B., *A Behavioral Theory of Labor Negotiations*, McGraw-Hill, New York, 1965.

Wannop W. and Cherry G., 'The development of regional planning in the UK', *Planning Perspectives*, 9(1), 1994.

Wils L., *Van Clovis tot Happart. De lange weg van de naties in de Lage Landen*, Garant, Leuven, 1992.

Woods D., 'The crisis of centre–periphery integration in Italy and the rise of regional populism: the Lombard League in comparative perspective', *Comparative Politics*, 27(2), 1995.

Wright V. and Cassese S. (eds), *La restructuration de l'Etat en Europe*, La Découverte, Paris, 1996.

Zaggario V., 'La tradizione meridionalista e il dibattito sulle autonomie nel secondo dopoguerra', in G. Mori (ed.), *Autonomismo meridionale: ideologia, politica e istituzioni*, Il Mulino, Bologna, 1981.

Index